D1591297

YELLOWSTONE & GRAND TETON CAMPING

BECKY LOMAX

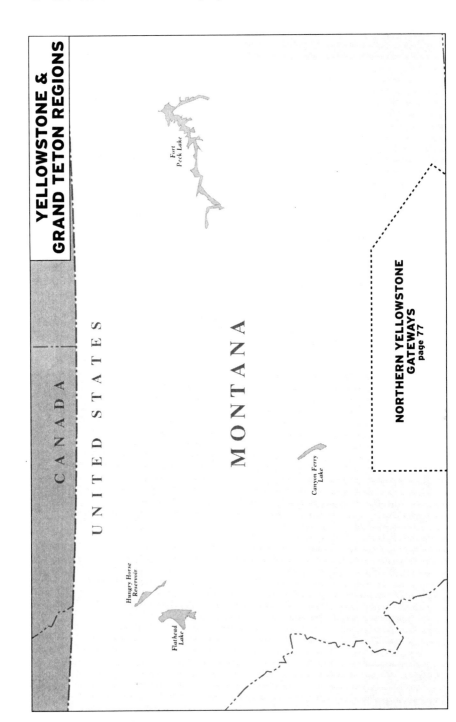

YELLOWSTONE &
GRAND TETON REGIONS

CANADA

UNITED STATES

MONTANA

Fort
Peck Lake

Hungry Horse
Reservoir

Flathead
Lake

Canyon Ferry
Lake

NORTHERN YELLOWSTONE
GATEWAYS
page 77

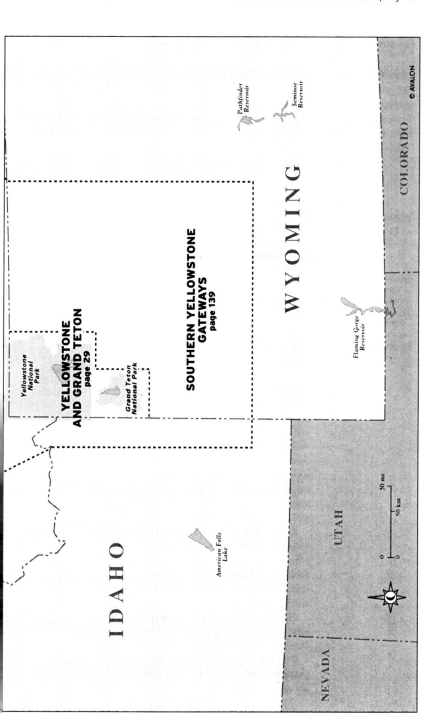

How to Use This Book

ABOUT THE CAMPGROUND PROFILES

The campgrounds are listed in a consistent, easy-to-read format to help you choose the ideal camping spot. If you already know the name of the specific campground you want to visit, or the name of the surrounding geological area or nearby feature (town, national or state park, forest, mountain, lake, river, etc.), look it up in the index and turn to the corresponding page. Here is a sample profile:

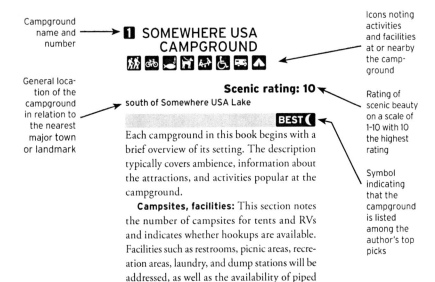

Campground name and number

General location of the campground in relation to the nearest major town or landmark

Icons noting activities and facilities at or nearby the campground

1 SOMEWHERE USA CAMPGROUND

Scenic rating: 10

south of Somewhere USA Lake

BEST (

Rating of scenic beauty on a scale of 1-10 with 10 the highest rating

Symbol indicating that the campground is listed among the author's top picks

Each campground in this book begins with a brief overview of its setting. The description typically covers ambience, information about the attractions, and activities popular at the campground.

Campsites, facilities: This section notes the number of campsites for tents and RVs and indicates whether hookups are available. Facilities such as restrooms, picnic areas, recreation areas, laundry, and dump stations will be addressed, as well as the availability of piped water, showers, playgrounds, stores, and other amenities. The campground's pet policy and wheelchair accessibility is also mentioned here.

Reservations, fees: This section notes whether reservations are accepted, and provides rates for tent sites and RV sites. If there are additional fees for parking or pets, or discounted weekly or seasonal rates, they will also be noted here.

Directions: This section provides mile-by-mile driving directions to the campground from the nearest major town or highway.

Contact: This section provides an address, phone number, and website, if available, for the campground.

ABOUT THE ICONS

The icons in this book are designed to provide at-a-glance information on activities, facilities, and services available on-site or within walking distance of each campground.

- 🥾 Hiking trails
- 🚲 Biking trails
- 🏊 Swimming
- 🎣 Fishing
- 🚤 Boating
- 🛶 Canoeing and/or kayaking
- 🏹 Hunting

- ❄ Winter sports
- ♨ Hot springs
- 🐾 Pets permitted
- 🛝 Playground
- ♿ Wheelchair accessible
- 🚐 RV sites
- ⛺ Tent sites

ABOUT THE SCENIC RATING

Each campground profile employs a scenic rating on a scale of 1 to 10, with 1 being the least scenic and 10 being the most scenic. A scenic rating measures only the overall beauty of the campground and environs; it does not take into account noise level, facilities, maintenance, recreation options, or campground management. The setting of a campground with a lower scenic rating may simply not be as picturesque that of as a higher rated campground, however other factors that can influence a trip, such as noise or recreation access, can still affect or enhance your camping trip. Consider both the scenic rating and the profile description before deciding which campground is perfect for you.

MAP SYMBOLS

░░░░░	Expressway	(80)	Interstate Freeway	✗	Airfield
┄┄┄	Primary Road	(101)	U.S. Highway	✖	Airport
░░░░░	Secondary Road	(21)	State Highway	○	City/Town
· · · · ·	Unpaved Road	(66)	County Highway	▲	Mountain
··············	Ferry		Lake	♠	Park
— ·· — ·	National Border		Dry Lake	⌒	Pass
— · — —	State Border		Seasonal Lake	◉	State Capital

Camping Tips

TRAVELING THE NORTHERN ROCKIES
Roads and Routes

When traveling the Northern Rockies of Montana, Wyoming, and Idaho, you're in big country with minimal roads: Interstates are few and far between. Dirt roads are as ubiquitous as pavement. Rough, narrow, paved two laners are common.

HIGHWAYS AND INTERSTATES

Only two interstate highways bisect the region. I-15 runs through Montana and Idaho, connecting Calgary with Salt Lake City, and I-90 crosses Montana en route from Seattle to Chicago and Boston. State highways crisscross the region, providing the main thoroughfares. Some can have four lanes, but most will be two laners. To navigate the area, use a current detailed map that shows pavement and gravel roads.

CROSSING THE CONTINENTAL DIVIDE AND HIGH PASSES

The Continental Divide skitters along the highest summits of the Rocky Mountains, making the division between water flowing to the Atlantic versus the Pacific. For campers, driving over the Continental Divide provides a challenge. In winter, some high passes are closed for several months, while others struggle with intermittent closures due to avalanches. The Beartooth Highway, Glacier National Park's Going-to-the-Sun Road, and much of Yellowstone National Park closes for winter, and remote Forest Service roads convert to snowmobile routes.

But even in summer, you can encounter snow on the higher passes through the mountains from Glacier to the Tetons. Wyoming's Beartooth Pass tops out at 10,947 feet, and Togwotee Pass is 9,658 feet. Both have amassed snow in August. The most notorious is Teton Pass on the south end of Grand Teton

National Park. Although it only touches 8,431 feet high, its 10 percent grade proves a grunt for RVs and those hauling camping trailers. Make a practice of downshifting into second gear for descents rather than burning your brakes.

Current pass conditions are available on each state's Department of Transportation website. Some even have webcams on the summits to check the weather.

DIRT ROADS

Many of the prized campgrounds in the Northern Rockies are accessed via dirt or gravel roads. The best roads—wide, graveled, double laners with regular maintenance—hold the washboards to a minimum. Others jounce along with large washboards, rocks, eroded streambeds, and small potholes. The worst contain monstrous chuckholes that can nearly swallow small cars and grab trailer hitches. Do not bring prized paint jobs on dirt roads! Take a hint from locals, who all drive rigs with dings and window chips. Rigs with four-wheel drive are helpful to get out of rough spots, but they are not required to reach any of the campgrounds in this book. If you are concerned about your vehicle's ability to navigate a certain dirt road, call the appropriate national forest for status.

DISTANCES

Many campers visiting the Northern Rockies for the first time expect to whiz between Glacier and Yellowstone National Parks in a few hours. The distance between the two is the same as driving from San Francisco to Los Angeles or from Boston to Baltimore, only without an interstate most of the way. To drive between the two parks, most campers take a full day without stopping or sightseeing.

GAS

Don't wait until you're empty to look for gas. Always plan ahead for filling up, as gas stations sometimes can be 60 miles or more away. Gas

ENTRY FEES

While many national forests and public lands require no entry fee, national parks, national historic sites, and some special federal sites charge entry fees. Rates vary by site.

NATIONAL PARKS

Entry for one private vehicle to Glacier, Grand Teton, or Yellowstone National Park costs $25 for a seven-day pass. No single-day passes are sold. Passes for Yellowstone or Grand Teton National Park are good for both parks. Entry on foot or by bicycle costs $12. A motorcycle can enter Glacier for $12, but entry to Yellowstone and Grand Teton costs $20.

Yellowstone has the same fees year-round, but Glacier reduces the entry fee in winter to $15, and Grand Teton reduces it to $5. You can enter all three national parks free on special days: Martin Luther King Jr. Day, National Park Week in late April, the birthday of the National Park Service in late August, National Public Lands Day in late September, and Veterans Day.

For those camping longer than seven days, annual passes are available, too, for each of the parks. A combined annual Yellowstone-Teton pass costs $50, and the Glacier annual pass costs $35. These are available for purchase at entrance stations.

INTERAGENCY PASSES

The **America the Beautiful Interagency Pass**, which costs $80, is a nontransferable annual pass that grants entrance to federal sites. This pass is valid at sites run by the National Park Service, Fish and Wildlife Service, Bureau of Land Management, Bureau of Reclamation, and the U.S. Forest Service. The pass does not cover camping fees or fees charged by concessionaires. The pass covers up to four adults and all children in a single, noncommercial vehicle. At walk-up entrance sites, the pass is good for the pass holder plus three adults. Children under 16 get free admission. Passes are available at entrance stations or online (store.usgs.gov/pass). The pass is available free for active military personnel and their dependents.

Seniors (U.S. citizens or permanent residents age 62 and older) can purchase lifetime nontransferable interagency passes for $10, available in person at park entrances. Bring proof of age (state driver's license, birth certificate, passport, etc.). The lifetime senior pass provides a 50 percent discount on some campgrounds.

U.S. citizens or permanent residents with permanent disabilities can get a free interagency pass, called an Access Pass, available only in person at entrance stations with proof of medical disability or eligibility for receiving federal benefits. The Access Pass provides a 50 percent discount on many campgrounds.

prices tend to be cheaper in Wyoming than in Montana or Idaho; they are also cheaper in cities compared to small rural stations.

REPAIRS

Repairs to vehicles and RVs are available. Even in the national parks or on remote national forest roads, mechanics can come take a look at your vehicle and tow it back to the shop. In some places, mobile repair services are available. Most repair services coming to your campsite will charge by the hour for their services rather than by the mile, to account for their time spent driving slow dirt roads and scenic byways to reach you.

RVs

Most RVers are well aware that different campgrounds have size restrictions based on the size of parking pads and configuration of the campground road. However, RVers will want to consider the road status in their choices of campgrounds, too. Dirt national forest roads do not usually post warnings on status. Call the local ranger station to check on conditions before driving. Most paved roads, except for the Logan Pass stretch of Glacier's Going-to-the-Sun Road, are suitable for any size RV. In Glacier, the Logan Pass stretch prohibits vehicles over 21 feet in length, taller than 10 feet, and wider than 8 feet.

MOTORCYCLES

Montana, Wyoming, and Idaho are popular for motorcycle touring. Many bikers haul their tents and mini trailers to camp in the national parks and ride the high scenic passes. None of the three states require helmets—except for those 17 years old and younger. Motorcyclists riding the high passes should be prepared for inclement weather and cold temperatures even in August.

Navigational Tools

MAPS

The dirt roads into many campgrounds in the Northern Rockies do not even appear on the state road maps. More detailed maps will provide you with a better view of where you are driving. Overall, U.S.G.S. seven-minute maps yield the most detail for driving forest roads, hiking, and camping; however, the dollars can rack up fast on a big trip requiring a load of maps. *National Geographic Trails Illustrated* maps (800/962-1643, www.natgeomaps.com) are available for Glacier, Grand Teton, and Yellowstone National Parks. Each national forest also sells huge maps with one-mile grids; find these at ranger stations or purchase online (www.nationalforeststore.com). Beartooth Publishing (406/585-7205 or 800/838-1058, www.beartoothpublishing.com) produces regional recreation maps for southern Montana, northwestern Wyoming, and eastern Idaho; maps include latitude and longitude grids, trail mileages, and campgrounds.

GPS, COMPASSES, AND PERSONAL LOCATING DEVICES

GPS units and compasses are useful for navigation but require knowledge on how to use them. Learn to use them before you depart on a trip where your safety may rely on them. Vehicle GPS units work well on most areas accessed by paved roads, but some remote Forest Service roads fail to appear on screen. Both vehicle and handheld GPS units rely on access to satellites; in deep canyons, you may not be able to pick up enough of a satellite signal for them to work. A compass, which always works, can provide a good backup.

While personal locating devices will

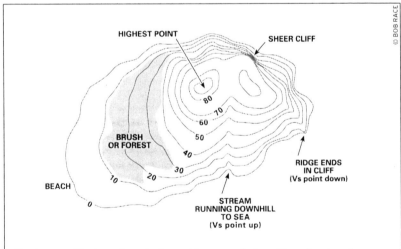

The **topographical map** is easier to read than many believe. Lines close together mean steep gradients; lines farther apart mean gentle gradients; V-shaped sets of lines pointing to higher elevations mean gulleys or stream-beds; V-shaped sets of lines pointing to lower elevations mean ridges.

transmit everywhere a GPS works, they require conscientious use. Across the West, rescue organizations are being called out for frivolous reasons or accidentally sent signals—risking the lives of the rescuers. Signals should only be transmitted in life-threatening situations. Personal locating devices should not be used as tickets to hike, climb, bike, or boat beyond one's abilities; go to only those places you would visit without one and plan self-rescue options.

Cell Phones

Visitors to the Northern Rockies expect cell phones to work everywhere as they do in virtually all populated areas. But dead zones are vast. Even though a cell tower sits near Old Faithful in Yellowstone National Park, much of the mountainous terrain across the Northern Rockies plummets into narrow canyons prohibiting signals. Don't expect to find reception deep in the forests, in canyons, or in the mountains. Most national forest and national park campgrounds do not get reception.

One of the best inventions for emergencies, cell phones allow immediate access to help. But do not rely on a cell phone as your sole means of rescue in case of an emergency. Whether you are backpacking in a wilderness or driving 20 dirt road miles snaking into a national forest, be prepared to rescue yourself.

When cell phones do work in campgrounds, use of them requires etiquette. Turn off ringers: Phone noise catapults hikers and campers from a natural experience back into the hubbub of modern life. If you must make a call, move away from campsites and other hikers to avoid disrupting their experience. On trails, refrain from using phones in the presence of other hikers. Be considerate of other campers and their desire to experience the outdoors rather than technology.

CLIMATE

The Northern Rockies from Glacier to Yellowstone sit on a collision course between Arctic Continental and Pacific Maritime weather. Storms race inland from the Pacific, with accompanying moderate temperatures and precipitation. They crash into weather systems from the north that bring cold temperatures, resulting in snow in the high mountains—even in August. Yet when maritime jet streams chug north into Canada, southern heat waves creep into Montana, Idaho, and Wyoming, shooting the summer thermometer into the 90s or above.

The Northern Rockies region is a land of weather extremes. North of Helena, Montana, Rogers Pass ranks in the top 10 coldest places in the world, alongside Antarctica and Siberia. From Glacier National Park to Helena, the Rocky Mountain Front frequently makes the record books for extreme winds, cold, and heat. Loma recorded the most extreme temperature change in a 24-hour period in the United States when the January thermometer yo-yoed over 100 degrees—from -54°F to 49°F. Lander, Wyoming, ranks in the top 10 snowiest cities in the country. Of all 50 states, Montana holds the record for the most variation in extremes—a 187-degree difference between its record high and low, and Great Falls holds the record for the most rapid temperature change recorded in the United States—47 degrees in seven minutes.

Although precipitation drops equally on both sides of the Continental Divide, wind produces more weather extremes on the east side. While winter winds often blow snow from slopes, providing forage for ungulates, they also have pushed trains off their tracks in East Glacier, Montana. Chinook winds—high warm winds with speeds reaching over 90 miles per hour—blow any time of the year, but they are most obvious in winter. Native Americans called them "snow eaters" for rapidly melting snow. In summer, high passes can rage with unpredictable winds, causing hikers to crawl on all fours across them.

Seasons

The mountains of Montana, Idaho, and Wyoming enjoy four distinct seasons, each with its own quirks. With the appropriate equipment and preparation, you can enjoy camping year-round, even in snow.

SPRING

Spring first enters the lower elevations beginning in late March and April. Winter snow melts, turning miles of dirt roads into mud. Despite March, April, and May typically being appealing off-season months to travel, in the Northern Rockies they are wet and cold, still clinging to winter. Weather bounces between soggy rains one day and 70-degree blue skies the next. Snow buries the high country, including scenic routes such as Going-to-the-Sun Road in Glacier National Park and the Beartooth Highway to Yellowstone National Park. May still brings tempestuous storms to the mountains, with rains and snows increasing the potential for avalanches and mudslides, but stretches of sunny days hint at summer. Spring temperatures range from the mid-50s to the mid-70s with nighttime lows 20-40°F.

SUMMER

Summer brings the most campers to the national parks and forests, but the mountainous terrain of the Northern Rockies often reels with its own weather agenda. While cool breezes are welcome on baking summer days, they can also bring snows to the mountains in August. During summer months, June habitually has monsoons, but July and August usher in warmer, drier skies. Temperatures run at a pleasant 70-80°F with very little humidity. Most areas will see several days each summer in the 90s (locals consider anything over 90°F to be sweltering), but rarely does the thermometer stretch up to triple digits. Nighttime lows dip into the 40s and 50s.

FALL

The first frosts usually descend in September. Autumn's cool nights usher in warm, bug-free days. While shades of gold paint aspen and larch trees, temperatures bounce through

extremes—from warm shorts-wearing weather during the day to below freezing at night. Plenty of 70-degree days keep summer outdoor recreation alive as schizophrenic weather jerks between rain with snow at higher elevations for a few days followed by clear, warming trends. Daytime highs vacillate between the 40s and 60s, and nighttime lows dip to the 20s.

WINTER

Although winter temperatures vary by elevation, most of the Northern Rockies hang in the 10-25°F range, producing voluminous snows. Yellowstone National Park sees about 150 inches of snowfall, but Logan Pass in Glacier National Park is buried under 350-700 inches of snow. Temperatures can spike above freezing, with its companion rain, or plummet below zero for several days with an arctic front.

DAYLIGHT AND TIME

Given the northern latitude and placement of Montana and Wyoming on the Mountain Time Zone's west edge, hours of daylight fluctuate wildly during the year. In June, more than 16 hours of daylight floods the mountains. First light fades in around 5am, and dark doesn't descend until almost 11pm. By late August, darkness drops by 9pm with daylight cruising on a shorter ride until December's slim 8.5 hours of daylight. Around the winter solstice, the sun rises around 8am and sets at 4:30pm. The Idaho Panhandle, which operates on Pacific time, sees both daylight and darkness an hour earlier.

ELEVATION

Because of the mountainous terrain, temperatures vary by elevation. Mountaintops are cooler than valley floors—up to 15 degrees cooler. Boaters may enjoy 82-degree weather camping on Montana's Flathead Lake in August, while hikers less than 60 air miles away in Glacier National Park hit trails with temperatures in the high 60s. Yellowstone National Park sits on a high-elevation plateau with most of the park above 7,500 feet, and the highest campgrounds on Wyoming's Beartooth Plateau top out at 9,600 feet. Campgrounds in these locations are substantially cooler than those at lower elevations, such as Montana's Missouri Headwaters State Park at 4,045 feet.

Weather

Locals have a saying about the weather in the Northern Rockies: "Wait five minutes, and the weather will change." The mountain terrain lends itself to wild swings in weather. You can begin hiking in shorts but by afternoon be pulling on gloves and fleece hats as gray clouds lob down sheets of sleet. Calm, glassy lakes can give way to four-foot whitecaps as storms blow in.

LIGHTNING AND THUNDERSTORMS

Afternoon thundershowers and lightning storms are common across much of the Northern Rocky Mountains. In some locations— particularly around Yellowstone National Park and Wyoming's Beartooth Plateau—they roll in daily in late afternoon, almost like clockwork. During lightning storms, boaters should exit the water, and those enjoying beaches should move to sheltered locations. Hikers should descend from summits, ridges, and exposed slopes, and stay away from isolated trees. Some thunderstorms bring hail; other dump pelting rains.

WINDS

The Continental Divide causes high winds. With eastern air masses trying to equalize with western jet streams, the result is strong winds optimal for wind farms. But the open, eastern slopes of the Continental Divide can pose tricky driving for large RVs, with wind gusts threatening to push them off the road. Likewise, treeless campgrounds on the prairie often bluster with winds. Montana's Rocky Mountain Front and the Absaroka Front receive the most notorious winds, on an average day blowing 7-20 mph with gusts up to 50 mph.

PRECIPITATION

While Montana, Wyoming, and Idaho are drier than the Pacific Northwest, their mountain areas receive substantial precipitation. The amount depends largely upon topography. Across the area, most snow falls November-March, but heavy snowstorms can occur as early as mid-September or as late as May— especially in the high mountains. Annual snowfall averages 300 inches in many of the mountain ranges—hence the region's numerous ski resorts. Valley floors receive about 50 inches of snowfall. Nearly half of the region's annual average precipitation falls from May through July in the form of valley rain, sleet, or snow. Heavy rains falling during the spring thaw contribute to early summer avalanches and flooding.

FOREST FIRES

Like snow, wind, or rain, lightning-caused fire is a natural process. It is healthy for the ecosystem, removing bug infestations, reducing deadfall and nonnative plants, releasing nutrients into the soil like a good fertilizer, and maintaining a natural mix of vegetation. Following decades of heavy fire suppression, forest fuels have built up across the Northern Rockies. Some forests suffer under severe attacks from pine beetles and blister rust. Those conditions kill trees and make them ripe for fire. You can check on current forest fire locations and their status at www.inciweb.org.

CAMPING CONCERNS
Camping Regulations and Red Tape
NATIONAL PARKS

National parks are set aside for their historical, geological, cultural, or biological significance, and geared toward public recreation. Hunting is not permitted; neither is picking wildflowers nor picking berries for commercial use. Dogs are not allowed on trails; neither are mountain bikes. Camping is limited to designated campgrounds with 7-14 days in one campsite, unless otherwise posted. Permits are needed for backcountry camping. National parks require entrance fees, and each campground requires fees.

Waterton Lakes National Park in Canada borders Glacier National Park and is used to access parts of Glacier. U.S. national park passes are not valid in Waterton. In fact, passports are required to drive to Waterton, and passports are required to boat or walk down Waterton Lake to hike from Goat Haunt USA.

NATIONAL FORESTS

National forests are used for their resources, with timber harvesting, commercial berry picking, mushroom harvesting, mining, and recreation permitted. Hunting is permitted with licenses administered by each state. Trails permit dogs and mountain bikes as long as no special designation says otherwise. Designated campgrounds usually allow stays up to 14-16 days in the same campsite; a few high-use areas employ shorter limits. Unless otherwise designated, primitive camping is usually permitted anywhere outside of developed campgrounds. Permits are not needed for backcountry camping. National forests usually do not charge entrance fees, but some specific visitor sites do. Some developed campgrounds require fees; others are free, as is primitive camping.

Wilderness areas are administered usually by the national forest that contains the wilderness. They permit no mechanical transports, including mountain bikes. Hunting is permitted. Fido can go along on the trail, and permits are not needed for backcountry camping, which is free.

OTHER GOVERNMENT LANDS

Bureau of Land Management and Bureau of Reclamation terrain operates much like national forest land, with most developed campgrounds charging fees. Entrance fees are usually not charged; however, some sites charge day-use fees. Stays are limited to 14 days in the same spot, unless posted otherwise. Free primitive camping is permitted outside of developed campgrounds.

Montana, Wyoming, and Idaho **state parks** vary in campgrounds and amenities under the auspices of each state. State parks charge fees for day use and camping. Most campground fees include day use, too. Camping is permitted in a Montana or Wyoming state park for 14 days; in Idaho, the limit is 15 days.

Camping with Children

Children learn to enjoy camping when they can participate in activities. Have them help with camp chores—building fires, collecting garbage, and bear-proofing the camp.

Kids can earn **Junior Ranger Badges** by completing self-guided activities in Glacier, Yellowstone, and Teton National Parks. Activities, which target ages 5-12, vary by park but are an excellent way to help children learn about the park and wildlife. Junior Ranger activity books or newspapers are available at all visitors centers in the parks. They can also be downloaded online under each national park (www.nps.gov). When kids return the completed newspaper to any visitors center, they are sworn in as Junior Rangers and receive park-specific badges.

Plan ahead with kids by taking along extra clothing and shoes. If kids can get wet, they will. Replacing wet soggy clothing with warm dry gear improves their attitude and their enjoyment of camping. When hiking, even for short walks, take along water and snacks to maintain the energy level for children.

Camping with Pets
NATIONAL PARKS

Pets are allowed in national parks, but only in limited areas. They are allowed in campgrounds, roadsides, and parking lots on a six-foot or shorter leash or in a cage. With the exception of Waterton Lakes National Park north of Glacier, pets are not permitted on national park trails, to protect fragile vegetation or thermal areas and to prevent conflicts with wildlife. Bears are a major argument for leaving the pooch home. Pets are also not permitted in visitors centers or at beaches. Pets can stay in your vehicle while you are viewing roadside attractions, but you must provide ventilation for the animal's survival.

NATIONAL FORESTS

National forests permit pets on most trails. (Read trailhead signs as some trails do not permit pets.) Keep in mind that many hikers in the Northern Rockies have heightened sensitivity to movement, as they're on alert for bears. To prevent bear conflicts and to avoid scaring other hikers with a dog charging down the trail, keep Fido on a leash. Pets are also allowed in campgrounds, but they must be leashed, rather than running free.

In bear country, store pet food, bowls, and toys in a hard-sided vehicle or bear box when not in use. Like humans, pets should leave no trace other than footprints. Clean up and dispose of all pet feces in the garbage.

Camping Ethics

Protection of public lands and campgrounds is up to those of us who use them. Be respectful of nature and campground facilities, taking care of them as if they were your own. Follow Leave No Trace ethics when camping in developed campgrounds or the backcountry.

LEAVE NO TRACE

Visitors to the Northern Rockies need to take an active role in maintaining the environment.

Plan ahead and prepare. Plan ahead for camping by keeping in mind fluctuating weather, and choose appropriate hiking routes for mileage and elevation gain. Carry hiking essentials.

Travel and camp on durable surfaces. In both developed and backcountry campgrounds, camp in designated sites only. Protect fragile trailside plants by staying on the trail, refusing to cut switchbacks, and walking single file on trails even in the mud. If you must walk off-trail, step on rocks, snow, or dry grasses rather than on wet soils and fragile plants.

Leave what you find. Flowers, rocks, and goat fur tufts on shrubs are protected resources in national parks. Even on other public lands, they should be left for others to enjoy. For lunch stops and camping, sit on rocks or logs where you find them rather than moving them to accommodate your camp.

Properly dispose of waste. Whatever you bring in, you must pack out or deposit in garbage receptacles. Do not burn garbage in fire pits. If toilets are not available, urinate on rocks, logs, gravel, or snow to protect fragile soils and plants from salt-starved wildlife. Bury feces 6-8 inches deep at least 200 feet from water. Pack out used toilet paper in your trash.

Minimize campfire impacts. Make fires in designated fire pits only. Use small, wrist-size dead and down wood, not live branches. Be aware that fires or firewood collecting is not permitted in many places in national parks.

Respect wildlife. Bring along binoculars, spotting scopes, and telephoto lenses to aid in watching wildlife. Keep your distance. Do not feed any wildlife, even ground squirrels. Once fed, they become more aggressive. Maintain a distance of a football-field length from bears and wolves and 25 yards from all other wildlife.

Be considerate of other visitors. Minimize use of electronics, generators, and other noisemakers in campgrounds, and keep dogs from barking. Follow posted quiet hours, departing and arriving as silently as possible before or after hours.

RECREATION
Hiking

The Northern Rockies are crisscrossed with hiking trails—some short day-hike destinations and others stringing long miles back into remote wilderness areas. Montana's Bob Marshall Wilderness and Yellowstone National Park each contain over 1,000 miles of trails, while Glacier National Park contains over 700 miles of trails. Outfitters are available for guided hiking and backpacking in Glacier, Grand Teton, and Yellowstone National Parks. Though links still remain to be built, the Continental Divide Trail forms the longest trail system, running through Wyoming's Wind River Range, Yellowstone National Park, several national forests and wilderness areas in Montana, and Glacier National Park.

Trails and Signs

Conditions on trails vary depending on the season, elevation, weather, and wildlife. In places where swinging or plank bridges are removed annually across rivers and creeks, crews reinstall them in late May or early June. Steep snowfields inhibit hiking at higher elevations until July. Avalanches and severe storms—wind microbursts, heavy snows, and torrential rains—can cause miles of downed trees across trails. Depending on the location, crews may or may not be available for immediate clearing. Some trails in Glacier, Grand Teton, and Yellowstone National Parks are closed temporarily because of increased bear activity. Yellowstone also has annual closures in feeding areas. To find out about trail conditions before hiking, stop at ranger stations and visitors centers for updates. In general, trails in the national parks are maintained in better condition than in national forests, which lack funding for bigger trail crews.

National park trails tend to be well signed with direction and mileage. Some signs, however, may be in kilometers, rather than miles. (To convert kilometers to miles, multiply the kilometers listed by 0.6.) National forests and wilderness areas tend to have less specific signage and fewer signs. Carry a good map and a compass or GPS to navigate the maze of trails. In the Northern Rockies, some trails have names while others use numbers with or without names. The numbers, which are assigned by the Forest Service, identify the trails on USFS maps and many topographical maps of the region.

In the national parks, where the concentration of bears is high, you may also see **bear warning signs.** Use extreme caution and all your bear country savvy when bears frequent a trail. Obey closures: They usually mean that

hikers on the Piegan Trail in Glacier National Park

a bear has been aggressive or is feeding on a carcass, which it will forcefully defend.

Backcountry Camping

Backcountry camping is by permit only in Glacier, Grand Teton, and Yellowstone National Parks. Backcountry campgrounds vary in size, but most separate sleeping sites from communal cooking areas. No food, garbage, toiletries, or cookware should ever be kept in the tent sites. Near the cook sites, a bear pole, bar, or box allows for safe food storage. Take along a 30-foot rope and stuff bags to hang your food in Glacier and Yellowstone; backpackers in Grand Teton are required to carry bear-resistant food containers, available for free. Many backcountry campsites do not allow fires. Carry a lightweight stove for cooking.

To plan backcountry camping trips by foot, horseback, or boat in Glacier, Grand Teton, or Yellowstone National Park, follow the directions in each park's Backcountry Trip Planner, available online (www.nps.gov/glac, www.nps.gov/grte, www.nps.gov/yell). Permits may be

HIKING ESSENTIALS

Hiking in the Northern Rockies of Montana, Wyoming, and Idaho demands preparedness. High elevations, unpredictable winds, fast-changing weather, and summer snowstorms can catapult a lazy day walk into a nightmare if one is not prepared. Take the following:

Extra clothing: Rain pants and jackets can double as wind protection while gloves and a lightweight warm hat will save fingers and ears. Carry at least one extra water-wicking layer for warmth. Avoid cotton fabrics that stay soggy and fail to retain body heat, opting instead for synthetics.

Extra food and water: Take lunch and snacks, like compact high-energy food bars. Low-odor foods will not attract animals. Heat, wind, and elevation dehydrate hikers quickly; always carry extra water. Don't drink directly from streams or lakes because of the bacteria; always filter or treat water sources before drinking.

Navigation: Although national park trails are well signed, national forest and wilderness trails are not. Take a detailed topographical map of the area to ascertain the distance traveled and location. A compass or GPS will also help, but only if you know how to use them.

Flashlight: Carry a small flashlight or headlamp with extra batteries. In an after-dark emergency, the light becomes invaluable.

First-aid kit: Two Band-Aids are not enough! Carry a fully equipped standard first-aid kit with blister remedies. Don't forget personal requirements such as bee-sting kits and allergy medications.

Sun protection: Altitude, snow, ice, and lakes all increase ultraviolet radiation. Protect yourself with 30 SPF sunscreen, sunglasses, and a sunhat or baseball cap.

Emergency bathroom supplies: To accommodate alfresco bathrooms, carry a small trowel, plastic bags, and toilet paper. Move at least 200 feet away from water sources. For urinating, aim for a durable surface, such as rocks, logs, gravel, or snow, rather than fragile plants, campsites, or trails. Bury feces 6-8 inches deep in soil. Pack the toilet paper out in a Ziploc bag.

Feminine hygiene: Carry heavy-duty Ziploc bags for packing tampons and pads out rather than burying them.

Insect repellent: Insect repellents containing 50 percent DEET work best with the mosquitoes and black flies. Purchase applications that rub or spray in a close range rather than aerosols that become airborne onto other people, plants, and animals.

Pepper spray: Use an eight-ounce can of pepper spray for charging bears, but do not bother unless you know how to use it and what influences its effectiveness. It is not to be used like bug repellent.

Cell phones: Take the cell phone along for emergencies, but don't rely on it for rescue. In many mountains and canyons, cell phones do not work. Plan to self-rescue. If you do carry a cell phone, turn it off to save the batteries for an emergency and to avoid offending fellow hikers who seek solitude, quiet, and the sounds of nature.

Miscellaneous: Pack along a knife, a few feet of nylon cord, and duct tape wrapped around a flashlight handle. Many hikers have repaired boots and packs with duct tape and a little ingenuity.

reserved by mail for $25-30 (a limited number of sites are assigned this way, and you still have to pay your per person fee when you pick up the actual permit), or you can pick up permits in person, no more than 24 hours in advance. Permits are not issued over the phone. Permits are free except in Glacier ($5 per person per night). Permits are not needed for backpacking in national forests or wilderness areas.

In addition to a rope for hanging food, backcountry campers should take a small screen or strainer for sifting food particles out of gray water, a water purifier, and a small trowel for human waste when a pit toilet is unavailable.

Mountaineering and Climbing

The peaks of Montana, Idaho, and Wyoming draw mountaineers for their rugged, challenging routes to the summits. The quality of the rock varies between crumbling sedimentary shales in the north and harder granitic rocks in the south, making the type of climbing different. Ice routes, too, are shrinking because of the rapid melting of the region's glaciers. Mountaineers shimmy routes up through most of the region's mountain ranges, but a few specific locales gain above-average reputations. Area-specific books include route descriptions of popular ascents.

While technical rock-climbing routes are available in Glacier National Park, the bulk of the summits are reached via Class 3 or 4 scrambles. Long, loose scree fields lead to tight goat walks along cliffs. Even though more technical routes exist, all six summits over 10,000 feet can be reached via scrambles. You're on your own, though, as the park has no permitted guides for off-trail scrambles.

Teton National Park harbors the region's best technical rock-climbing opportunities. With over 50 major routes to the summit, the Grand Teton tops the Northern Rockies' highest elevation at 13,770 feet. Two companies in Jackson offer instruction and guided trips to Teton summits—including the Grand. Other popular rock-climbing routes string down the Wind River Mountains, particularly Cirque of the Towers in the Popo Agie Wilderness.

With the glaciers across the Northern Rockies fast melting into extinction, the routes that utilize ice are changing. However, winter ascents on skis and ice climbing are available.

Bicycling
ROAD BIKING
Road bicyclists relish the Northern Rockies for the long dramatic climbs over the Continental Divide and the miles of pedal-free descents. The **TransAmerica Trail** cuts through the region as does the **Lewis and Clark Trail**, among other long-distance rides. Route descriptions and maps are available from Missoula's Adventure Cycling Association (800/721-8719, www.adventurecycling.org).

Narrow, curvy roads with no shoulders and

drivers gawking at scenery instead of the road all shove the biker into a precarious position. Wear a helmet and bright colors to ensure your safety.

Two scenic byways rank with bicyclists for their challenge and their scenery. In Glacier National Park, the 52-mile **Going-to-the-Sun Road** is a biker must-do. Early-season up-and-back riding is available in spring and fall while plowing and road construction has the route closed to vehicles. Once the road is open (mid-June-mid-Sept.), bicycling restrictions close two narrow sections of the road on the west side 11am-4pm until Labor Day. Eastbound riders must be at Logan Pass by 11am or dismount and wait.

Starting from Red Lodge, Montana, the 68-mile **Beartooth Highway** climbs a lung-busting route up to 10,947 feet to cross Beartooth Pass on a high tundra plateau. Riding westbound toward Yellowstone National Park lets you get the full wow of the snowcapped peaks of the Absaroka Range. The route, which bounces from Montana into Wyoming and back into Montana, passes scads of lakes, which produce mosquito swarms into August that plague bicyclists. Snow buries the highway much of the year, but it usually is open late May to mid-October.

For riders looking for flat spins instead, Idaho's 72-mile paved **Trail of the Coeur d'Alenes** runs from Mullan to Plummer, following rivers, passing wetlands brimming with wildlife, and crossing the Chacolet Bridge. Interpretive signs, picnic areas, and rest stations dot the route, which changes so little in elevation that you're never sure if you're riding uphill or down. The trail is usually snow-free April-November. Several resort locations also have extensive paved bike trail systems, including Sun Valley and Jackson Hole.

Glacier, Yellowstone, and Grand Teton National Parks maintain a few campsites at most of their campgrounds for bicyclists. The shared first-come, first-served campsites ($5-8 per person) have bear boxes for storing food and room for several small tents.

bicyclists on Going-to-the-Sun Road in Glacier National Park

MOUNTAIN BIKING

As single-track mountain bike trails are sprouting up around the region faster than weeds, rail trail projects are converting defunct tracks into wide bike paths. Idaho's 15-mile **Route of the Hiawatha** (208/744-1301, www.ridethehiawatha.com), the region's most popular mountain bike trail, crosses seven trestles and rides through nine dark tunnels, with the longest (1.7 miles) running under the Idaho-Montana state line. The Route of the Hiawatha (open late May-early Oct.) also offers a shuttle for those who only want to ride downhill. Eastern Idaho's 42-mile **Railroad Right of Way Trail** also runs from Warm River to West Yellowstone.

Many national forest trails permit bicycles, except in wildernesses or areas with special designations. Mountain bikes are not permitted on national park trails, except for special routes designated in each national park. Ski resorts, such as Big Sky, Whitefish, Sun Valley, and Jackson Hole, also have mountain biking trails, some with lift-served access for downhill riding.

Fishing

The movie *A River Runs Through It* catapulted Montana's rivers into the national consciousness with dreams of clear waters and wild trout. But that's the true nature of fly-fishing in the Northern Rockies, which harbor 18 blue-ribbon trout streams populated with rainbow, brown, brook, Yellowstone cutthroat, westslope cutthroat, and bull trout—many wild. Lowland lakes also fill with lake trout (mackinaw), kokanee salmon, northern pike, and bass.

NATIONAL PARK FISHING

Each of the national parks has different licensing regulations for fishing. Glacier requires no license. Yellowstone requires a fishing permit for anglers 16 years and older ($18 for three days, $25 for seven days, or $40 for a season); anglers 15 and younger may fish free under a supervising adult's permit or their own permit. Grand Teton requires a Wyoming fishing license. Waterton requires a national park fishing license (one day C$10 or annual C$35).

Buy national park fishing licenses at ranger stations and visitors centers.

Each park has slightly different fishing regulations with seasons, catch-and-release laws, closure locations, and creel limits designed to protect the resources. You'll need to be able to identify species that are catch-and-release only—especially the endangered bull trout. Fishing regulations are available online and at ranger stations and visitors centers.

STATE FISHING LICENSES

Outside the national parks, state fishing licenses are required. Some states offer discounts for seniors and those who are disabled. Kids often can fish free. Licenses are available online and at sporting goods stores. The one exception is on Indian reservations; each has its own tribal fishing permits and rates.

Montana fishing licenses (http://fwp. mt.gov) cost $13 for two days or $26 per season for resident adults ages 15-61. Teens ages 15-17 can get a season license for $16. Resident seniors age 62 and older and kids ages 12-14 only need an $8 conservation license. Nonresident licenses for ages 15 and older, including seniors, cost $25 for two days, $54 for 10 days, or $60 for the season. Additional permits are required for warm-water game fish, paddlefish, and bull trout.

Idaho fishing licenses (http://fishand-game.idaho.gov) for residents cost $11.50 for a single day and $5 for each consecutive day; for the season, they cost $14 for ages 14-17 and $26 for adults. Nonresident licenses cost $13 for one day and $6 for each consecutive day, or season licenses cost $22 for ages 14-17 and $99 for adults. Nonresidents can also purchase a three-day salmon/steelhead license for $38.

Wyoming fishing licenses (http://wgfd. wyo.gov) cost $6 per day for residents; for the season, they cost $3 for youth and $24 for adults. For nonresidents, a one-day adult license costs $14 and an annual license costs $92. Nonresident youth pay $15 for an annual license.

© BECKY LOMAX

Kids can enjoy fishing in the Northern Rockies.

Boating

Small reservoirs dot the Northern Rockies, but big lakes command most of the boating interest from visitors. Montana's Flathead Lake is the largest freshwater lake west of the Mississippi. Montana, Wyoming, and Idaho require boats to be registered. Rates vary depending on the state and the size of boat. Boats may also need to undergo checks in various waters for aquatic invasive species.

In **Montana,** motorized boats, personal watercraft, and sailboats over 12 feet long must be registered. Nonmotorized smaller sailboats, rowboats, rafts, canoes, and kayaks are exempt. Boats from out of state or country may be used in Montana for up to 90 consecutive days without registering.

Wyoming requires motorized boats to be registered. Motorboats that are properly registered in another state may be used on Wyoming's waters for up to 90 consecutive days without registration.

Idaho requires boats with mechanical

propulsion to be registered. Boats currently registered in another state may be used on Idaho's waterways for 60 consecutive days or less without registering.

National parks have their own boating permits, but costs vary depending on the park. Glacier and Waterton parks issue free permits to boats that pass the aquatic invasive species inspection. Boat permits cost $5-10 in Yellowstone or $20-40 in Grand Teton.

WATERSKIING

Water-skiers from warm-water areas often are shocked by their first contact with the chilly Northern Rockies. Water is cold—frigid in places. The ice-fed deep lakes maintain a chill even in summer. Surface water may only heat up in August into the low 60s, if that. Bring a wetsuit for more enjoyable waterskiing. Yellowstone does not permit waterskiing, and Jet skis are not allowed in Glacier, Yellowstone, or Grand Teton parks.

Swimming

You can swim in any lake in the Northern Rockies; however, buoy-rimmed swimming areas with lifeguards are rare. In most lakes, you swim at your own risk. Prepare for frigid cold water, even in midsummer, as snowmelt and glacial runoff feed the lakes. Plus, they are only ice-free for a portion of the year.

Use caution when swimming in rivers. Slick algae-covered rocks and swift-moving currents can be lethal. In Glacier National Park, drowning is the number one cause of accidental death.

Rafting

The Northern Rockies spill with Class III-V white water, frothy waves with big holes. Other Class I-II rivers make for more leisurely float trips. Thirteen major rivers contain Class III and above white-water sections that you can run on your own if you have the expertise or go with local guides. In Montana, head for the Clark Fork, Middle Fork of the Flathead, Yellowstone, Gallatin, Madison, or Stillwater River for white-water thrills. Where Wyoming's Shoshone, Green, and Snake Rivers squeeze through canyons, you can bounce

© BECKY LOMAX

rafting on the Middle Fork of the Flathead River in Montana

through rapids. In Idaho, the Lochsa, Selway, and Main Salmon provide single-day options for white water, but the Middle Fork of the Salmon requires a multiday trip through the Frank Church-River of No Return Wilderness. Most of these rivers have nearby drive-to campgrounds available, and some are lined with primitive campgrounds for overnight float trips. Check on current water levels through state hydrology departments or American Whitewater (www.american-whitewater.org).

Floating most of these rivers on an overnight trip does not require a permit. However, Idaho's Selway, Middle Fork of the Salmon, and Main Salmon Rivers do. These are acquired via an annual computerized lottery drawing. You can apply for all three rivers with one application (877/444-6777, www.recreation.gov). Permits are not available by phone, except for acquiring permits from cancelled launches after the annual drawing.

Outfitters guide trips on most of the Northern Rockies' major rivers and some of their tributaries. Trips include half-day, full-day, and multiday excursions. Locate outfitters in the towns nearest the rivers. Check with state agencies to be sure they are licensed.

Canoeing and Kayaking

The Northern Rockies also harbor lakes and slow-moving rivers—gems for multiday paddling trips. In Montana, the Missouri River through Gates of the Mountains offers paddling along the route of Lewis and Clark, plus hiking and camping. Connected lakes, such as Idaho's Priest Lake and Upper Priest Lake, include camping on islands as well as paddling the two-mile Thoroughfare to the upper lake. A paddle route around Montana's Flathead Lake makes use of six state parks. Glacier, Yellowstone, and Teton National Parks offer large lakes with overnight paddling campgrounds.

Canoes and kayaks are available to rent in select places, but to guarantee you have a boat, bring your own or call ahead to reserve

the rental. Rentals and guided paddle trips are available in Yellowstone and Grand Teton National Parks; Glacier has only rentals.

National parks require permits for non-motorized watercraft. Glacier requires a free self-inspection permit. Permits cost $5-10 in Yellowstone or $10-20 in Grand Teton.

GEAR SELECTION AND MAINTENANCE

Camping in the Northern Rocky Mountains requires planning for all types of weather and conditions. The proper equipment can make the difference between enjoying a trip when the temperatures plummet or the air drips soggy and hating the experience.

Tents

Tents come in a variety of shapes, sizes, weights, and prices—tailored to different types of camping. Any reputable outdoor store will provide comparative ratings for their tents. Considering elevation, erratic weather, and the potential for snow even in August, tents for the Northern Rockies should be double walled—with a tent wall and a rain fly that covers the complete tent to the ground. Purchase a tent with sealed seams to prevent water seeping into the tent. Bug netting is also essential for the voracious mosquitoes and black flies that proliferate during June and July. While many campers go without footprints or tarps below their tents, in wet, muddy conditions or snow, ground cloths can keep the tent floor dry. They also will prolong the life of a tent. Three-season tents work the best in the Northern Rockies for camping in summer, spring, or fall. But for winter camping, invest in a four-season tent.

After use, dry tents completely before storing to prevent mildew. They also should be stored in a dry location rather than a damp garage, attic, or crawl space. If possible, store them loose rather than folded or rolled up tight to prevent breakdown of the fabric on the folds.

© BECKY LOMAX

Daypacks should be large enough to carry essentials, first aid, and extra clothing.

Sleeping Bags and Pads

Sleeping bags are sold with synthetic or goose down insulation. Either works well in the Northern Rockies, although goose-down bag owners need to take extra precaution to keep the bags dry to prevent the down from losing its insulation value. Invest in a waterproof stuff sack to keep sleeping bags dry. Bags for summer camping should be rated to 20°F; however, if you plan on camping in spring or fall in the Northern Rockies, you'll be more prepared for the weather mood swings with a bag rated to zero. Mummy bag cuts as opposed to rectangular bags will allow your body to heat up the space faster.

A sleeping bag alone will not keep you warm without an insulating layer between the ground and your body. Sleeping pads range from a thin 0.5-inch layer of foam to large thick air mattresses that require a compressor to inflate. Assess your needs before purchasing. If backpacking, go for the lightest weight in foam or inflatable. If car camping, you can afford to pack along more weight. Self-inflating

and blow-up air mattresses allow you to camp more quietly than if you must turn on an air compressor.

Both sleeping bags and pads should be stored loose to extend their life as long as possible. A tall closet works well for hanging both. Launder sleeping bags according to the manufacturer's instruction.

Day Packs

If you plan on hiking on your camping trip, bring along a day pack. While you can get away with carrying just a water bottle for a one-hour hike, you should be prepared for the weather to change on longer day hikes. Mountain weather can mutate from blue skies to rain squalls, raging winds, hail, and even snow during summer. Bring a day pack that can fit extra clothing—rain jacket and pants, warm hat, gloves, and a light fleece layer. Your pack should also be able to fit lunch, snacks, first-aid kit, sunscreen, bug juice, headlamp, and water. Consider the size of optional items you may enjoy, such as a camera and binoculars.

Good day packs will include small padded hip belts to keep the weight from pulling on your neck. Hip belts also work for attaching pepper spray holders for bears. Try day packs on for size in the store, as different brands work better for different body types. Air out packs after use and store them in a dry location.

Food and Cooking Gear

Cooking while camping can be as simple as boiling water for quick instant freeze-dried meals or as involved as slow roasting on the fire. Your mode of travel will most likely dictate choices in cooking. If backpacking, bicycling, kayaking, or canoeing, quick-cooking meals require less gas, they weigh less, and they need fewer pots. Slow roasting on the fire requires aluminum foil, aluminum pots, or Dutch ovens. Traveling by RV, car, or boat allows for more room to pack along meals that are entertaining to cook. Virtually any recipe can be adapted to cooking outdoors with a little ingenuity. In bear country, low-odor foods mean less scent to attract wildlife.

Stoves and cooking pots also come in a variety of sizes to suit different uses. Smaller versions are available for backpacking, kayaking, and canoeing, while larger, heavier options are only suitable for vehicle-assisted camping. Most stoves are heated with white gas or propane, easy to find in the Northern Rockies. Butane canisters are convenient, but replacements may not be as easy to find, and they add to landfills. Most outdoor lightweight cooking pots are now available with nonstick surfaces.

Water Treatment

While the water in developed campgrounds is usually safe to drink, most streams and lakes in the West run the risk of carrying giardia and cryptosporidium, the two most common cysts. At campgrounds where potable water is not available, purify or boil water to kill potential trouble causers.

Boiling water requires no extra equipment—just a stove and extra fuel. The Wilderness Medical Society recommends heating the water to a rapid boil for one minute to kill microorganisms.

Water filters and purifiers pump water by hand through filters that are rated to strain out certain sizes of critters. A 1.0-micron filter will remove giardia and cryptosporidium, but a 0.2-micron filter will also remove bacteria while a 0.0004-micron purifier will remove viruses, too.

Chemical treatments include the use of chlorine or iodine tablets, crystals, or liquid. Follow the manufacturer's instructions for their use, most of which require waiting 30 minutes before drinking. While many campers dislike the taste left from iodine, it can work as a backup in an emergency.

UV light is now available in a compact instrument about the size of an electric toothbrush for killing microorganisms. Immerse the light tube into the water for 60 seconds. Batteries are required.

What to Wear

LAYERS

Dress in layers to adapt to the quick-changing

© SABRINA YOUNG

a standard Coleman propane stove

mountain conditions and weather. Mornings can start with blue skies and temperatures for T-shirts and shorts, but by afternoon, winds can usher in storm fronts delivering hail and even snow. The opposite can happen, too, with frosty mornings warming by afternoon. Layers allow adapting to the changing conditions by putting on additional clothing for protection from the elements or taking a layer off to cool down. Prepare for mountain extremes by packing a fleece or wool hat and gloves.

SUN PROTECTION
The sun's intensity increases at high elevations. With much of the Northern Rocky Mountains stretching above 6,000 feet in elevation, protection from the glaring sun is important for preventing blistering sunburns. Add white snowfields and glaciers to the elevation, and the sun's rays wax more intense. Ball caps or sun hats protect the face from the sun's scorching rays, and sunglasses will protect the eyes from burns and snow blindness.

RAIN GEAR
Breathable rain gear is essential camp clothing for the Northern Rockies. Breathable rain fabrics let you recreate outdoors without getting as wet beneath your jacket as outside of it. Both rain shells and pants are useful, especially when hiking in brushy meadows laden with moisture. Armpit zippers let you adjust the ventilation of shells. Hoods allow for closing off the neck area to chilling wet winds, and ankle zippers on pants allow for putting them on and taking them off without removing your hiking boots.

SHOES, SOCKS, AND FOOT CARE
Footwear needs to adapt to the activities you plan to do while camping. Hikers need boots with a sturdy tread, which are available in lightweight, waterproof, and leather options. Ill-fitting shoes and incorrect socks cause blisters—preventable by shoe choice and fit. Squished toes and loose heels are the biggest culprits for blisters. To prevent toes from

blistering by rubbing on each other, a shoe with a larger toe box is essential. If heels fit too loosely, two remedies can prevent blisters: Wearing one liner sock inside a heavier sock allows socks to rub against each other rather than against the heels, and footbeds (either custom or market-ready) will absorb excess space and provide more support for the foot.

Appropriate socks can also prevent blisters. Although cotton socks feel good, they aren't the best choice for hiking. Cotton absorbs water from the feet and holds it, providing a surface for friction. Synthetic, silk, or wool blend socks wick water away from the skin. Socks should fit smoothly over the feet with no added bunching. A comfortable fit, but not loose, is paramount for preventing blisters.

Those including water sports in their itineraries should also bring sturdy water sandals or shoes that will protect the feet on rough algae-slick rocks. Flip-flops do not protect the feet; use sandals or water shoes with a thick, solid tread. During spring and fall, booties will keep the feet warm in chilly waters.

SAFETY AND FIRST AID
Plants
POISON IVY
Montana, Wyoming, and Idaho have pockets of poison ivy. Recognize the below-knee-height plant by its three leaves, often tinged with red and clustering in river corridors. If your skin comes into contact with poison ivy, wash immediately with soap and water. Do not scratch infected areas as it can spread. Avoid contact with eyes, mouth, and open sores. If you have a reaction, an antihistamine can relieve symptoms. Seek medical help.

NETTLES AND COW PARSNIP
Lush, forested slopes of the Northern Rockies sprout with two irritating plants. Stinging nettles vary in height 2-4 feet. Recognize them by the serrated-edged leaves and minuscule flowers hanging on a drooping stem. If skin comes into contact with nettles, you can use sting-relief products such as those for

mosquito bites. Calamine lotion also provides relief. Some people react to cow parsnip. Recognize the plants by their 10-inch-diameter heads of white flowers and gigantic leaves shaped like maple leaves. Reactions can vary from redness to blistering. For the latter, seek medical help.

Mosquitoes and Ticks

Bugs are irritants, but more importantly, they can carry diseases such as West Nile virus and Rocky Mountain spotted fever. Protect yourself by wearing long sleeves and pants as well as using bug repellents in spring and summer when mosquitoes and ticks are common. Also, avoid areas heavily trafficked by ungulates (deer, sheep, elk), which transport ticks. If a tick bites you, remove it and disinfect the bite; keep your eye on it for lesions or a rash, consulting a doctor if either appears.

Wildlife

BEARS

Safety in bear country starts with knowledge and appropriate behavior. With the exception of Alaska and Canada, the Northern Rockies harbor the highest density of grizzly bears, and black bears find likable habitat here, too. For safety while watching bears, maintain the distance of a football field between you.

Hike safely by making vocal noise on the trails. Do not rely on the bells sold in gift shops to alert bears to your presence. Guides jokingly call them "dinner bells." Bells are ineffective and incur wrathful glares from hikers who loathe them. To check the bells' effectiveness out hiking, see how close you are to oncoming hikers before you hear their ringing. Sometimes, it's too close! Bear bells are best as a souvenir, not as a substitution for human noise on the trail. Talk, sing, hoot, and holler. You'll feel silly at first, but after a while, you'll realize it's something everyone does.

Many hikers carry **pepper spray** to deter aggressive, attacking bears. They are not repellents like bug sprays to be sprayed on the human body, tents, or gear. Instead, spray the capsicum derivative directly into a bear's face, aiming for the eyes and nose. While pepper sprays have repelled some attacking bears, wind and rain may reduce effectiveness, as will the product's age. Small, purse-sized pepper sprays are not adequate for bears; carry an eight-ounce can, which can be purchased in most outdoor stores in the Northern Rockies, and practice how to use it. Pepper spray is not protection: Carrying it does not lessen the need for making noise in bear country. Pepper sprays are not allowed by airlines unless checked in luggage, and only brands with USEPA labels may cross through Canadian customs.

Bears are dangerous around food—be it a carcass a bruin may be guarding in the woods or a cooler left in a campsite. Protecting bears and protecting yourself starts with being conscious of food, including wrappers and crumbs. Tidbits dropped along the trail attract wildlife, as do "biodegradable" apple cores chucked into the forest. Pick up what you drop and pack out all garbage, so you will not be leaving a Hansel and Gretel trail for bears.

MOUNTAIN LIONS

Mostly unseen because of their nocturnal wanderings, these large cats are a sight to behold in daylight. They rarely prey on humans, but they can—especially small kids. While hiking, make noise to avoid surprising a lion. Hike with others, and keep kids close. If you do stumble upon a lion, do not run. Be calm. Group together and look big, waving arms overhead. Look at the cat from peripheral vision rather than staring straight on as you back slowly away. If the lion attacks, fight back with everything: rocks, sticks, or kicking.

BISON, MOOSE, AND OTHER WILDLIFE

Bison can be as dangerous as bears. Gorings frequently occur despite the docile appearance of the animals. Moose also can be lethal with both antlers and hooves. For safety, maintain a distance of 25 yards from most wildlife and 100 yards from bears and wolves.

First Aid

DEHYDRATION

Many first-time visitors find the Northern Rockies to be surprisingly arid, despite the green appearance. Fight fluid loss by drinking plenty of water—especially when hiking. Altitude, sun exposure, wind, and exercise can all lead to dehydration, which manifests in yellow urine (rather than clear), lightheadedness, headaches, dizziness, rapid breathing and heart rate, and fatigue. If you feel a headache coming on, try drinking water. If you hike with children, monitor their fluid intake. For mild dehydration, sports drinks can restore the balance of body fluids, electrolytes, and salt. Severe cases of dehydration may need intravenous fluids; treat these as a medical emergency and get to a hospital.

GIARDIA

Lakes and streams can carry parasites such as *Giardia lamblia,* which if ingested causes cramping, nausea, and severe diarrhea for an exceptionally long period of time. Tap water in the park campgrounds and picnic areas has been treated (you'll definitely taste the strong chlorine in some systems), but if you drink untreated water from streams and lakes, you run the risk of ingesting the cysts. Seek medical attention if you suspect a case of giardia.

WATER HAZARDS

Contrary to popular opinion, grizzly bears are not the number one cause of death and accidents in the Northern Rockies—drowning is. Be cautious around lakes, streams, and waterfalls. Waters are swift, frigid, full of submerged obstacles, and unforgiving. Be especially careful on rocks and logs around fast-moving streams; moss and algae can make the rocks slippery.

Yellowstone's gorgeous hydrothermic features can be deadly, too. In many, water bubbles above boiling, and what looks like solid ground may only be a thin crust that can give way with the weight of a human. Stay on designated boardwalks and trails. Toxic gases spew in some of the geyser basins. If you feel sick, leave the area immediately.

ALTITUDE

The Northern Rockies climb in elevation. Some visitors from coastal regions may feel the effects of altitude—a lightheadedness, headache, or shortness of breath—in high zones like Logan Pass in Glacier, the Yellowstone plateau, and the Beartooth Highway. In most cases, slowing down a hiking pace helps, along with drinking lots of fluids and giving the body time to acclimatize. If symptoms are more dramatic, descend in elevation as soon as possible.

Altitude also increases the effects of UV radiation. Above the tree line, you can actually feel cool but still redden with sunburn. Use a strong sunscreen to prevent burning. Sunglasses and a hat will also add protection.

CREVASSES AND SNOWBRIDGES

While ice can look solid to step on, it harbors unseen caverns beneath. Crevasses (large vertical cracks) are difficult to see, and snowbridges can collapse with the weight of a person. Unless you have training in glacier travel, stay off the ice. Even Glacier National Park's tiny ice fields have caused fatalities. Snowfields also demand respect. Steep slopes can run out into rocks, trees, or over cliffs. If sliding for fun, choose a location with a safe runout. Do not travel across steep snowfields unless appropriately equipped with an ice axe and the knowledge of how to use it.

HYPOTHERMIA AND FROSTBITE

Because mountain weather can deteriorate from a summer balm to a winter snowstorm, hypothermia is a very real threat. At onset, the body's inner core loses heat, thus reducing mental and physical functions. It's insidious and progressively subtle: Watch for uncontrolled shivering, incoherence, poor judgment, fumbling, mumbling, and slurred speech. Exhausted, physically unprepared, and ill-clad

CAMPING IN BEAR COUNTRY

Prime grizzly bear habitat and black bear territory makes up most of the Northern Rocky Mountains. Where bears are plentiful, campgrounds require strict food- and garbage-management practices. Even in areas with less frequent bear visitation, properly storing food and garbage prevents problems with other wildlife, such as deer, squirrels, jays, and rodents.

• When not in immediate use, store all food, meat, cooking appliances, utensils, pots, pans, canned foods, toiletries, and empty or full food storage containers in a closed, hard-sided vehicle during the day and at night. Coolers and beverage containers should also be stored inside vehicles, as should garbage.

• For campers traveling on bicycles, motorcycles, or open vehicles, many campgrounds provide brown metal food lockers or **bear boxes** for storing food. Use these to store food, cooking gear, toiletries, and garbage, but do not leave the garbage in the bear box. Dispose of it properly in a bear-resistant trash container. In case bear boxes are not available, carry 30 feet of rope for hanging food supplies. Hang food 20 feet from the ground and 10 feet from the trunk of a tree.

• Store all pet items that may attract or provide a reward to wildlife inside vehicles. This includes pet food, empty food dishes, and toys. Stock feed should also be stowed in hard-sided vehicles.

• When hiking or walking in the woods, make noise. To avoid surprising a bear, use your voice. Sing loudly, hoot, holler, or clap your hands. Bears tend to recognize human sounds as ones to avoid and usually scoot off if they hear people approaching. Consciously make loud noise in thick brushy areas, around blind corners, near babbling streams, and against the wind.

• Hike with other people in broad daylight, avoiding early mornings, late evenings,

hikers are most at risk. You can avoid becoming hypothermic by donning rain gear and warm layers. Don't let yourself get wet. Also, leave the cotton clothing back in the car; instead wear moisture-wicking layers that you can adjust to stay dry.

If someone in your party is hypothermic, get him or her sheltered and into dry clothing. Warm liquid can help heat the body, but be sure it's nonalcoholic and noncaffeinated. Build a fire for warmth. If the victim cannot regain body warmth, crawl into a sleeping bag for skin-to-skin contact with the victim. Seek medical help.

Frostbite, which usually affects extremities when exposed to very cold temperatures, causes the tissues to freeze, resulting in hard, pale, and cold skin. As the area thaws, the flesh becomes red and painful. Prevent frostbite by watching the hands, feet, nose, and ears for discoloration and wearing appropriate clothing. Warm the hands in armpits, and cover the nose and ears with dry, gloved hands. If frostbitten, do not rub the affected skin, let thawed areas refreeze, or thaw frozen areas if a chance of refreezing exists. Seek medical help.

BLISTERS

Blister prevention starts with recognition of "hot spots" or rubs. Before any blister forms, apply Moleskin or New Skin to the sensitive area. Both act as another layer of skin. Moleskin adheres to the skin, like a thick Band-Aid, with its fuzzy covering absorbing friction. New Skin, looking and smelling like fingernail polish, rubs off gradually, absorbing friction instead of the skin. Be aware that New Skin must be reapplied frequently and should not be used on open sores. In a pinch, duct tape can be slapped on potential trouble spots.

and night. Avoid hiking alone. Keep children near.

- Avoid bears' feeding areas. Since bears must gain weight before winter, eating is imperative. Often, bears will pack in 20,000 calories in a day. In the early season, glacier lily bulbs attract grizzlies for their high nutritional value. By midseason, cow parsnip patches provide sustenance, in between high-protein carrion. If you stumble across an animal carcass, leave the area immediately and notify a ranger. In August, huckleberry patches provide high amounts of sugar. Detour widely around feeding bears.

- Never approach a bear. Watch its body language: A bear that stands on hind legs may just be trying to get a good smell or better viewpoint. On the other hand, head swaying, teeth clacking, laid-back ears, a lowered head, and huffing or woofing are signs of agitation. Clear out!

- If you do surprise a bear, back away. Contrary to all inclinations, do not run! Instead, walk backward slowly, talking quietly and turning sideways or bending your knees to appear smaller and non-threatening. Avoid direct eye contact, as the animal kingdom interprets eye contact as a challenge; instead, avert your eyes. Leave your pack on; it can protect you if the bear attacks.

- In case of an attack by a bear you surprised, use pepper spray if you have it. Protect yourself and your vulnerable parts by assuming a fetal position on the ground with your hands around the back of your neck. Play dead. Only move again when you are sure the bear has vacated the area.

- If a bear stalks you as food, which is rare, or attacks at night, fight back, using any means at hand. Grab pepper spray, shout, hit with sticks, or throw rocks to show the bear you are not an easy food source. Try to escape up something, like a building or tree.

Once a blister occurs, apply Second Skin, a product developed for burns that cools the blister off and cushions it. Cover Second Skin with Moleskin, which absorbs future rubbing and holds the Second Skin in place. Also, marketed under several brand names, specialty blister bandages promote healing. Apply the adhesive bandage carefully with hand heat to mold it to the foot surface. Leave it in place until the blister begins to callus. Check placement often, as these bandages and moleskin tend to migrate away from the blister.

HANTAVIRUS

The hantavirus infection is contracted by inhaling the dust from deer mice urine and droppings. Once infected, you'll feel flu-like symptoms set in; seek medical attention if you suspect contact with the virus. To protect yourself, avoid areas thick with rodents, their burrows, and woodpiles. Store all food in rodent-proof containers. If you find rodent dust in your gear or tent, spray with a mix of water and bleach (1.5 cups bleach to one gallon water).

CAMPING EQUIPMENT CHECKLIST

GROUP GEAR
- 30-foot bear pole rope
- Aluminum foil
- Camp chairs
- Camp table
- Can opener
- Coffee cone and filters
- Cooking utensils
- Cooler
- Corkscrew
- Dishwashing tubs
- Duct tape
- Eating utensils
- Firewood
- Food
- Fuel for stove
- Garbage bags
- Ground tarp or tent footprint
- Hatchet
- Kindling and newspaper
- Lanterns
- Lighter and matches
- Maps, GPS, and compass
- Mugs, plates, bowls
- Parachute cord for tarps
- Pot holder
- Pots and pans with lids
- Rain tarps
- Salt, pepper, and spices
- Soap and sponge
- Stove
- Tent with rain-fly
- Toilet paper and trowel
- Utility knife
- Water filter
- Water jugs
- Ziploc bags

SAFETY
- First-aid kit
- Insect repellent
- Pepper spray
- Sunscreen

PERSONAL GEAR
- Bandana
- Batteries
- Flashlight or headlamp
- Fleece top and pants
- Gloves
- Hiking boots
- Rain jacket and pants
- Sleeping bag and pad
- Sunglasses
- Sun hat or ball cap
- Swimsuit
- Toiletries
- Warm hat and gloves
- Water bottle
- Water sandals

RECREATIONAL GEAR
- Binoculars and spotting scopes
- Camera
- Cribbage board
- Day pack
- Fishing rod and tackle
- Kayak, raft, or canoe
- Mountain bike and helmet
- Paddles and personal flotation devices
- Playing cards
- Trekking poles

YELLOWSTONE AND GRAND TETON

Located a full day's drive south of Glacier National Park, Yellowstone and Teton National Parks attract about three million visitors a year—most packed into a short summer season when sightseeing and hiking bring you face to face with bison, pronghorn antelope, and grizzly bears. Yellowstone and Grand Teton National Parks are prime wildlife watching areas. Bring the binoculars for enhanced viewing. Yellowstone holds 12 drive-up campgrounds. To the south, Grand Teton offers six large campgrounds. Surrounding Yellowstone, three small towns neighbor northern entrances: West Yellowstone, Gardiner, and Cooke City. While RV parks and national forest campgrounds ring the park's perimeters, camping inside the parks lets you smell the fuming caldera and hear the howl of wolves at night.

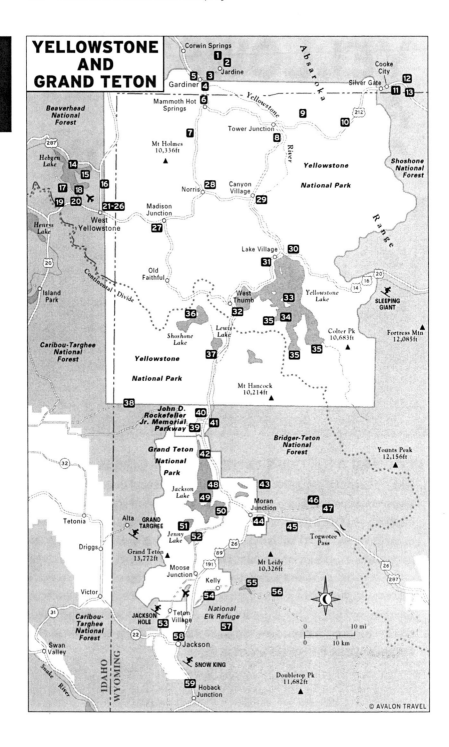

1 BEAR CREEK

Scenic rating: 5

in the Absaroka Mountains in Gallatin National Forest

In Montana's Absaroka Mountains, Bear Creek Campground, elevation 7,200 feet, sits on the edge of the Absaroka-Beartooth Wilderness. The narrow, forested Bear Creek Valley climbs up to peaks topping out above 10,000 feet. Mountain bikes and ATVs can tour the Forest Service roads on the slopes of Ash Mountain east of the campground, but not into the wilderness. Bear Creek Trail, which departs from a trailhead 0.3 mile north of the campground, follows the creek 2.4 miles to trail #620, which accesses Knox and Fish Lake as well as the ridgeline north of Ash Mountain.

In a scrappy mixed fir and pine forest, the remote campground is for those seeking absolute solitude with only the sounds of nature—jays squawking, squirrels chattering, and a burbling creek. The campsites line up along the creek with flat spaces for tents. The first two sites are well-used, but the more difficult to reach sites are overgrown. Small lupine and paintbrush meadows weave through the campground.

Campsites, facilities: The campground has four primitive RV or tent campsites. RVs are limited to 21 feet. With large potholes and no turnaround space on the campground road, trailers are not recommended, and a high-clearance vehicle will help. Scout all campground roads before driving them. Facilities include rock fire rings and a pit toilet. No drinking water is available. Bring your own, or treat creek water. Pack out your trash. Pets are permitted.

Reservations, fees: Reservations are not accepted. Camping is free. Open mid-June–October, depending on snow.

Directions: From Gardiner, drive northeast on Jardine Road for 5.4 miles. (The pavement ends quickly.) In Jardine, turn right over the worn wooden bridge onto Bear Creek Road (Forest Road 493) and climb on the potholed, single-lane road with turnouts for five miles to a Y. Take the left fork for 0.2 mile and turn left into the campground. Warning: The campground road is extremely narrow.

GPS Coordinates: N 45° 6.661' W 110° 36.016'

Contact: Gallatin National Forest, Gardiner Ranger Station, P.O. Box 5, Hwy. 89 S., Gardiner, MT 59030, 406/848-7375, www.fs.usda.gov/gallatin.

2 TIMBER CAMP

Scenic rating: 7

in the Absaroka Mountains in Gallatin National Forest

At 7,182 feet Montana's Absaroka Mountains, Timber Camp enjoys a high subalpine meadow on the slopes of Ash Mountain, which tops out over 10,000 feet. Because of the forest and the steep terrain, the peak is not visible from the campground. Across the road from the campground, a Forest Service spur road climbs up the west slope, a road explored by mountain bikers and ATVers. Within three miles in both directions on the road, hikers can access trails into the Absaroka-Beartooth Wilderness. Bear Creek Trailhead sits to the north, Pine Creek Trailhead to the south.

Ultra-quiet campsites tuck under mature Douglas firs for protection from weather and partial shade. The campsites surround a large open meadow bursting with July wildflowers—cow parsnips, lupines, sticky geraniums. Rough, unnumbered sites with forest duff spaces for tents are spread out for privacy, but they are in sight of each other because of the open meadow. A creek runs along the camp's north side. Prepare for copious mosquitoes.

Campsites, facilities: The primitive campground has five RV or tent campsites. RVs are limited to 21 feet. Facilities include picnic tables and fire rings with grills at three sites, rock fire rings at two sites, and a pit toilet. No drinking water is available. Bring your own, or treat creek water. Pack out your trash. Pets are permitted.

Reservations, fees: Reservations are not accepted. Camping is free. Open mid-June-October, depending on snow.

Directions: From Gardiner, drive northeast on Jardine Road for 5.4 miles (the pavement ends quickly). In Jardine, turn right over the worn wooden bridge onto Bear Creek Road (Forest Road 493) and climb for 4.2 miles. The road narrows to a potholed single lane with turnouts. Turn left into the campground. Scout out the spur roads into the campsites—some have deep muddy holes.

GPS Coordinates: N 45° 5.743' W 110° 36.323'

Contact: Gallatin National Forest, Gardiner Ranger Station, P.O. Box 5, Hwy. 89 S., Gardiner, MT 59030, 406/848-7375, www.fs.usda.gov/gallatin.

🄳 EAGLE CREEK
🚶 🚲 🛶 🚤 ⚓ 🏠 ♿ 🚐 ⛺

Scenic rating: 8
in the Absaroka Mountains in Gallatin National Forest

Within three miles of Yellowstone National Park, Eagle Creek offers an inexpensive place to camp in Montana with expansive views of the park's north slopes. Eagle Creek is the closest Forest Service campground to the park's north entrance. Surrounded by an arid sagebrush slope, the habitat often draws wildlife, such as elk. Bring binoculars! Hiking is available north of Jardine at Bear Creek, from Gardiner along the Yellowstone River, and in Yellowstone at Mammoth Hot Springs. Gardiner is also the local headquarters for rafting and fishing outfitters, and the Yellowstone River, which flows through town, provides white water for rafting and kayaking.

The campground sits on an open hillside, providing little shade and no privacy between most of the campsites. Site 7 is the exception, tucked into aspens. Eagle Creek runs along the west side of the campground, surrounded by brush, aspens, and willows. The grassy campground—green in July, brown by August—is roomy enough for tents, but many of the sites are sloped. Stock corrals sit adjacent to the main campground road; two campsites ring the dusty parking lot. Views from the campground extend across the valley to Mammoth Hot Springs and Yellowstone National Park's rugged northern peaks.

Campsites, facilities: The campground has 16 RV or tent campsites. RVs are limited to 40 feet. Facilities include picnic tables, fire rings with grills, bear boxes, stock facilities, and vault toilet (wheelchair-accessible). No drinking water is available. Bring your own; to treat creek water. Pack out your trash. Leashed pets are permitted.

Reservations, fees: Reservations are not accepted. Campsites cost $7. An extra vehicle costs $3. Cash or check. Open year-round.

Directions: From Gardiner, climb the hairpins northeast on Jardine Road for 2.1 miles. (The pavement ends in 0.3 mile.) Turn left into the campground.

GPS Coordinates: N 45° 2.581' W 110° 40.840'

Contact: Gallatin National Forest, Gardiner Ranger Station, P.O. Box 5, Hwy. 89 S., Gardiner, MT 59030, 406/848-7375, www.fs.usda.gov/gallatin.

🄴 ROCKY MOUNTAIN CAMPGROUND
🚶 🚲 🛶 🚤 ⚓ 🏠 ♿ 🚐 ⛺

Scenic rating: 8
in downtown Gardiner

Located at 5,357 feet in elevation, Rocky Mountain Campground sits in downtown Gardiner, Montana within walking distance to shopping, restaurants, ranger station, visitors centers, art galleries, and groceries. The campground is four blocks from the Roosevelt Arch, the north entrance to Yellowstone National Park. Gardiner is a hub for guided fishing, rafting, kayaking, zipline, and horseback-riding outfitters. Four raft companies guide trips on the Yellowstone River, which slices through town. Several fly shops can provide advice on the best places to fish the river and what flies to use when. From town, a trail traverses east along the Yellowstone River. Mountain bikers head to the five-mile abandoned railroad bed paralleling the Yellowstone River between Gardiner and the park boundary at Reese Creek.

On a bluff in Gardiner, the sunny campground commands views of the town, Yellowstone River, and north slopes of Yellowstone National Park. The park has two types of campsites: standard and deluxe. Many of the sites rim the edge of the bluff, with the views, and a few tuck under the shade of large trees. The campsites, which are stacked up in parking-lot fashion lacking in privacy, are grassy with gravel parking pads. Traffic noise is audible. Toilet and shower facilities were renovated in 2011.

Campsites, facilities: The campground has 71 RV campsites. RVs are limited to 45 feet. The campground has 28 pull-through campsites, 50 sites that accommodate rigs with four slide-outs, and full hookups for water, sewer, and electricity up to 50 amps. Facilities include flush toilets (wheelchair-accessible), showers, launderette, picnic tables, community campfire area, drinking water, wireless Internet, cable TV, propane, miniature golf, and disposal station. Leashed pets are permitted, but only two per campsite.

Reservations, fees: Reservations are accepted. Campsites cost $52-58. Rates are for two people; $3 for each additional person. Seniors can get a discount, and rates in shoulder seasons are cheaper. Add on 7 percent Montana bed tax. Cash, check, or credit card. Open mid-April-mid-October.

Directions: In Gardiner on Highway 89, turn northeast onto Jardine Road. Drive 0.1 mile up the hill and turn right.

GPS Coordinates: N 45° 1.975' W 110° 42.167'

Contact: Rocky Mountain Campground, 14 Jardine Rd., Gardiner, MT 59030, 406/848-7251 or 877/534-6931, www.rockymountain-campground.com.

⑤ YELLOWSTONE RV PARK

Scenic rating: 7

in Gardiner

At 5,200 feet, Yellowstone RV Park overlooks the Yellowstone River just outside downtown Gardiner, Montana. Views across the canyon sometimes lend sightings of wildlife—moose, antelope, bighorns, elk, deer, ospreys, and bald eagles. The campground is 1.3 miles from the Roosevelt Arch, the north entrance to Yellowstone National Park. Gardiner is a hub for fishing, rafting, kayaking, zipline, and horseback-riding outfitters. Four raft companies guide trips on the Yellowstone River. Several fly shops can provide advice on the best places to fish the river and what flies to use when. From town, a trail traverses east along the Yellowstone River. Mountain bikers head to the five-mile abandoned railroad bed paralleling the Yellowstone River between Gardiner and the park boundary at Reese Creek.

The campground has two rows of RV sites—one overlooks the river and the other lines up like a parking lot. The campsites are open, sunny, and speckled with a few low trees. A rail fence runs along the river canyon to mark where the slope drops to the water. A dirt road with gravel parking pads loops through the lawn sites but kicks up dust. Views span the brown, barren sagebrush canyon sweeping up from the river. With the campground squeezed between the river and the highway, the sounds of both permeate the campsites. Winds frequently blow through the canyon.

CAMPING IN YELLOWSTONE

Yellowstone, the nation's first national park, spills from mountains to high plateaus, covering more land than Delaware and Rhode Island combined. Its forests and prairies hold 12 drive-up campgrounds. Inside Yellowstone National Park, the Grand Loop Road forms a figure-eight through the caldera, where shaggy brown bison graze next to steam billowing from hot pools. Small campgrounds cluster in the north, while large campgrounds verging on the size of small towns populate the Old Faithful, canyon, and lake areas. For those looking to escape crowds, remote boat-in campsites rim the arms of Yellowstone and Shoshone Lakes.

- **To camp closest to geysers, hot pools, and mud pots:** Head to Mammoth, Norris, Madison, or Canyon Campgrounds.
- **To camp near the famed wildlife watching of Lamar Valley:** Aim for Tower, Slough Creek, or Pebble Creek Campgrounds in the northeast corner.

- **To explore the park's lakes:** Go to Grant, Fishing Bridge, Bridge Bay, or Lewis Lake in the southeast corner. (Fishing Bridge offers hookups for RVs.) Better yet, hit the backcountry office in Bridge Bay for permits for remote, quiet boat-in campsites flanking Yellowstone Lake's 110 miles of shoreline, or kayak or canoe into Shoshone Lake. On both lakes, be ready for afternoon winds.

- **To cast into blue-ribbon trout streams:** Anglers should camp at Madison Junction to fish the Madison River or at Fishing Bridge, Canyon, or Tower Fall to fish the Yellowstone River.

Yellowstone's northern entrances harbor three small towns, West Yellowstone, Gardiner, and Cooke City, that provide RV parks, nearby national forest campgrounds, and services for campers, plus outfitters for rafting, horseback riding, and fishing.

Campsites, facilities: This campground has 46 RV campsites and can accommodate tents in 10 of them. RV pull-throughs can fit rigs up to 70 feet. Hookups are available for water, sewer, and electricity up to 50 amps. Facilities include picnic tables, flush toilets (wheelchair-accessible), showers, drinking water, cable TV, launderette, and wireless Internet. Leashed pets are permitted.

Reservations, fees: Reservations are accepted. Campsites cost $40-45. Rates are based on a maximum of six people per site. Add on 7 percent Montana bed tax. Cash, check, or credit card. Open May-October.

Directions: From downtown Gardiner where the bridge crosses the Yellowstone River, drive northwest on Highway 89 for one mile to the campground entrance to the south.
GPS Coordinates: N 45° 2.324' W 110° 43.438'
Contact: Yellowstone RV Park and Campground, 117 Hwy. 89 S., Gardiner, MT 59030,

406/848-7496, www.ventureswestinc.com/YellowstoneRVPark.htm.

6 MAMMOTH

Scenic rating: 8
on the upper Grand Loop in Yellowstone National Park

BEST (

Located on an arid slope at 6,039 feet at Mammoth Hot Springs, Mammoth Campground offers a sweeping view of the dry, sagebrush canyon and Mount Everts. With elk hanging around the lawns, the town—historical Fort Yellowstone—contains restaurants, gift shops, Albright Visitor Center, medical clinic, horseback trail rides, showers at Mammoth Hotel, gas, post office, and Yellowstone's park headquarters. More services are available about 10 miles north in Gardiner, including guided rafting, kayaking, fishing, and ziplines. Boardwalks, stairs, and trails loop through steaming Mammoth Hot Springs travertine terraces. The narrow, curvy Upper Terrace Drive (no buses, RVs, or trailers) arcs through more mineral terraces. Other trails lead to the Beaver Ponds, Sepulcher Mountain, and Lava Creek. Mountain bikers can ride the six-mile Bunsen Peak Road looping around 8,564-foot Bunsen Peak. The Gardner River offers trout fishing and is a good river for beginning and young anglers. For soaking in a natural hot springs, visit Boiling River after high water recedes in July. Located off the entrance road north of the campground, a 0.5-mile hike leads to the volunteer-maintained hot pools.

If Mammoth Campground were any other place, most people would bypass it. The sagebrush and grass campsites with gravel parking pads have little privacy, little shade, and are exposed to winds and weather. Views include other campsites. Because the campground is tucked in a hairpin on the highway, you'll hear and see vehicles both above and below the campground. Nevertheless, it is a popular campground for exploring the park's northwest corner; in summer, plan to arrive early to claim a campsite. RVs have the advantage of pull-through at most sites.

Campsites, facilities: Mammoth Campground has 85 RV or tent campsites. RVs are limited to 75 feet. Fifty-one campsites have tent platforms. Facilities include picnic tables, fire rings with grills, flush toilets, drinking water, amphitheater for interpretive programs, and garbage service. Leashed pets are permitted. Wheelchair-accessible facilities include toilets and five campsites.

Reservations, fees: Reservations are not accepted. Campsites cost $20. Shared hiker and biker campsites cost $5 per person. Cash or check. Open year-round.

Directions: From the north entrance to Yellowstone National Park, drive south for five miles on the north entrance road, or from park headquarters in Mammoth, drive 0.7

© BECKY LOMAX

Trails lead through travertine terraces at Mammoth Hot Springs.

mile toward Gardiner. Turn west into the campground.

GPS Coordinates: N 44° 58.377' W 110° 41.600'

Contact: Yellowstone National Park, P.O. Box 168, Yellowstone, WY 82190-0168, 307/344-7381, www.nps.gov/yell.

7 INDIAN CREEK

🚶 🚲 🛶 🏕 ♿ 🚐 ⛺

Scenic rating: 8

on the upper Grand Loop in Yellowstone National Park

BEST (

Sitting at 7,298 feet in elevation, Indian Creek perches at the confluence of the Gardner River, Obsidian Creek, and Indian Creek in Yellowstone's northwest corner. North of the campground, the Grand Loop Road passes the marshy meadows of Gardners Hole and Swan Lake, which offers excellent wildlife-watching opportunities for elk and bears.

Anglers can fish for small brook trout in the Gardner River and the two creeks. Mountain bikers can ride the six-mile Bunsen Peak Road looping around 8,564-foot Bunsen Peak. A separate hiking trail goes to its summit. From the campground, a trail runs 12.8 miles west to Bighorn Pass. Several miles south on the road, other trailheads depart for Grizzly Lake (2.9 miles), Trilobite Lake (7.9 miles), and Mt. Holmes (10 miles).

Indian Creek sat in the midst of the 1988 wildfire that ripped through Yellowstone. While silvered trunks litter hillsides, fast-growing lodgepoles have converted the slopes to green again. A loose lodgepole forest lends partial shade to the campground as grassy meadows add sunny spots. Views of the surrounding peaks include the 10,023-foot Antler Peak to the west. Indian Creek is smaller in size and located away from Yellowstone's big hubs, so this campground is quieter and more relaxing than the park's larger campgrounds. The campsites are also spaced out a little more for privacy, and those adjacent to larger meadows can offer evening and morning wildlife-watching.

Campsites, facilities: The campground has 75 RV or tent campsites. Ten campsites can accommodate RVs up to 40 feet; 35 campsites can fit RVs up to 30 feet. Generators are not permitted. Facilities include picnic tables, fire rings with grills, vault toilets, drinking water, firewood and ice for sale, bear boxes, and garbage service. Leashed pets are permitted. Wheelchair-accessible toilets and campsites are available.

Reservations, fees: Reservations are not accepted. Campsites cost $15. Shared hiker and biker campsites cost $5 per person. Cash or check. Open mid-June-early September.

Directions: From Mammoth, drive 8.5 miles south on the Grand Loop Road, or from Norris Junction, drive 12.5 miles north. Turn west and drive 0.3 mile to the campground.

GPS Coordinates: N 44° 53.200' W 110° 44.093'

Contact: Yellowstone National Park, P.O. Box 168, Yellowstone, WY 82190-0168, 307/344-7381, www.nps.gov/yell.

8 TOWER FALL

Scenic rating: 7
on the upper Grand Loop in Yellowstone National Park

Located at 6,535 feet on the east side of the Grand Loop, Tower Fall Campground sits above the Tower Falls Complex in Yellowstone National Park. The area buzzes in summer with visitors stopping at the popular attraction, which includes a general store, picnic tables, and a one-mile trail to view the 132-foot falls and the Yellowstone River. Fishing is available in the river. A trail also tours up Tower Creek. Roosevelt Lodge, 2.5 miles north, offers horseback trail rides, stagecoach rides, nightly western cookout dinners, gas, convenience store, restaurant, and showers. To the south, mountain bikers can climb three miles on a dirt road up Mt. Washburn, at 10,243 feet the tallest mountain in Yellowstone. Hikers can also ascend to the lookout at the summit via the south side trail.

On a bluff above the Grand Loop Road, the campground sits on an arid north-facing hillside in a sparse, mixed forest of firs and pines that only shade some of the campsites. Dry grasses, dust, and forest duff make up the campsite floors, which are surrounded by green wild grasses in early July but brown in August. The open campground permits views of neighboring campers; sites around the outside of the loop have more privacy. Sites at the lower end of the campground overlook employee housing. Most of the campsites include views of forested and sagebrush slopes. Evening ranger programs may be offered in summer. Plan to arrive by 11am to claim a spot.

Campsites, facilities: The campground has 31 RV or tent campsites. RVs are limited to 30 feet, but parking pads work better for smaller RVs, such as truck campers, minivans, and trailer popups. Facilities include picnic tables, fire rings with grills, vault toilets (wheelchair-accessible), drinking water, bear boxes, and garbage service. Generators are not allowed. Leashed pets are permitted.

Reservations, fees: Reservations are not accepted. Campsites cost $12. Shared hiker and biker campsites cost $5 per person. Cash or check. Open late May-September.

Directions: From Tower-Roosevelt Junction, drive three miles south on the Grand Loop Road, or from Canyon Village, drive 16 miles north. Turn west and drive 0.3 mile up the hill to the campground. The campground road has one hairpin turn.

GPS Coordinates: N 44° 53.403' W 110° 23.381'

Contact: Yellowstone National Park, P.O. Box 168, Yellowstone, WY 82190-0168, 307/344-7381, www.nps.gov/yell.

9 SLOUGH CREEK

Scenic rating: 8

in the Absaroka Mountains in Yellowstone National Park

BEST(

At 6,249 feet, Slough Creek is prized for its small size, quiet creekside ambiance, and wildlife watching. The campground sits in the foothills of the Absaroka Mountains at the confluence of Slough Creek and Buffalo Creek. Fly-fishing anglers go after Yellowstone cutthroat trout in the creeks. Trails run up both creek drainages in the Absaroka Mountains, although they travel above the creeks rather than adjacent to them. A few miles west of the entrance road, a trail ascends Specimen Ridge overlooking the Lamar Valley. For wildlife watching, the entrance road to the campground provides several pullover spots to set up scopes to survey the wide-open sagebrush meadow hillsides littered with glacial erratics. You can often see bison, pronghorn, bears, bighorn sheep, and sometimes wolves. Nearby, a convenience store, gas, showers, restaurant, cowboy cookout, horseback trail rides, and stagecoach rides are at Tower-Roosevelt Junction.

This campground is for those who enjoy solitude away from crowds, so plan to arrive early to claim a site. Its remote location off the main park roads guarantees silence so that you can hear wolves howl and owls hoot at night. Various sunny and shaded campsites are available, most lining up along the creeks. Sites 16 and above are better suited for tents but not limited to them. The campground rims a huge sagebrush and wildflower meadow that can be good for spotting elk, bison, and foxes. Some sites are more private than others, tucked behind trees or brush, but from most, you'll see other campers. The park service spruced up the campground landscaping in 2013.

Campsites, facilities: The campground has 23 RV or tent campsites. RVs are limited to 30 feet, but check the site first before pulling in. Generators are not permitted. Facilities include picnic tables, fire rings with grills, vault toilets (wheelchair-accessible), bear boxes, drinking water, garbage service, and campground host. Leashed pets are permitted.

Reservations, fees: Reservations are not accepted. Sites cost $15. Cash or check. Open mid-June-October.

Directions: From Tower-Roosevelt Junction, drive 5.8 miles east on the northeast entrance road, or from the northeast entrance station, drive 23.2 miles west. Turn north onto the dirt road and drive 2.3 miles to the campground. GPS Coordinates: N 44° 56.915' W 110° 18.410'

Contact: Yellowstone National Park, P.O. Box 168, Yellowstone, WY 82190-0168, 307/344-7381, www.nps.gov/yell.

10 PEBBLE CREEK

Scenic rating: 8

in the Absaroka Mountains in Yellowstone
National Park

BEST (

At 6,900 feet, Pebble Creek Campground cuddles under high mountains, in contrast to Yellowstone's other campgrounds. The Absaroka
Mountains—snowcapped well into June—rise
to 10,000 feet around the Soda Butte Valley
that descends from the campground. In summer, Soda Butte Creek lines with anglers casting flies because of its reputation for prime
trout fishing. Pebble Creek has fishing, too.
Soda Butte Valley and the adjacent Lamar
Valley offer outstanding wildlife watching for
bears, bison, elk, pronghorn, bighorn sheep,
coyote, and wolves. Guides often refer to the
area as the Serengeti of the West. Yellowstone
Association Institute (406/848-2400, www.
yellowstoneassociation.org), headquartered in
the Lamar Valley, offers educational programs
for all ages. For hikers, the 12-mile Pebble
Creek Trail loops northeast to the Warm Creek
Trailhead near the northeast park entrance.
Nearby, a short 0.6-mile trail tours around
Trout Lake and the Thunderer Cutoff Trail ascends 3.7 miles to Chaw Pass before dropping
15-miles down Cache Creek and the Lamar
River to the Soda Butte Trailhead.

Pebble Creek squeezes its sunny campsites
close together in two loops in a sparse aspen
and lodgepole forest mixed with a wildflower
meadow that blooms in July with cow parsnips,
pink sticky geraniums, and yarrow. While
views include neighboring campers, they also
sweep up to the rugged, glacier-carved high
peaks surrounding the campground. Even
though the campground is removed from the
more hectic areas of the park, vehicles stream
by during the day. But at night, it quiets. The
park service spruced up the campground's
landscaping in 2013.

Campsites, facilities: The campground has
30 RV or tent campsites. RVs are limited to
midsized rigs. Facilities include picnic tables,
fire rings with grills, vault toilets (wheelchair-
accessible), drinking water, garbage service,
bear boxes, and campground hosts. Generators
are not allowed. Leashed pets are permitted.
Reservations, fees: Reservations are not accepted. Sites cost $15. Shared hiker and biker
campsites cost $5 per person. Cash or check.
Open mid-June-September.
Directions: From Tower-Roosevelt Junction,
drive 20 miles east on the northeast entrance
road, or from the northeast entrance station,
drive nine miles west. Turn north onto the dirt
road and drive 0.1 mile to the campground.
GPS Coordinates: N 44° 55.004' W 110°
6.839'
Contact: Yellowstone National Park, P.O. Box
168, Yellowstone, WY 82190-0168, 307/344-
7381, www.nps.gov/yell.

11 SODA BUTTE

Scenic rating: 8

in the Absaroka-Beartooth Mountains in
Gallatin National Forest

Sitting at 7,791 feet, Soda Butte Campground
is the last Forest Service campground for
those heading west into Yellowstone National Park, 4.5 miles from the northeastern
entrance. Located one mile east of Cooke
City, Montana with 10,000-foot-high Sheep
Mountain to the north, the campground is
convenient for hooking up with local outfitters for fly-fishing, hunting, or horse-packing
trips into the Absaroka-Beartooth Wilderness
about two miles north. Several nearby trails
head into the wilderness, but mountain bikes
are permitted only to the border. A 3.5-mile
trail leads to Lady of the Lake. Other nearby
trails climb to several strings of lakes in the
wilderness. Rafters and kayakers head to the
Clarks Fork of the Yellowstone for whitewater, and you can drive the scenic Beartooth
Highway over and back in a day. A four-mile

scenic drive also leads up a Forest Service road to Daisy Pass.

Thinning of beetle-killed trees has opened up much of this campground to sunlight and views. Cow parsnip, sticky pink geranium, lupine, and grass meadows cover most of the campground, interspersed with a few lodgepole pines and spruces that lend privacy to a few sites. The busy highway runs above the campground, but quiets at night, and you can hear Soda Butte Creek burbling. Neighboring campers are visible. Unfortunately, this campground was the site of a tragic bear attack on tenters in 2010, so it no longer permits tents or tent trailers.

Campsites, facilities: This campground has 27 RV and tent campsites. RVs are limited to 48 feet. Facilities include picnic tables, fire rings with grills, vault toilets (wheelchair-accessible), drinking water, bear boxes, garbage service, and campground hosts. Bring your own firewood. Leashed pets are permitted.

Reservations, fees: Reservations are not accepted. Campsites cost $9. An extra vehicle costs $3. Cash or check. Open July-September, depending on snow.

Directions: From Cooke City, drive the Beartooth Highway (Hwy. 212) about one mile east, or from the Chief Joseph Highway (Hwy. 296) junction drive 14 miles west. Turn south at milepost 4.5 into the campground. GPS Coordinates: N 45° 1.388' W 109° 54.947'

Contact: Gallatin National Forest, Gardiner Ranger Station, P.O. Box 5, Hwy. 89 S., Gardiner, MT 59030, 406/848-7375, www.fs.usda.gov/gallatin.

12 COLTER

Scenic rating: 9

in the Absaroka-Beartooth Mountains in Gallatin National Forest

At an elevation of 8,044 feet, Colter Campground sits two miles east of Cooke City, Montana, and six miles from the northeast entrance to Yellowstone National Park. Surrounding peaks climb over 10,000 feet high, and the 900,000-acre Absaroka-Beartooth Wilderness is two miles to the north. Hiking and mountain-biking trails depart 0.2 mile west. The route heads 3.5 miles to Lady of the Lake, and farther to other lakes in the wilderness area. Other nearby trails ascend into the wilderness to pass reams of lakes. Mountain bikers can only travel as far as the wilderness boundary. Rafters and kayakers head to the Clarks Fork of the Yellowstone River for whitewater, and you can drive the scenic Beartooth Highway over and back in a day. Outfitters for horseback riding, fishing, and hunting are available nearby.

Campsites are spread out in this sunny campground in a loose forest of lodgepoles, spruces, and subalpine firs surrounded by wildflower meadows and new growth forest. Sites in the open garner broad views of the meadows and mountains while others tuck into the shade and privacy of trees. Sites on the spur have more privacy than the loop. Noise from the road seeps into the campground, but the route is not a major trucking thoroughfare, so it quiets at night. Reconstruction following logging spruced up the campground with gravel parking pads, gravel campsites, and new facilities. Due a bear attack on tenters in 2010 in the neighboring campground, tents and tent trailers are no longer permitted.

Campsites, facilities: The campground has 18 RV or tent campsites. The largest gravel parking pad can fit RVs up to 66 feet, but the Forest Service recommends RV combinations less than 48 feet because of the access road. Facilities include picnic tables, fire rings with grills, bear boxes, vault toilets (wheelchair-accessible), drinking water, garbage service, and campground hosts. No firewood is available; bring your own. Leashed pets are permitted.

Reservations, fees: Reservations are not accepted. Campsites cost $9. An extra vehicle costs $3. Cash or check. Open July-September, depending on snow.

Directions: From Cooke City, drive the Beartooth Highway (Hwy. 212), about two miles east, or from the Chief Joseph Highway (Hwy. 296) junction, drive 13 miles west. Turn north at milepost 5.6 into the campground. (The sign is off the highway and difficult to see.) GPS Coordinates: N 45° 1.685' W 109° 53.645'

Contact: Gallatin National Forest, Gardiner Ranger Station, P.O. Box 5, Hwy. 89 S., Gardiner, MT 59030, 406/848-7375, www. fs.usda.gov/gallatin.

13 CHIEF JOSEPH

Scenic rating: 7

in the Absaroka-Beartooth Mountains in Gallatin National Forest

On the west end of the Beartooth Scenic Byway, Chief Joseph Campground, elevation 8,037 feet, sits four miles east of Cooke City, Montana, and seven miles from the northeast entrance to Yellowstone National Park. The campground is named after the Nez Perce chief who led his people across Idaho, Wyoming, and Montana while being chased by the U.S. Army. Across the road from the campground are interpretive sites for the Nez Perce National Historic Trail, wildlife nature trail, and Flume Interpretive Trail and Picnic Area. The latter also has a fishing pier, wheelchair-accessible trail, giant rushing waterfall, historical mining artifacts, view of Granite Peak (Montana's highest peak) and access to the Russell Creek Trail that enters the 900,000-acre Absaroka-Beartooth Wilderness. Nearby, a two-mile trail also leads to Curl Lake. Other short hikes lead to Rock Island Lake and Vernon Lake. Mountain bikers can access the local forest roads and trails only up to the wilderness boundary. Fishing, rafting, and kayaking is available in the Clarks Fork of the Yellowstone River, also across the highway from the campground, and you can drive the scenic Beartooth Highway over and back in a

© BECKY LOMAX

The Flume Trail near Chief Joseph Campground leads to historic power generation sites.

day. Outfitters for horseback riding, fishing, and hunting are available nearby.

Tucked into a mature lodgepole pine and spruce forest, Chief Joseph has more large trees than neighboring Soda Butte or Colter Campgrounds. Its one small loop sits close to the highway, so road noise is pervasive; however, it dwindles substantially at night. Reconstruction spruced up the campground with gravel parking pads and campsites plus new facilities, and hazard tree removal in 2013 allowed more sunlight into the shady campground. Tents and tent trailers are not permitted.

Campsites, facilities: The campground has six RV or tent campsites. The largest gravel parking pad can fit RVs up to 60 feet, but the Forest Service advises a limit of 42 feet because of the access road. Facilities include picnic tables, fire rings with grills, vault toilet (wheelchair-accessible), drinking water, bear boxes, garbage service, and campground hosts. No firewood is available; bring your own. Leashed pets are permitted.

Reservations, fees: Reservations are not accepted. Campsites cost $9. An extra vehicle costs $3. Cash or check. Open July-September.

Directions: From the Beartooth Scenic Byway (Highway 212), about four miles east of Cooke City or 11 miles west of the Chief Joseph Highway 296 junction, turn south at milepost 7 into the campground.

GPS Coordinates: N 45° 1.047' W 109° 52.247'

Contact: Gallatin National Forest, Gardiner Ranger Station, P.O. Box 5, Hwy. 89 S., Gardiner, MT 59030, 406/848-7375, www.fs.usda.gov/gallatin.

14 YELLOWSTONE HOLIDAY RV

Scenic rating: 8

on Hebgen Lake

Located on the north shore of Hebgen Lake at 6,555 feet, Yellowstone Holiday RV Campground sits a 15-minute drive from West Yellowstone and the west entrance to Yellowstone National Park. Flanked by the Madison Mountains, Montana's Hebgen Lake is popular for boating, paddling, waterskiing, sailing, and fishing. The campground includes a marina that has a cement boat ramp, boat slips, fuel, trailer parking, and a fish-cleaning station. The marina also rents fishing boats, kayaks, canoes, and paddleboats and sells fishing licenses.

The campground sits on a low open plateau on the lake, within view of the highway, lake, and mountains, which are snowcapped in June. Mowed lawn surrounds the sunny campsites with little shade or protection from afternoon winds. What you give up in privacy, you get back in a broad panorama of views. Most of the sites are back-ins near the water; pull-through sites are behind a set of cabins near the highway. Sites 6, 8, 9, and 11 claim prime waterfront.

Campsites, facilities: The campground has 36 RV campsites. Eight pull-through sites can accommodate big rigs. Hookups include water, sewer, and electricity up to 50 amps. Facilities include picnic tables, fire rings, flush toilets, showers, launderette, general store, propane, marina, horseshoes, volleyball, swimming beach, and camper kitchen. Leashed dogs are permitted.

Reservations, fees: Reservations are accepted. RV sites cost $43-60. Rates less during shoulder seasons. Add on 7 percent Montana bed tax. Cash, check, or credit card. Open mid-May-early September.

Directions: From West Yellowstone, drive north on Highway 191 for eight miles and then turn west onto Highway 287 for five miles. The entrance sits on the south side of the road.

GPS Coordinates: N 44° 48.202' W 111° 12.950'

Contact: Yellowstone Holiday, 16990 Hebgen Lake Rd., West Yellowstone, MT 59758, 406/646-4242 or 877/646-4242, www.yellowstoneholiday.com.

15 RAINBOW POINT

🏊 🛶 ⛴ 🎣 🏕 ♿ 🚐 ⛺

Scenic rating: 8

on Hebgen Lake in Gallatin National Forest

Located at 6,550 feet, Rainbow Point Campground sits on Rainbow Bay, an east arm of Montana's Hebgen Lake, the site of Montana's largest earthquake in 1959. From the beach at the campground, views look northwest to the Madison Range. The campground, about 10 miles north of West Yellowstone and 11 miles from the west entrance to Yellowstone National Park, has a boat launch, which includes a cement ramp, docks, and trailer parking. The lake is popular for swimming, paddling, waterskiing, boating, and fishing—known for its dry fly trout fishing (Montana fishing license needed). Rainbow Bay is more sheltered from winds than the main lake, making it more appealing for canoeing and kayaking. The 16-mile-long lake is also surrounded by summer homes.

Four loops of of the quiet campsites tuck into a thick shady forest of tall lodgepole pines that admit only filtered sunlight. Tree trunks act as privacy fences between the close campsites because little understory can grow beneath the trees. The loops are set back from the lake with only a few sites at the front of loops A and B catching glimpses of blue water across the road and between the trees. Paths lead from the loops to the beach. Big, flat spaces for tents are available.

Campsites, facilities: The campground has 85 RV and tent campsites. RVs are limited to 40 feet. Facilities include picnic tables, fire rings with grills, vault and pit toilets, drinking water, garbage service, electrical hookups at 15 campsites in Loop C, bear boxes, boat launch, firewood for sale, and campground hosts. Leashed pets are permitted. A wheelchair-accessible toilet and one campsite are available.

Reservations, fees: Reservations are accepted (877/444-6777, www.recreation.gov).

Campsites cost $16, plus $6 more for those with electrical hookups. An extra vehicle costs $6. Cash or check. Open mid-May-mid-September.

Directions: From West Yellowstone, drive north on Highway 191 for five miles and turn west onto the two-lane paved Rainbow Point Road (Forest Road 6954) for 3.2 miles. Then turn north onto the gravel Rainbow Point Road (Forest Road 6952) for 1.7 miles. The road veers right to the boat launch, but continue straight to reach the campground. GPS Coordinates: N 44° 46.725' W 111° 10.466'

Contact: Gallatin National Forest, Hebgen Lake District Office, P.O. Box 520, West Yellowstone, MT 59758, 406/823-6961.

16 BAKER'S HOLE

🥾 🚴 🛶 🏕 ♿ 🚐 ⛺

Scenic rating: 7

on the Madison River in Gallatin National Forest

Baker's Hole Campground, which sits at 6,600 feet, is three miles north of West Yellowstone, Montana and four miles from the west entrance to Yellowstone National Park. The campground is strung along a narrow strip of forest in between the highway and the Madison River. In this stretch, the river slows to a crawl as it winds in convoluted oxbows through willow wetlands that provide habitat for moose and birds, plus churn out hordes of mosquitoes. The Madison River is famed for its trout fishing, and West Yellowstone is the headquarters for fishing outfitters. The 1.4-mile Riverside Trail for mountain bikers and hikers tours the river from West Yellowstone.

Located adjacent to the highway, the campground picks up vehicle noise—especially from commercial trucks. Across the road is the Yellowstone Airport, which sees three commercial flights arrive and depart daily in the summer. A paved road loops through the campground, which is forested with short lodgepole pines and blooming with fireweed. Some campsites have views of the mountains, and several campsites overlook the river. Sites, which vary from shady to sunny, are spread out for privacy, but the lack of undergrowth means you'll see a neighboring campsite or two.

Campsites, facilities: The campground has 73 RV and tent campsites. RVs are limited to 75 feet. Facilities include picnic tables, fire rings with grills, electrical hookups at 33 campsites, vault and pit toilets (wheelchair-accessible), drinking water, garbage service, bear boxes, firewood for sale, campground hosts, and a fishing platform. Leashed pets are permitted.

Reservations, fees: Reservations are not accepted. Campsites cost $14, plus $6 for those sites with electricity. An extra vehicle costs $6. Cash or check. Open mid-May-mid-September.

Directions: From West Yellowstone, drive north on Highway 191 for almost three miles. At milepost 2.9, turn east onto the paved road into the campground.

GPS Coordinates: N 44° 42.249' W 111° 6.083'

Contact: Gallatin National Forest, Hebgen Lake District Office, P.O. Box 520, West Yellowstone, MT 59758, 406/823-6961.

🔟 MADISON ARM RESORT

🚴 🏊 🛶 🚐 ⛵ 🐕 🚃 ⛺

Scenic rating: 7

on Hebgen Lake

Madison Arm Resort sits on the south shore of the Madison Arm of Montana's Hebgen Lake at 6,557 feet in elevation. Its sandy beach and marina tuck into a small bay protected by islands of sand that grow larger as the water level in the lake drops throughout the summer. The lake is popular for boating, paddling, fishing, waterskiing, sailing, and swimming. Anglers go after rainbow and brown trout (Montana fishing license needed), and the resort rents out 14-foot aluminum boats with eight horsepower motors, canoes, paddleboats, kayaks, and water-bikes. A buoyed swimming area is available, along with a cement boat ramp and boat slips. The store sells fishing licenses. Bicyclists ride the dirt forest roads in the area. The resort sits 8.5 miles from West Yellowstone and 9.5 miles from the west entrance to Yellowstone National Park.

A forest of tall lodgepole pines surrounds the campground. Tent campsites are along the waterfront between trees, and RV campsites sit back in the trees and open areas. The quiet campground packs its campsites close together; privacy is available only inside the tent or RV. Also, back-in sites can pose difficulties for some RVs squeezing in. The resort tends to get families returning year after year.

Campsites, facilities: The resort has 22 tent campsites and 52 RV campsites with hookups for water, sewer, and up to 30-amp electricity. Pull-through sites can fit large RVs. Facilities include picnic tables, fire rings, flush toilets, showers, launderette, convenience store, propane, firewood for sale, boat rentals, and wireless Internet. Leashed pets are permitted.

Reservations, fees: Reservations are accepted. RV hookups cost $39-42. Tent campsites cost $29. Rates are for two people. Each additional person incurs $5. Add on the 7 percent Montana bed tax. Cash, check, or credit card. Open mid-May-September.

Directions: From West Yellowstone, drive north on Highway 191 for three miles. Turn west onto the dusty gravel Madison Arm Road (Forest Road 291) for 5.3 miles to the resort entrance on the right.

GPS Coordinates: N 44° 44.142' W 111° 11.159'

Contact: Madison Arm Resort, 5475 Madison Arm Rd., West Yellowstone, MT 59758, 406/646-9328, www.madisonarmresort.com.

18 LONESOMEHURST

Scenic rating: 8

on Hebgen Lake in Gallatin National Forest

Located at 6,550 feet, Lonesomehurst Campground sits on the South Fork Arm, a narrow bay on the southern end of Montana's Hebgen Lake. The long beach offers plenty of places to swim and beach boats. The boat launch includes a cement ramp, docks, and trailer parking. The lake is popular for swimming, paddling, waterskiing, boating, and fishing, and known for its dry fly trout fishing (Montana fishing license needed). South Fork Arm is more sheltered from winds than the main lake, making it more appealing for canoeing and kayaking. The campground sits about 10 miles from of West Yellowstone and 11 miles from the west entrance to Yellowstone National Park.

Scatter conifers dot the sunny, quiet campground surrounded by arid grass and sagebrush meadows. Campsites along the east side of the one campground loop overlook the lake, and all campsites have territorial views, which include the Madison Range across the lake. The open terrain means that you'll see neighboring campers.

Campsites, facilities: The campground has 27 RV and tent campsites. Five sites have electrical hookups. RVs are limited to 45 feet. Facilities include picnic tables, fire rings with grills, vault and pit toilets (wheelchair-accessible), drinking water, garbage service, bear boxes, boat launch, firewood for sale, and campground hosts. Leashed pets are permitted.

Reservations, fees: Reservations are accepted (877/444-6777, www.recreation.gov). Campsites cost $16, plus $6 more for those with electrical hookups. An extra vehicle costs $6. Cash or check. Open mid-May–mid-September.

Directions: From West Yellowstone, drive Highway 20 for seven miles west and turn north onto Denny Creek Road. Drive 3.5 miles, jogging right and left around farms to the campground entrance on the right.

GPS Coordinates: N 44° 44.063' W 111° 13.903'

Contact: Gallatin National Forest, Hebgen Lake District Office, P.O. Box 520, West Yellowstone, MT 59758, 406/823-6961.

19 LIONSHEAD RV PARK

Scenic rating: 7

outside West Yellowstone

At 6,718 feet in Montana, Lionshead RV Park is seven miles west of West Yellowstone and eight miles from the west entrance to Yellowstone National Park. For those looking for the convenience of being near town with its activities, but who want a place less crowded and noisy, this campground provides an alternative to the West Yellowstone hubbub. The campground is behind a motel and restaurant. Denny Creek flows past the back of the campground, with two bridges allowing access to a trail and constructed fishing ponds. Other fishing is available within 10 miles at Hebgen Lake or the Madison River. Horseback rides are nearby, too.

Most of the RV area is open without trees, but the tent sites rim the perimeter shaded in pines. A gravel road loops through the campground, which has mowed-lawn campsites set very close together with little privacy and pull-through sites available. The proximity to the highway means vehicle noise enters the campground.

Campsites, facilities: This campground has 175 RV campsites and 20 tent campsites. RVs are limited to 80 feet. Hookups include water, sewer, and electricity up to 50 amps. Facilities include picnic tables, fire rings, grills, flush toilets (wheelchair-accessible), showers, drinking water, launderette, convenience store, propane, playground, pizza café, and camping kitchen. Leashed pets are permitted.

Reservations, fees: Reservations are accepted. RV hookups cost $35-70. Tent campsites

cost $25-35. Rates are for four people. For additional adults, add $6 each, and for kids add $4 each. Additional vehicles cost $15. Add on 7 percent Montana bed tax. Cash, check, or credit card. Open late May-mid-September.
Directions: From West Yellowstone, drive seven miles west on Highway 20 to the campground, on the north side of the road.
GPS Coordinates: N 44° 41.242' W 111° 15.124'
Contact: Lionshead RV Resort, 1545 Targhee Pass Hwy., West Yellowstone, MT 59758, 406/646-7662 or 877/935-5690, www.lionsheadrv.com.

20 YELLOWSTONE KOA

Scenic rating: 7
outside West Yellowstone

Sitting at 6,590 feet outside West Yellowstone, Montana, the Yellowstone KOA offers a place to camp away from the crowded West Yellowstone streets but convenient for exploring the town and Yellowstone National Park. The west entrance to the park sits seven miles east of the campground. Horseback rides and weekend rodeos are available nearby, along with fishing at Hebgen Lake or the Madison River.

The campground fills every niche of the property with close-set campsites. With its location outside of town and surroundings of open prairie, views encompass the mountains of the Madison Range. Pines near almost every campsite provide shade for the sunny, mowed-lawn campground, and tent sites are divided with split rail fences and pines. You can hear vehicles passing on the two-lane highway, but traffic dwindles at night. A paved road loops through the campground, but the parking pads are gravel.
Campsites, facilities: This KOA has 168 RV campsites and 84 tent campsites. Some of the campsites can accommodate big rigs, and

hookups include sewer, water, and electricity up to 50 amps. Thirteen tent sites also have water and electricity. Facilities include picnic tables, fire rings, flush toilets (wheelchair-accessible), showers, drinking water, launderette, convenience store, indoor pool, hot tub, camping kitchen, pancake breakfasts, nightly barbecue dinners, espresso kiosk, mini-golf, playground, basketball, dog walk, game room, surrey bike rentals, propane, and wireless Internet. Leashed pets are permitted.
Reservations, fees: Reservations are accepted. RV hookups cost $32-74. Tent campsites cost $22-41. Rates cover two people. Each extra person incurs $5. Kids under five stay for free. Add on 7 percent Montana bed tax. Cash, check, or credit card. Open late May-September.
Directions: From West Yellowstone, drive Highway 20 west for six miles to the campground entrance to the north.
GPS Coordinates: N 44° 41.204' W 111° 13.008'
Contact: Yellowstone Park KOA, 3305 Targhee Pass Hwy., West Yellowstone, MT 59758, 406/646-7606 or 800/562-7591, www.yellowstonekoa.com.

21 RUSTIC WAGON RV CAMPGROUND

Scenic rating: 4
in West Yellowstone

In West Yellowstone, Montana, the Rustic Wagon RV Campground sits on the opposite side of town from the busy shopping, restaurant, and tourist district. Yet, with town being only seven blocks wide, it still offers the convenience of walking to the visitors center, Yellowstone IMAX Theatre, Grizzly and Wolf Discovery Center, and Museum of the Yellowstone. The town is also headquarters for outfitters for horseback riding, white-water rafting, and fishing. The west entrance gate to Yellowstone National Park is one mile to the east. Hiking four miles or mountain biking 1.4 miles is available on the Riverside Trail, which tours along the Madison River about 1.5 miles east of the campground. Trout fishing is also available in the Madison River.

With its location on the west end of town, the campground is removed from the busy crowds downtown and quieter than the town's east side. The narrow campsites are close together. Spruce and pine trees help give it seclusion from the surrounding residential and commercial properties. Vehicle noise from the highway seeps in, but its side street is not busy. Tent campsites are in a grassy area.

Campsites, facilities: The campground has 45 RV campsites and 10 tent campsites. RV combinations are limited to 70 feet, and hookups have sewer, water, and electricity up to 50 amps. Facilities include picnic tables, flush toilets, showers, launderette, cable TV, patios, wireless Internet, horseshoes, playground, and basketball. Leashed pets are allowed in RV sites, but not in tent sites.

Reservations, fees: Reservations are accepted. RV hookup sites cost $46-50. Tent sites cost $39. Rates cover two people. For each additional person older than three, add $4. Add on 10 percent tax. Cash, check, or credit card. Open year-round with pull-through sites plowed in winter.

Directions: In West Yellowstone at the junction of Highways 20 and 191, drive west on Highway 20 (Firehole Avenue) and then angle north, staying on Highway 20 as it departs Firehole Avenue. Drive three blocks, turn north onto Iris Street, and immediately turn right onto Gibbon Street. The campground entrance is on the left.

GPS Coordinates: N 44° 39.856' W 111° 6.721'

Contact: Rustic Wagon RV Campground and Cabins, 637 Hwy. 20, West Yellowstone, MT 59758, 406/646-7387, www.rusticwagonrv.com.

22 WAGON WHEEL RV

Scenic rating: 4

in West Yellowstone

At 6,663 feet in elevation, the Wagon Wheel RV Campground sits in downtown West Yellowstone, Montana surrounded by residential and commercial properties. The campground spans the length of one block. It is three blocks from the center of town and shopping, restaurants, groceries, and gas. The only reason for staying in town is for the convenience of walking to the visitors center, Yellowstone IMAX Theatre, Grizzly and Wolf Discovery Center, and Museum of the Yellowstone. The campground also sits less than one mile from the west entrance to Yellowstone National Park. Hiking four miles or mountain biking 1.4 miles is available on the Riverside Trail, which tours along the Madison River less than a mile east of the campground. Anglers head to the Madison River for trout fishing. The town is headquarters for outfitters for horseback riding, white-water rafting, and fishing.

The location in downtown West Yellowstone means the campground comes with traffic noise and crowds—although its location off the main drags gives it some seclusion and quiet. The campsites are narrow and squeezed close together. Tall spruces and pines grant shade and a semblance of privacy to the RV sites, which have gravel pull-through or back-in parking pads and patios. Grassy tent sites are in a private area.

Campsites, facilities: The campground has 36 RV campsites and 15 tent campsites. RV combinations are limited to 60 feet. Hookups are available for water, sewer, and electricity up to 30 amps. Facilities include picnic tables, flush toilets, showers, drinking water, launderette, recreation room, cable TV, and wireless Internet. Leashed pets are allowed in the RV sites, but not in the tent sites.

Reservations, fees: Reservations are accepted. RV hookup sites cost $46-50. Tent sites cost $39. Rates cover two people. For each additional person older than three, add $4. Add on 10 percent tax. Cash, check, or credit card. Open mid-May-September.

Directions: In the center of West Yellowstone at the junction of Highway 20 and Highway 191, drive west on Highway 20 (Firehole Avenue) for three blocks. Turn right (north) onto Faithful Street and drive two blocks to Gibbon Avenue. Turn left and immediately left again into the campground.

GPS Coordinates: N 44° 39.829' W 111° 6.408'

Contact: Wagon Wheel RV Campground and Cabins, 408 Gibbon Ave., West Yellowstone, MT 59758, 406/646-7872, www.wagonwheelrv.com.

23 HIDEAWAY RV PARK

Scenic rating: 7

in West Yellowstone

Located 10 blocks from the west entrance to Yellowstone National Park, Hideaway RV Park, at 6,664 feet, allows convenient access to the park and the town of West Yellowstone, Montana. Shopping, restaurants, the visitors center, the Yellowstone IMAX Theatre, the Grizzly and Wolf Discovery Center, and the Museum of the Yellowstone are within three to seven blocks. The town is also headquarters for outfitters for horseback riding, white-water rafting, and fishing. The Riverside Trail along the Madison River offers hiking (four miles) and mountain biking (1.4 miles) about one mile east of the campground. Trout fishing is available in the Madison River. The campground is one block from a city park with a children's playground and a half block from a launderette.

Hideaway is West Yellowstone's smallest campground, and its location on the north edge of town in a residential area removes it from the busy tourist blocks. A gravel road loops through the campground, which has gravel pull-through or back-in parking pads. Tall conifers lend partial shade to many of the campsites, which are close together.

Campsites, facilities: The campground has 14 RV campsites and one tent campsite. RVs are limited to 45 feet, and hookups include water, sewer, and electricity up to 50 amps. Facilities include picnic tables, flush toilets, showers, patios, cable TV, and wireless Internet. Leashed pets are permitted.

Reservations, fees: Reservations are accepted. RV sites cost $32-37. The tent site costs $24. Rates cover two people. Extra people over six years old incur $3 each. Add on 10 percent tax. Cash, check, or credit card. Open mid-May-September.

Directions: From downtown West Yellowstone at the intersection of Highways 20 and 191, drive west on Highway 20 (Firehole Avenue) for two blocks. Turn north onto Electric Street and drive 2.5 blocks to the entrance on the left.

GPS Coordinates: N 44° 39.862' W 111° 6.263'

Contact: Hideaway RV Park, 320 Electric St., West Yellowstone, MT 59758, 406/646-9049, www.hideawayrv.com.

24 PONY EXPRESS RV PARK

Scenic rating: 4

in West Yellowstone

The Pony Express RV Park, at 6,668 feet, sits literally on the edge of West Yellowstone, Montana across the street from Yellowstone National Park. The west entrance gate to the park is five blocks away, along with the visitors center, Yellowstone IMAX Theatre, Grizzly and Wolf Discovery Center, and Museum of the Yellowstone. Shopping, restaurants, gas, and groceries are also within five blocks. The town is headquarters for outfitters for horseback riding, white-water rafting, and fishing.

The Riverside Trail along the Madison River offers hiking (four miles) and mountain biking (1.4 miles) less than 0.5 mile east of the campground. Trout fishing is also available in the Madison River.

Located at a motel, this small campground squeezes campsites close together in an open lot. Some of the campsites look across Boundary Street into the park, but the view is of a forest—no geysers, mountains, or rivers. The territory comes with a certain amount of noise because of its location in downtown, but perched on the edge of town off the main drags, it is quieter than other locations. A handful of trees dot the campground with minimal shade.

Campsites, facilities: The campground has 16 RV campsites. RVs are limited to 38 feet. Hookups include sewer, water, and electricity up to 50 amps. Facilities include picnic tables, flush toilets, showers, launderette, wireless Internet, cable TV, and pull-through sites. Leashed pets are permitted.

Reservations, fees: Reservations are accepted. Campsites cost $40 ($30 in winter). Add on 10 percent tax. Open April-November with full hookups and during winter for dry camping.

Directions: In downtown West Yellowstone, from the intersection of Highway 20 and Highway 191, turn east on Firehole Avenue and drive 1.5 blocks. The entrance is on the left.

GPS Coordinates: N 44° 39.742' W 111° 5.916'

Contact: Pony Express Motel and RV Park, 4 Firehole Ave., West Yellowstone, MT 59758, 406/646-9411 or 800/217-4613, www.yellowstonevacations.com.

25 YELLOWSTONE CABINS AND RV PARK

Scenic rating: 4

in West Yellowstone

At 6,669 feet, Yellowstone Cabins and RV Park offer the conveniences of being right in the middle of West Yellowstone, Montana. The west entrance gate to the Yellowstone National Park is less than one mile west, and you can walk to the visitors center, Yellowstone IMAX Theatre, Grizzly and Wolf Discovery Center, and Museum of the Yellowstone. Shopping, restaurants, gas, and groceries are also within five blocks. The town is headquarters for outfitters for horseback riding, white-water rafting, and fishing. The Riverside Trail along the Madison River offers hiking (four miles) and mountain biking (1.4 miles) less than 0.5 mile east of the campground. Trout fishing is also available in the Madison River.

Conifers shade this campground that is connected with a small cabin and motel complex. The campsites are gravel and grass. Given its location on the highway, traffic is a constant sound.

Campsites, facilities: The campground has eight RV campsites. RVs are limited to 38 feet. Hookups include sewer, water, able TV, and electricity up to 50 amps. Facilities include flush toilets and showers. Leashed pets are permitted.

Reservations, fees: Reservations are accepted. Campsites cost $35. Add on 10 percent tax. Open May-mid-October.

Directions: In downtown West Yellowstone, from the intersection of Highway 20 and Highway 191, drive west on Highway 20 (Firehole Avenue) for four blocks and turn south into the campground right after Geyser Street.

GPS Coordinates: N 44° 39.762' W 111° 6.537'

Contact: Yellowstone Cabins and RV Park, 504 Highway 20, West Yellowstone, MT 59758, 406/646-9350 or 866/646-9350, www.yellowstonecabinsandandrv.com

26 YELLOWSTONE GRIZZLY RV PARK

Scenic rating: 4

in West Yellowstone

Located on West Yellowstone's southern

edge away from the crowded tourist streets, Yellowstone Grizzly RV—the area's newest campground—is bordered on two sides by Montana's Gallatin National Forest. The west entrance to Yellowstone National Park, shopping, restaurants, visitors center, the Yellowstone IMAX Theatre, the Grizzly and Wolf Discovery Center, Museum of the Yellowstone, and all outfitters for rafting, horseback riding, and fishing are within five blocks. The Riverside Trail along the Madison River offers hiking (four miles) and mountain biking (1.4 miles) about one mile east of the campground. Trout fishing is available in the Madison River.

The campground—West Yellowstone's largest—was expanded in 2006. Landscaped gardens, lawns, aspens, and lodgepole pines cover the campground, but the trees are still young and provide only partial shade. The RV sites, with paved back-in or pull-through parking pads, cement walkways, and patios, are positioned right next to each other, but they are roomy enough for slide-outs and awnings. The tent campsites ring a grassy area across from the playground and clubhouse, which has outdoor kitchen sinks.

Campsites, facilities: The campground has 261 RV campsites and 16 tent campsites. RVs are limited to 80 feet, and hookups include for water, sewer, and electricity up to 100 amps. Facilities include picnic tables, barbecue grills (bring your own charcoal), flush toilets (wheelchair-accessible), showers, drinking water, patios, cable TV, wireless Internet, dog walk, game room, playground, convenience store, launderette, and horseshoes. Leashed pets are permitted.

Reservations, fees: Reservations are accepted. RV campsites cost $55-65 for up to six people with each extra person costing $5. Tent campsites cost $40 for four people with each extra person costing $10. A 10 percent tax is added on. Cash, check, or credit card. Off-season rates are lower in May and October. Open May-late October.

Directions: In downtown West Yellowstone from the junction of Highway 20 and Highway 191, drive west on Highway 20 for two blocks to Electric Street. Turn south and drive 0.5 mile. The campground entrance sits on the west side of the road opposite Gray Wolf Avenue.

GPS Coordinates: N 44° 39.330' W 111° 6.271'

Contact: Yellowstone Grizzly RV Park, 210 S. Electric St., West Yellowstone, MT 59758, 406/646-4466, www.grizzlyrv.com.

27 MADISON

🚶 🚴 🏊 🏕 ♿ 🚐 ⛺

Scenic rating: 9

on the lower Grand Loop in Yellowstone National Park

BEST (

Centrally located in Yellowstone National Park, Madison Campground offers the quickest access to the big geyser basins, including Old Faithful 16 miles south. Between the campground and Old Faithful, basins line up with geysers, mud pots, hot springs, and fumaroles. Firehole Lake Drive tours past the Great Fountain Geyser, which spurts 200 feet high, and Fountain Paint Pots contain multicolored blurping mud. Upper, Lower, and Biscuit Geyser Basins link by boardwalks to colorful, steaming hot pools. The Old Faithful basin contains the most geysers and volcanic features, including the famous Old Faithful Geyser and the Old Faithful Visitor Education Center. Mountain bikers can ride several trails connecting geyser basins, including Fountain Flat Drive to Fairy Falls Trailhead and the Daisy Geyser cut-off to Biscuit Basin. The campground sits at 6,806 feet near the confluence of the Gibbon and Firehole Rivers, where they become the Madison River, each with superb fly-fishing. Near the campground, bison or elk usually hang out in the meadows along the river, accessed via a network of trails from the campground. In fall, the male elk bugle as they round up their harems. Hikers can climb three miles up Purple Mountain for a view of the Firehole and lower Gibbon Valleys.

© BECKY LOMAX

The Madison River attracts anglers for trout fishing.

Madison Campground has ten loops, in a loose forest of tall pine trees for partial shade. With no understory—only tree trunks—campsites are visible to each other. At the campground's west end, the tenting G and H loops are more open and sunny, but also garner peek-a-boo views of National Park Mountain. Paved roads with paved parking pads (back-in and pull-through) weave through the campground. Although the campground picks up daytime traffic noise from the busy west entrance road, it quiets after dark.

Campsites, facilities: Madison has 278 campsites—213 for RVs or tents and 65 for tents only. RVs are limited to 40 feet. Facilities include picnic tables, fire rings with grills, flush toilets, drinking water, sporadic tent pads, bear boxes, garbage services, disposal station, firewood and ice for sale, amphitheater and ranger station for interpretive programs, and campground hosts. Leashed pets are permitted. A wheelchair-accessible toilet and one campsite are available.

Reservations, fees: Reservations are recommended (307/344-7901 same day, 307/344-7311 or 866/439-7375 advance, www.YellowstoneNationalParkLodges.com). Sites cost $23, plus sales tax and utility fee. Shared hiker and biker campsites cost $5 per person. Cash, check, or credit card. Open May-late October.

Directions: From the west entrance to Yellowstone National Park, drive 14 miles east on the west entrance road to the campground entrance is on the south side of the road. GPS Coordinates: N 44° 38.738' W 110° 51.672'

Contact: Yellowstone National Park, P.O. Box 168, Yellowstone, WY 82190-0168, 307/344-7381, www.nps.gov/yell.

28 NORRIS

Scenic rating: 8

on the lower Grand Loop in Yellowstone National Park

Sitting at 7,555 feet on the upper Grand Loop Road's southwest corner, Norris Campground sits near Norris Geyser Basin. A 10-minute walk connects the campground with the basin's boardwalks and trails. The geyser basin houses hot pools, steam vents, and Steamboat—the world's tallest geyser, which spouts to 380 feet. Porcelain Basin loops 1.6-mile through an austere landscape of colorful minerals, and Back Basin is a two-mile loop that houses the geysers, including the predictable Echinus, which begins eruptions with boiling water filling its basin. At the campground, the Museum of the National Park Ranger contains exhibits about early rangers, and anglers can fish for small brook trout in the confluence of the Gibbon River and Solfatara Creek. Hiking trails depart from the campground east to Ice Lake (4.3 miles) and north along Solfatara Creek. Another Ice Lake trailhead sits 3.5 miles east of Norris Junction. Don't carry a fishing rod to the barren lake.

Plan on arriving by 11am in midsummer to claim a site at this popular campground. Set in a loose pine and fir forest where you can see plenty of neighboring campers and surrounded by the large Norris meadows, the campground provides an excellent location for spotting moose, elk, bears, and bison. Choose from among sunny or shaded campsites. Large, flat spaces are available for tents at some sites. Loop A offers campsites that are more level and overlook the meadows while Loops B and C pitch on the hillside, sometimes posing a challenge for RVs.

Campsites, facilities: Norris has 100 RV or tent campsites. Two campsites are available for RVs up to 50 feet; five sites are available for RVs up to 30 feet. Three campsites are walk-in tent sites. Facilities include picnic tables, fire rings with grills, flush toilets, drinking water, bear boxes, garbage service, amphitheater for interpretive programs, and firewood and ice for sale. Leashed pets are permitted. A wheelchair-accessible toilet and campsites are available.

Reservations, fees: Reservations are not accepted. Campsites cost $20. Shared hiker and biker campsites cost $5 per person. Cash or check. Open mid-May–September.

Directions: From Norris Junction, drive 0.8 mile north on the Grand Loop Road, or from Mammoth, drive 20.2 miles south. Turn east and drive 0.2 mile into the campground. GPS Coordinates: N 44° 44.269' W 110° 41.623'

Contact: Yellowstone National Park, P.O. Box 168, Yellowstone, WY 82190-0168, 307/344-7381, www.nps.gov/yell.

29 CANYON

🏃 🚴 ⛴ 🐕 ♿ 🚐 ⛺

Scenic rating: 9

at Grand Canyon of the Yellowstone in Yellowstone National Park

BEST (

Canyon Campground, elevation 7,944 feet, sits just off the busy junction of Grand Loop Road and Norris Canyon Road at Canyon Village, which houses the Canyon Visitor Education Center, groceries, shopping, post office, restaurants, gas, vehicle repairs, and disposal station. The education center features live earthquake monitoring and other exhibits. The main attraction is the Grand Canyon of the Yellowstone, an immense colorful 1,200-foot-deep chasm with the Yellowstone River plunging down two huge waterfalls. Trails rim both sides of the canyon with overlooks at several points, accessed via connected trails or separate parking accesses. Multiple switchbacks and stairways climb down to platforms at the falls. Artist Point is the most photographed viewpoint. A bike lane runs on the road from the campground to canyon. Nearby, the trailhead goes two miles to Cascade Lake and further to Grebe Lake. At Dunraven Pass, hikers can climb the tallest peak in Yellowstone—Mt. Washburn. An evening drive south through Hayden Valley provides wildlife watching for bison, elk and sometimes wolves. Upstream and downstream from the canyon, the Yellowstone River offers fishing, but check restrictions as some sections are closed to fishing. Horseback trail rides are also available from Canyon Village.

The large Canyon Campground winds up a lodgepole forested hill with eleven loops. Four loops are for tents only. Leveling RVs and fitting into tight spots can prove challenging. Some private nooks tuck into the trees, but without shrubs neighbors are visible through the trunks. Although all loops have restrooms, showers (two included for each site with fee) are located in the launderette at the bottom of the hill, 0.75-mile away from Loops K and L. In midsummer, the campground fills every day; plan to arrive by 11am to claim a campsite.

Campsites, facilities: The campground has 200 RV and tent campsites and 73 campsites for tents only. RVs over 30 feet can fit in a limited number of campsites, but make reservations for large rigs to get a site. Facilities include picnic tables, fire rings with grills, flush toilets, drinking water, bear boxes, showers, firewood and ice for sale, amphitheater for interpretive programs, garbage service, launderette, disposal station, and campground

© BECKY LOMAX

The Yellowstone River flows through the Grand Canyon of the Yellowstone and tumbles with several falls.

hosts. Leashed pets are permitted. Wheelchair-accessible toilets and campsites are available.

Reservations, fees: Reservations are recommended (307/344-7901 for same day, 307/344-7311 or 866/439-7375 for advance, www.YellowstoneNationalParkLodges.com). Campsites cost $27, plus sales tax and a utility fee. Shared hiker and biker campsites cost $5 per person. Cash, check, or credit card. Open June-early September.

Directions: From Canyon Village Junction, drive 0.2 mile east on North Rim Drive. Turn left into the campground.

GPS Coordinates: N 44° 44.157' W 110° 29.319'

Contact: Yellowstone National Park, P.O. Box 168, Yellowstone, WY 82190-0168, 307/344-7381, www.nps.gov/yell.

30 FISHING BRIDGE RV

🥾 🛶 🏊 🚌 ⛵ 🏕 ♿ 🚐

Scenic rating: 7
on Yellowstone Lake in Yellowstone National Park

At 7,751 feet in thick forest, Fishing Bridge flanks the north side of Yellowstone Lake. Contrary to its name, fishing is not permitted from the famous Fishing Bridge on the Yellowstone River; however, it is allowed about one mile downstream and on Yellowstone Lake. All native species are catch-and-release only. The one-mile Pelican Creek Nature Trail tours a marsh along Pelican Creek, where you can see American white pelicans and end at a black-sand beach on the lake. Fishing Bridge also has a grocery store, visitors center, restaurant, gas, and RV repair shop. A boat launch is available five miles southwest at Bridge Bay, although hand-carried watercraft can launch from picnic areas on the lake's north shore. Boat permits, available at visitors centers and backcountry offices, are required.

In a thick lodgepole forest, a paved road passes through the long campground loops, which all have paved, back-in campsites. Sites are close together, so privacy is minimal. Small patches of grass between the parking pads make up the campsites. Some campsites have one fir or lodgepole pine tree that offers a little shade; others are open and sunny. Little log tipis are available in a kids' play area. Located back in the woods, the campground is quiet once the generators turn off. The air at Fishing Bridge smells of sulfur.

Campsites, facilities: Fishing Bridge has 346 RV campsites for hard-sided vehicles only. No popup tent trailers or tent campers are allowed. RVs are limited to 40 feet. Hookups include water, sewer, and electricity up to 50 amps. Facilities include flush toilets (wheelchair-accessible), coin-op showers, launderette, garbage service, firewood for sale, and disposal station. Leashed pets are permitted.

Reservations, fees: Reservations are recommended (307/344-7901 for same day, 307/344-7311 or 866/439-7375 for advance, www.YellowstoneNationalParkLodges.com). RV sites cost $50, plus sales tax and a utility fee. Cash, check, or credit card. Open late May-late September.

Directions: From Yellowstone's east entrance, drive 27 miles west on the east entrance road, or from Fishing Bridge Junction, drive one mile east. Turn north into the campground. GPS Coordinates: N 44° 33.820' W 110° 22.167'

Contact: Yellowstone National Park, P.O. Box 168, Yellowstone, WY 82190-0168, 307/344-7381, www.nps.gov/yell.

31 BRIDGE BAY

Scenic rating: 9

on Yellowstone Lake in Yellowstone National Park

Located at 7,784 feet on the west side of Yellowstone Lake, Bridge Bay Campground and Marina sits on an idyllic sheltered lagoon off Bridge Bay. Bridge Bay includes a ranger station, store, and boat launch with docks, boat slips, trailer parking, and cement ramps. One-hour tours of Yellowstone Lake are available several times daily; the *Lake Queen* loops around Stevenson Island to see bald eagles and ospreys fish. Boat rentals (rowboats and motorboats), charter fishing and tour services, and a shuttle service to backcountry campsites are available. Paddlers will enjoy the shelter of the lagoon and bay, but should plan to avoid the lake's notorious afternoon winds. All boats require permits, available at the marina; no waterskiing or Jet Skiing. Separate one-mile trails for hikers and mountain bikers lead to Natural Bridge, a rhyolite rock arch 51 feet above Bridge Creek. You can climb to the top of the arch, but to protect the feature should not cross it. Bicyclists can also tour the scenic lakeshore drive around Gull Point.

Bridge Bay is Yellowstone's largest campground; in high summer it can hold a population bigger than many small towns in the Northern Rockies. Its huge front loops circle on a gentle, sunny sloped meadow above the lake. Many campsites overlook the water and Absaroka Mountains in the distance, but also include view of neighboring campers. Expect June's green grassy meadows to turn brown by August. Denser conifers cast more shade on back loop campsites. While Bridge Bay bustles during the day with marina traffic, it quiets at night.

Campsites, facilities: The campground has 432 RV or tent campsites. RV combinations are limited to 40 feet. As large RV parking pads are limited, RVs over 30 feet should reserve sites. Facilities include picnic tables, fire rings with grills, flush toilets, drinking water, bear boxes, garbage service, disposal station, firewood and ice for sale, amphitheater for evening ranger programs, and campground hosts. Leashed pets are permitted. Wheelchair-accessible toilets and campsites are available.

Reservations, fees: Reservations are recommended (307/344-7901 for same day, 307/344-7311 or 866/439-7375 for advance,

www.yellowstonenationalparklodges.com).
Campsites cost $23, plus tax and utility fee.
Shared hiker and biker campsites cost $5 per
person. Cash, check, or credit card. Open late
May-early September.

Directions: From the Fishing Bridge Junction
on Grand Loop Road, drive 3.5 miles south,
or from the West Thumb Junction, drive 17.5
miles north. Turn west into Bridge Bay for
0.2 mile, and turn right into the campground
entrance.
GPS Coordinates: N 44°32.195' W 110°
25.995'

Contact: Yellowstone National Park, P.O. Box
168, Yellowstone, WY 82190-0168, 307/344-
7381, www.nps.gov/yell.

32 GRANT VILLAGE

Scenic rating: 8
on Yellowstone Lake in Yellowstone National
Park

BEST (

On Yellowstone Lake, Grant Campground
sits at 7,733 feet on the south shore of West
Thumb—a huge bay larger than other lakes
in the park. Of the campgrounds around Yellowstone Lake, it is the closest to Old Faithful,
about 20 miles away. The sprawling Grant
Village complex houses a visitors center, restaurant, interpretive sightseeing tours, lodge,
general store, gas, showers, launderette, post
office, and marina that includes cement
ramps, docks, slips, and trailer parking. The
cold lake whips up a notorious chop in the
afternoons, so paddlers and anglers will want
to plan accordingly, but mornings and evenings can yield appealing water. All boats need
permits, available at the backcountry office at
the visitors center; no waterskiing or Jet Skiing. Nearby, West Thumb Geyser Basin has a
0.5-mile boardwalk trail to access hot springs,
Abyss Pool, and the Fishing Cone offshore,
where anglers used to cook their catch over
the steam. Also, hikers can grab a panoramic

view of the park's largest lake and Absaroka
Mountains by climbing the one-mile Yellowstone Lake Overlook Trail.

A paved road with paved parking pads
loops through this giant campground with
a midsummer population larger than some
Wyoming towns. In contrast to the other
large Yellowstone Lake campgrounds across
the highway from beaches, this one sits in
a lodgepole forest adjacent to the shoreline.
Trails lead to a large pebble and sand beach
for sunbathing or swimming. The campsites
sit close together under the partial shade of a
loose, sunny lodgepole forest. With no understory, you can see neighbors.

Campsites, facilities: The campground has
430 RV or tent campsites. RV combinations
are limited to 40 feet. With limited large RV
parking pads, RVs over 30 feet should reserve
sites. Facilities include picnic tables, fire rings
with grills, flush toilets, drinking water, bear
boxes, firewood for sale, garbage service, and
campground hosts. Showers, launderette, and
disposal station are available 0.5 mile south
in Grant Village. Leashed pets are permitted.
Wheelchair-accessible toilets and campsites
are available.

Reservations, fees: Reservations are recommended (307/344-7901 for same day,
307/344-7311 or 866/439-7375 for advance,
www.YellowstoneNationalParkLodges.com).
Campsites cost $27, plus tax and utility fee.
Shared hiker and biker campsites cost $5 per
person. Cash, check, or credit card. Open late
June-late September.

Directions: From West Thumb Junction,
drive south on Rockefeller Parkway for 1.8
miles, or from the park's south entrance, drive
22 miles north. Turn east into Grant Village
and drive one mile. Turn left and drive 0.5
mile to the campground.
GPS Coordinates: N 44° 23.654' W 110°
33.828'

Contact: Yellowstone National Park, P.O. Box
168, Yellowstone, WY 82190-0168, 307/344-
7381, www.nps.gov/yell.

33 FRANK ISLAND
🏕 🚣 ⛴

Scenic rating: 8
on Yellowstone Lake in Yellowstone National
Park

At 136 square miles, Yellowstone Lake is the second-largest freshwater lake in the world that is above 7,000 feet. That means cold water, 40-50°F, in summer. Frank Island is a unique place to camp in Yellowstone, but camping here does require a self-contained boat with a galley, berth, toilet, and anchor. The island itself is for day visitation only, but it's a good place to see bald eagles or ospreys. Because of nesting, shore landings are not permitted prior to August 15, except at the dock and picnic area, on the north side of the spit in the south bay, where a dock is available. Anglers fish for native cutthroat trout. All boats require permits, available at Bridge Bay or Grant Village; no waterskiing or Jet Skiing.

Boaters may camp at two anchorage locations within the eastern double cove of the island: one in the north bay and one in the south bay. Anchorage sites must be at least 100 feet from shore and 300 feet from the dock. The coves, which face east, are open to the lake's notorious afternoon winds, which can whip up five-foot waves, but also garner views of the Absaroka Mountains. Powerboats are limited to 45 mph on the lake.

Campsites, facilities: Overnight camping is not permitted on the island, but two anchorage spots are available. No facilities are provided at the anchorage sites, and only one boat, with a maximum of eight people, is permitted per site.

Reservations, fees: Reservations are accepted for backcountry campsites. Applications (available online) may be submitted with a nonrefundable $25 after January 1; reservation confirmations are issued starting April 1. Reservations are recommended for the coveted lake permits. At 48 hours or less before your trip, pick up free permits for backcountry

campsites in person at Bridge Bay, Grant Village, or the south entrance backcountry office. Open June-October, depending on seasonal conditions.

Directions: To reach Frank Island, launch power boats from Bridge Bay for the 10-mile crossing.

GPS Coordinates: N 44° 24.795' W 110° 21.267'

Contact: Yellowstone National Park, P.O. Box 168, Yellowstone, WY 82190-0168, 307/344-7381, www.nps.gov/yell.

34 YELLOWSTONE LAKE
🥾 🏕 🚣 ⛴ 🏕 ⛰

Scenic rating: 9
on Yellowstone Lake in Yellowstone National
Park

Yellowstone Lake—the second-largest freshwater lake above 7,000 feet in the world—offers boat-in and hike-in camping on its east shore, three southern arms, and several bays east of West Thumb. You can launch boats from Grant Village or Bridge Bay; hand-carried watercrafts can also launch from Sedge Bay picnic area. The chilly (45°F) lake is notorious for daily afternoon winds with big whitecaps, so plan trips accordingly. Bridge Bay Marina (307/242-3893) provides a boat shuttle service for hikers and boaters mid-May-mid-September. For canoers and kayakers, the shuttle can save travel over open water. All boats require permits, available at Bridge Bay and Grant Village; no waterskiing or Jet Skiing. Many campsites link to hiking trails, and the park service advocates fishing for lake trout to help restore the cutthroat trout fishery.

These popular shoreline campsites are prized for their quiet, solitude, scenery, and wildlife-watching. The campsites sit back in the trees for protection, most within a few hundred feet of the shoreline. Some of the beaches garner views of the Absaroka Mountains to the east. Three locations with docks have three campsites each.

Campsites, facilities: Yellowstone Lake has 32 primitive tent campsites. Sites are limited to 8-12 people, depending on restrictions. Facilities include fire rings where campfires are permitted, bear boxes or poles, and pit toilets at some. Bring a 35-foot rope for hanging food, garbage, toiletries, and cooking gear. No drinking water is available; treat lake water. Pack out your trash. Pets are not allowed.

Reservations, fees: Reservations are accepted for backcountry campsites. Applications (available online) may be submitted with a nonrefundable $25 after January 1; reservation confirmations are issued starting April 1. Reservations are recommended for the coveted lake permits. At 48 hours or less before your trip, pick up free permits for backcountry campsites in person at Bridge Bay, Grant Village, or the south entrance backcountry office. Open June-October, depending on seasonal conditions; some campsites are closed because of bears until mid-July.

Directions: For launching from Grant Village, drive south from West Thumb Junction on Rockefeller Parkway for 1.8 miles, or from the park's south entrance, drive 22 miles north. Turn east into Grant Village, drive 0.9 mile, and turn right, following the signs to the boat launch. To launch from Bridge Bay, drive south from Fishing Bridge Junction on Grand Loop Road for 3.5 miles, or from the West Thumb Junction drive 17.5 miles north. Turn west into Bridge Bay for 0.2 mile to the marina.

GPS Coordinates for Bridge Bay: N 44° 32.026' W 110° 26.426'

GPS Coordinates for Grant Village: N 44° 23.520' W 110° 32.882'

Contact: Yellowstone National Park, P.O. Box 168, Yellowstone, WY 82190-0168, 307/344-7381, www.nps.gov/yell.

35 FLAT MOUNTAIN, SOUTH, AND SOUTHEAST ARMS

Scenic rating: 9

on Yellowstone Lake in Yellowstone National Park

BEST (

Yellowstone Lake offers paddlers and hikers access to three remote southern bays with views of the Absaroka Mountains, still snowcapped in early summer. Only hand-propelled watercraft are permitted; a few campsites allow sailboats to anchor. Launch from Grant Village to paddle 19 miles to Flat Mountain Arm or 33-35 miles into South Arm; launch from Sedge Bay picnic area on the lake's northeast corner to paddle the east shore for 20 miles into Southeast Arm. Watch for daily afternoon winds that whip the chilly (45°F) lake water into a chop of whitecaps. Bridge Bay Marina (307/242-3893) provides a boat shuttle service for hikers and boaters mid-May-mid-September. For canoers and kayakers, the shuttle saves paddling over open water. Hiking trails follow the shoreline, and the lake holds trout for fishing. All boats require permits, available at Bridge Bay or Grant Village; no waterskiing or Jet Skiing.

The popular campsites are prized for their quiet, solitude, scenery, wildlife-watching, and restrictions that exclude motorboats. The campsites are set back in the trees for protection, but most are within a few hundred feet of the shoreline; one site requires a 0.25-mile walk.

Campsites, facilities: Yellowstone Lake has 10 primitive tent campsites spread between the nonmotorized bays. Sites are limited to 8-12 people, depending on restrictions. Facilities include fire rings where campfires are permitted, bear boxes or poles, and pit toilets at some. Bring a 35-foot rope for hanging food, garbage, toiletries, and cooking gear. No drinking water is available; treat lake water. Pack out your trash. Pets are not allowed.

Reservations, fees: Reservations are accepted

for backcountry campsites. Applications (available online) may be submitted with a nonrefundable $25 after January 1; reservation confirmations are issued starting April 1. Reservations are recommended for the coveted lake permits. At 48 hours or less before your trip, pick up free permits for backcountry campsites in person at Bridge Bay, Grant Village, or the south entrance backcountry office. Open June-October, depending on seasonal conditions; seven campsites are closed because of bears until mid-July.

Directions: For launching from Grant Village, drive south from West Thumb Junction on Rockefeller Parkway for 1.8 miles, or from the park's south entrance, drive 22 miles north. Turn east into Grant Village, drive 0.9 mile, and turn right, following the signs to the boat launch. To launch from Bridge Bay, drive south from Fishing Bridge Junction on Grand Loop Road for 3.5 miles, or from the West Thumb Junction drive 17.5 miles north. Turn west into Bridge Bay for 0.2 mile to the marina.

GPS Coordinates for Bridge Bay: N 44° 32.026' W 110° 26.426'

GPS Coordinates for Grant Village: N 44° 23.520' W 110° 32.882'

Contact: Yellowstone National Park, P.O. Box 168, Yellowstone, WY 82190-0168, 307/344-7381, www.nps.gov/yell.

36 SHOSHONE LAKE

Scenic rating: 8

on Shoshone Lake in Yellowstone National Park

BEST (

Campers access the solitude of Shoshone Lake's primitive campgrounds by hiking, canoeing, or kayaking. Motorized boats are not permitted. Launch boats from the ramp at Lewis Lake Campground to paddle across the lake and up the Lewis River Channel between the two lakes. The last channel requires wading in frigid water while dragging boats. Because of the long paddle, select a south shore site for the first night. Afternoon high winds on the lake are a daily occurrence, so plan to paddle early. All boats, including kayaks and canoes, need permits, available at Lewis Lake Campground. For hikers, the Howard Eaton, DeLacy, Dogshead, and Lewis Channel Trails connect to the trail that circles Shoshone Lake.

The remote, quiet popular campsites sprinkle along the north, west, and south shores of the lake, snuggled into the edge of the forest for protection from weather. Some campsites are for hikers only, some for boaters only, and some for both.

Campsites, facilities: The lake is rimmed with 21 tent campsites that each hold eight people maximum. Five campsites are accessed by trail only, 13 by boat only, and three via trail or water. These are primitive campsites, with no fires permitted. Facilities include pit or composting toilets and a bear pole or bar. Bring a 35-foot rope for hanging food, garbage, toiletries, and cooking gear. Pack out your trash. No pets are permitted.

Reservations, fees: Reservations are accepted for backcountry campsites. Applications (available online) may be submitted with a nonrefundable $25 after January 1; reservation confirmations are issued starting April 1. Reservations are recommended for the coveted lake permits. At 48 hours or less before your trip, pick up free permits for backcountry campsites in person at Bridge Bay, Grant Village, or the south entrance backcountry office. Open June 15-October, depending on seasonal conditions and bear restrictions.

Directions: From the south entrance to the park, drive 11 miles north, or from West Thumb Junction, drive 11 miles south. Turn west into the Lewis Lake boat launch.

GPS Coordinates: N 44° 22.378' W 110° 42.250'

Contact: Yellowstone National Park, P.O. Box

168, Yellowstone, WY 82190-0168, 307/344-7381, www.nps.gov/yell.

37 LEWIS LAKE

Scenic rating: 8

on Lewis Lake in Yellowstone National Park

BEST (

At 7,830 feet, Lewis Lake is the third-largest lake in the park. Its appeal rests in its quieter ambiance and less visited location. Adjacent to the campground, a boat dock, cement ramp, and trailer parking allow for launching onto the lake for pleasure boating or fishing for brown trout (no waterskiing or Jet Skiing). Lewis Lake is also the gateway to Shoshone Lake via the Lewis Lake Channel, but only canoes and kayaks are permitted up the channel into the larger lake. All boats require permits, available at Lewis Lake Campground. Driving north from the Tetons, this is the first Yellowstone National Park campground you'll reach tucked at the southeast corner of the lake. At the lake's northeast corner (about four miles away), two trails depart in opposite directions. An 11-mile loop goes up the Lewis Channel to Shoshone Lake and returns via the Dogshead Trail. Across the highway, a 7.5-mile trail heads to Heart Lake. For sightseers, Lewis Falls sits about one mile south on the road.

By park standards, Lewis Lake is one of the smaller campgrounds, although it is still larger than most Forest Service campgrounds. On a hillside, campsites are spaced out for privacy under the conifer canopy with choices of varying degrees of sunny or shaded sites. Narrow parking pads may pose difficulties for those not used to backing in RVs. Most of the daytime activity concentrates around the boat launch and beach with nights bringing quiet. This campground is the one of the last to fill in the park, but in peak season, all the sites can be taken by early afternoon.

Campsites, facilities: The campground has 85 RV or tent campsites. RVs are limited to 25 feet. Facilities include picnic tables, fire rings with grills, vault toilets, drinking water, garbage service, bear boxes, and boat launch. Generators are not permitted. Leashed pets are permitted. Wheelchair-accessible toilets and campsites are available.

Reservations, fees: Reservations are not accepted. Sites cost $15. Shared hiker and biker campsites cost $5 per person. Cash or check. Open mid-June-October.

Directions: From the south park entrance, drive 11 miles north on the Rockefeller Parkway, or from West Thumb Junction, drive 11 miles south. Turn west into the Lewis Lake boat launch and campground entrance.

GPS Coordinates: N 44° 16.875' W 110° 37.644'

Contact: Yellowstone National Park, P.O. Box 168, Yellowstone, WY 82190-0168, 307/344-7381, www.nps.gov/yell.

38 CAVE FALLS

Scenic rating: 9

on the Falls River in Caribou-Targhee National Forest

BEST (

At 6,200 feet in Caribou-Targhee National Forest, Cave Falls Campground requires a long drive through Idaho farmland and forest to reach this remote corner of Wyoming and Yellowstone National Park. The road ends in Yellowstone at Cave Falls—a cascade only 20 feet high, but spanning 250 feet wide. A five-minute walk leads to the falls, and a path climbs above to look down on it. A 1.5-mile trail leads farther to Bechler Falls (1.5 miles). The Falls and Bechler Rivers are home to rainbow trout. Depending on where you are fishing, you'll need a Wyoming or Yellowstone

© BECKY LOMAX

Cave Falls, a 250-foot-wide waterfall, tucks into the remote southwest corner of Yellowstone National Park.

fishing license. The Bechler Ranger Station in Yellowstone sits about two miles west, where multiple trails tour rivers in this remote corner of the park.

Set along the Falls River in the national forest, the campground lines up most of its campsites overlooking the river. You can prop a chair on the high bank's edge and watch the roaring river as the sunset glows on the rocky outcroppings opposite. Paths drop down the steep bank to the water, too. A tall forest of aspens, subalpine firs, and lodgepoles alternates with meadows of arrowleaf balsamroot and huckleberries. Campsites have a mix of shade, sun, and flat tent spaces. Plan on enjoying solitude.

Campsites, facilities: The campground has 22 RV or tent campsites. RVs are limited to 24 feet. Facilities include picnic tables, fire rings with grills, pedestal grills, vault toilets (wheelchair-accessible), drinking water, and bear boxes. Pack out your trash. Leashed pets are permitted.

Reservations, fees: Reservations are not accepted. Campsites cost $10. Extra vehicles cost $6. Cash or check. Open June-mid-September.

Directions: From five miles north of Ashton on Highway 47 in Idaho, drive east on Cave Falls Road (Greentimber Road or Forest Road 582) for 18 miles. At mile 5.5, the pavement ends and the bumpy ride begins. You'll hit pavement again at mile 16, where the road narrows and enters Wyoming. Turn right, drop 0.1 mile to the pay station, and swing right to the campsites. From Flagg Ranch, the 52-mile rugged, narrow, dirt Grassy Lake Road takes 2.5 hours to Cave Falls Campground.

GPS Coordinates: N 44° 7.874' W 111° 0.896'

Contact: Caribou-Targhee National Forest, Island Park Ranger District, 3726 Hwy. 20, Island Park, ID 83429, 208/558-7301, www.fs.usda.gov/ctnf.

39 GRASSY LAKE PRIMITIVE

Scenic rating: 8

in Rockefeller Parkway and Caribou-Targhee National Forest

BEST (

An old Native American and wagon route, the 52-mile Grassy Lake Road through remote wilderness connects Flagg Ranch, Wyoming with Ashton, Idaho, topping out at 7,306 feet. In winter, snowmobiles and dog sleds travel the route. In summer, once the road dries (usually by August), those with tenacity and sturdy rigs drive it. (Trailers are not recommended.) The dirt road is rocky and narrow, has few turnouts, offers fewer views than one would expect, and will take 2.5 hours to drive. Mountain bikers can ride the road, too. Grassy Lake has a boat ramp and can be fished, paddled, or motored. On its east end, the Snake River is known for its trout fishery and can be floated with rafts and kayaks. Budget cuts in 2013 closed the designated campsites along this route; call for updates.

Eight tiny camps—prized for their quiet and solitude—are about one mile apart with large tent spaces. Facing east within 10 minutes from Flagg Ranch, camps 1-4 command outstanding views of the Snake River and Teton Wilderness peaks. Camps 1 and 2 sit on the river in sagebrush, willow, and grass bottomlands. Camps 3 and 4 sit on partly shaded open-forest bluffs overlooking the river. With forest and meadow views, camps 5-8 line the road as it climbs toward Grassy Lake. Camp 5 sits the farthest back from the road in green lodgepoles. Camps 6-8 sit closer to the road in forested settings, broken by meadows of yarrow and asters. Other primitive campsites sit at Grassy Lake and Lake of the Woods.

Campsites, facilities: Eight tiny campgrounds with 14 RV or tent campsites between them line the first 10 miles from Flagg Ranch to Grassy Lake on Rockefeller Parkway. Camp 1 has four sites, camps 2-4 have two sites each, and camps 5-8 have one site each. Only small RVs are recommended. Facilities include picnic tables, fire rings with grills, vault toilets, bear boxes, and garbage service. Bring your own water. Seven additional primitive campsites sit in Caribou-Targhee National Forest at Grassy Lake and Lake of the Woods. The only facilities include rock fire rings. Leashed pets are permitted.

Reservations, fees: Reservations are not accepted. Camping is free. Open June-September.

Directions: From Flagg Ranch, Grassy Lake Road (Ashton-Flagg Ranch Road) heads west, crossing the Snake River. From Ashton, Idaho, the road begins two miles southeast of Ashton, heading east.

GPS Coordinates for the site nearest Flagg Ranch: N 44° 6.244' W 110° 41.233'

Contact: Grand Teton National Park, P.O. Drawer 170, Moose, WY 83102, 307/739-3300, www.nps.gov/grte/.

40 HEADWATERS

Scenic rating: 7

at Flagg Ranch in Rockefeller Parkway

At 6,849 feet at Flagg Ranch, Headwaters Campground is the only developed campground in Rockefeller Parkway between Yellowstone National Park and Grand Teton National Park. On the Snake River, the large tourist center (lodge, restaurant, grocery, and gas station) offers guided fly-fishing, lake kayaking, horseback riding, rafting trips, and interpretive programs. Skilled whitewater rafters, kayakers, and canoeists can put in at Southgate Launch, 0.5 mile south of the south entrance of Yellowstone, for three miles of Class III white water to the campground. The water mellows in the 10 miles from the ranch to Lizard Creek on Jackson Lake but requires route-finding through braided channels and paddling against strong lake winds. A non-motorized boat park permit is required ($10 for seven days), available at Moose and Colter Bay Visitor Centers. From the campground, you can fish the river, mountain bike Grassy Lake Road heading west, and hike to Huckleberry Lookout from Sheffield Creek one mile south.

The forested campground sits near the Snake River, with paths connecting to the riverfront. Campsites vary from fully shaded under large spruces and firs to partly sunny with mountain views. RV campsites have gravel pull-throughs wide enough for slide-outs and awnings. Because of the lack of understory, views include neighboring campers. The eastern loops sit closest to the highway, but traffic dwindles at night, and commercial trucking isn't permitted.

Campsites, facilities: The campground has 54 tent campsites and 96 RV campsites with hookups for sewer, water, and electricity up to 50 amps. RVs are limited to 60 feet. Facilities include picnic tables, fire rings, flush toilets, showers, drinking water, garbage service, launderette, and convenience store. Leashed pets are permitted. A wheelchair-accessible toilets and campsites are available.

Reservations, fees: Reservations are recommended. RV campsites cost $64 or $32 with park access passes. Tent campsites cost $35. Add on tax. Rates are for two adults. For each additional adult, add $5. Cash, check, or credit card. Open late May-September.

Directions: From Jackson Lake Junction in Grand Teton National Park, drive north on Highway 26/191/89 for 21 miles. From the south entrance to Yellowstone National Park, drive three miles south. Turn west into Flagg Ranch.

GPS Coordinates: N 44° 6.305' W 110° 40.091'

Contact: Headwaters Camping and RV, P.O. Box 187, Moran, WY 83013, 307/543-2861 or 800/443-2311, www.gtlc.com/headwaters-lodge.aspx

41 SHEFFIELD CREEK

Scenic rating: 8

near Teton Wilderness in Bridger-Teton National Forest

At 7,000 feet, Sheffield Creek Campground cuddles next to a small tributary of the nearby Snake River below the 9,615-foot Huckleberry Mountain in the Teton Wilderness. Sheffield Creek Trail (#027) climbs 2,600 feet in 5.5 miles from the campground to the Huckleberry Lookout, which is listed on the National Register of Historic Places. Outstanding views from the lookout include Jackson Lake, the Tetons, Yellowstone National Park, and Teton Wilderness. Mountain bikers can ride the Grassy Lake Road, departing from nearby Flagg Ranch. Fishing, rafting, kayaking, and canoeing are available on the Snake River, but be sure to get the appropriate permits from Grand Teton National Park.

Sheffield Creek offers sunny campsites with huge territorial views of the surrounding mountains, valley, and the Tetons to the south. A small stream runs west of the campground—one that you must drive through on the access road as no bridge crosses it. June may have too much water to cross; scout the water depth. Some years, the access isn't good until August. Because the campground is located in a grizzly bear recovery area, it may be closed temporarily to tents, tent campers, and tent trailers, allowing only hard-sided RVs, during high bear activity. Call to check on status first. Sheffield is a popular trailhead but quiets at night.

Campsites, facilities: The campground has five RV or tent campsites. RVs are limited to 30 feet. Facilities include picnic tables, fire rings with grills, vault toilet (wheelchair-accessible), horse facilities, drinking water, and bear box and food pole. Pack out your trash. Leashed pets are permitted.

Reservations, fees: Reservations are not accepted. Campsites cost $5 per unit (RV, trailer,

CAMPING IN GRAND TETON

Grand Teton National Park, which connects to Yellowstone via the John D. Rockefeller, Jr. Memorial Parkway, hosts high rugged spires shooting up from sagebrush meadows. A paved bike trail tours the valley floor while a myriad of hiking trails climb to high vistas in the mountains. Boaters can enjoy several lakes, including the biggest, **Jackson Lake.** A few smaller lakes allow for the quiet of only canoes and kayaks. On the park's south end, the National Elk Refuge is home to 5,000 wintering elk, and the town of Jackson offers shopping, art galleries, and restaurants. The area houses outfitters for rafting, fishing, hiking, horseback riding, mountaineering, and rock climbing.

The park strings its six large campgrounds along the east side of the mountain range and Jackson Lake. **Flagg Ranch** services campers on the parkway between the two parks. The surrounding Caribou-Targhee and Bridger-Teton National Forests also offer a few campgrounds within 15 minutes of the park. Of Teton's campgrounds, **Jenny Lake** is by far the most popular, due to its access to hiking trails that climb up canyons toward the Teton Crest and the tour boat that runs across the lake. **Signal Mountain, Colter Bay,** and **Lizard Creek Campgrounds** rim the east shores of Jackson Lake, a large dammed reservoir on the Snake River. **Gros Ventre Campground** borders the National Elk Refuge. Boaters, canoers, and kayakers can enjoy remote campsites on Jackson Lake and the smaller, more wind-protected Leigh Lake.

Colter Bay in Grand Teton offer hookups for RVs, while Jenny Lake caters to tent camping only and does not permit RVs.

or tent). Cash or check. Open late May-September. If weather permits, the campground can remain open later in fall, but without services.

Directions: From Jackson Lake Junction in Grand Teton National Park, drive north on Highway 26/191/89 for 20 miles. From the Flagg Ranch, drive one mile south. Turn east onto the dirt road south of the bridge over the Snake River and drive 0.3 mile southeast into to the campground.

GPS Coordinates: N 44° 5.592' W 110° 39.814'

Contact: Bridger-Teton National Forest, Buffalo Ranger District, Hwy. 26/287, Moran, WY 83013, 307/543-2386, www.fs.usda.gov/btnf.

42 LIZARD CREEK

Scenic rating: 9

on Jackson Lake in Grand Teton National Park

At the north end of Jackson Lake, Lizard Creek Campground, elevation 6,823 feet, stares across the lake at the jagged teeth of the northern Teton Mountains. While the campground offers enjoyment of the lakeshore (with several walk-in tent sites right on it), sometimes the lake level can drop so low that huge mudflats surrounds the campground. The lake harbors cutthroat and lake trout, but fishing from the campground varies depending on water levels. The campground has no boat launch, but with high water levels, you can launch hand-carried boats, rafts, kayaks, and canoes at a pullout about one mile south of the campground. Boat permits are required, available at Colter Bay Visitors Center.

The partly sunny hillside campground is prized for its quiet location and outstanding views. It offers less harried enjoyment of the lake compared to other lakefront campgrounds. A thick spruce, fir, and lodgepole forest aids privacy, which is greater in the upper loop. Many of the lower loop prime campsites overlook the lake and the Tetons. Most of the walk-in tent sites, located in the lower loop, sit on the lake. Claim a campsite early in the day.

Campsites, facilities: The campground has 43 RV or tent campsites and 17 walk-in tent campsites. RV size is limited to 30 feet. Facilities include picnic tables, fire rings with grills, drinking water, flush toilets, garbage service, bear boxes, hiker-biker shared campsites, amphitheater for interpretive programs, and campground hosts. Generators are permitted in the upper loop, but not the lower loop. Only one vehicle is permitted per site. Leashed pets are permitted. A wheelchair-accessible campsite is available.

Reservations, fees: Reservations are not accepted. Campsites cost $21. Shared hiker and biker campsites cost $5. Cash or check. Open early June-early September.

Directions: From Jackson Lake Junction, drive 14 miles north on Highway 89/191/287, or from the south entrance to Yellowstone, drive 10 miles south. Turn south onto the paved road for 0.1 mile into the campground.

GPS Coordinates: N 44° 0.350' W 110° 41.135'

Contact: Grand Teton National Park, P.O. Drawer 170, Moose, WY 83102, 307/739-3300, www.nps.gov/grte/.

43 PACIFIC CREEK

Scenic rating: 8

near Teton Wilderness in Bridger-Teton National Forest

Pacific Creek Campground perches at 7,000 feet on the edge of the Teton Wilderness—a 585,238-acre wilderness bordering Yellowstone and Grand Teton National Parks. The campground serves as a leap off point into the wilderness with the trail following Pacific Creek upstream. Anglers can find pools for fly-fishing for trout on the stream. For a day hike destination, hikers and anglers head eight miles to Gravel Lake, 0.4-mile-long lake southeast of rugged Pinyon Peak. The trail also provides hunting access in fall for big game.

Pacific Creek offers a mix of sunny and shady campsites under cottonwoods with territorial views of the surrounding

mountains—even the tops of the Tetons in the distance. Pacific Creek flows east of the campground. Because the campground is located in a grizzly bear recovery area, it may be closed temporarily to tents, tent campers, and tent trailers, allowing only hard-sided RVs, during high bear activity. Call to check on status first. The trailhead is located here, so hikers and horse packers may come through the camp. Other than that, it's a quiet location.

Campsites, facilities: The campground has five RV or tent campsites. RVs are limited to 30 feet. Facilities include picnic tables, fire rings with grills, vault toilet, horse facilities, drinking water, and bear box and food pole. Pack out your trash. Leashed pets are permitted. Several free primitive campsites are also located on Pacific Creek after leaving the national park boundary.

Reservations, fees: Reservations are not accepted. Campsites cost $10 per unit (RV, trailer, or tent). Cash or check. Open late May-September. If weather permits, the campground can remain open later in fall, but without services.

Directions: From Moran Junction, head into Grand Teton National Park and turn north onto Rockefeller Parkway for 1.2 miles. From Jackson Junction, drive Rockefeller Parkway for 2.9 miles east. At the gravel Pacific Creek Road, turn north for eight miles to the campground entrance at the terminus.

GPS Coordinates: N 43° 56.357' W 110° 26.572'

Contact: Bridger-Teton National Forest, Buffalo Ranger District, Hwy. 26/287, Moran, WY 83013, 307/543-2386, www.fs.usda.gov/btnf.

44 TETON RANGE RESORT

Scenic rating: 8

in Moran

The Teton Range Resort, formerly called

Grand Teton RV, is a campground for convenience located just west of Moran Junction where one road goes north into Yellowstone National Park and the other road heads south into Grand Teton National Park. At 6,800 feet, the location away from the high-impact tourist areas and its views give it appeal. The campground sits behind a convenience store, restaurant, and gas station. Buffalo Fork circles in and around the campground. Anglers can wade-fish the stream, and when water levels are high enough, canoers can paddle it.

A handful of trees dot this sunny campground, but the trade-off is the view: From many campsites, the entire Teton Mountain range is visible across the horizon to the west. The ex-KOA campground is older, dusty, showing wear and tear, and the pool and hot tub were still closed in 2013.

Campsites, facilities: This campground has 160 RV campsites and 14 tent campsites. Sites can fit the largest RVs. Hookups are available for water, sewer, and electricity up to 50 amps. Facilities include picnic tables, fire rings, flush toilets, showers, drinking water, launderette, playground, convenience store, rental cars, and wireless Internet. Leashed pets are permitted.

Reservations, fees: Reservations are accepted. RV hookups cost $70-100. Tents cost $30-50. Rates cover four people; for each extra person, add $8; kids under six stay for free. Add on sales tax. Cash, check, or credit card. Open year-round.

Directions: From the Moran Junction, drive east on Highway 287 for 5.6 miles and turn south into the campground.
GPS Coordinates: N 43° 49.889' W 110° 24.123'

Contact: Teton Range Resort, 17800 Highway 287, Moran, WY 83013, 307/733-1980 or 800/563-6469, www.yellowstonerv.com.

45 HATCHET

Scenic rating: 7

near Moran Junction in Bridger-Teton National Forest

While Hatchet Campground isn't worth a visit as a destination in itself, its location provides a last-minute place to camp before reaching Grand Teton National Park and access to scenic fly-fishing and floating. The campground, elevation 6,800 feet, sits 0.2 mile west of the Buffalo Ranger Station and at the base of the dirt Hatchet Road, which climbs south along the foothills with dramatic views across the valley to the toothy Teton Mountains. The road, good for scenic drives, ATVs, hunting access, and mountain biking, also offers primitive campsites with big views overlooking the valley and the Tetons. The Buffalo Fork River parallels the highway heading west to its confluence with the Snake River—both trout fisheries. Paddling Jackson Dam to Pacific Creek on the Snake offers five miles of scenic, calm water. Buffalo Fork is closed to floating. Nonmotorized boats need a permit ($10 per week, $20 per season), available at the ranger station.

Rimmed with lodgepole pines and aspens, the sunny campground tucks its small campsites and small tent spaces around one loop. The best sites sit on the outside of the ring. Fireweed, wild roses, serviceberries, and sagebrush add to a short understory for some privacy. Sites 1 and 9 gaze north toward mountains, but unfortunately the highway is in sight, too. Given the campground's proximity to the highway, road noise is inevitable.

Campsites, facilities: The campground has nine RV or tent campsites. Sites can fit mid-sized RVs only. Facilities include picnic tables, fire rings with grills, pit toilets (wheelchair-accessible), drinking water, garbage service, and bear boxes. Leashed pets are permitted.

Reservations, fees: Reservations are not accepted. Campsites cost $10. Cash or check.

Open late May-September; however, if weather permits, campground stays open through fall without services.
Directions: From Moran Junction, drive east on Highway 26/287 for 8.3 miles. Turn south onto Hatchet Road (Forest Road 30160) and immediately left into the campground.
GPS Coordinates: N 43° 49.463' W 110° 21.323'
Contact: Bridger-Teton National Forest, Buffalo Ranger District, Hwy. 26/287, Moran, WY 83013, 307/543-2386, www.fs.usda.gov/btnf.

46 BOX CREEK

Scenic rating: 6
near Teton Wilderness in Bridger-Teton National Forest

Located in a valley of outfitters, Box Creek Campground at 7,000 feet is not a destination campground in itself, but one for access to the Teton Wilderness—a 585,238-acre wilderness bordering Yellowstone and Grand Teton National Parks. The trailhead campground is used mostly by horse-packers, with corrals, hitch rails, and stock ramps available. The Box Creek Trail climbs about five miles to 8,600 feet on Gravel Ridge. From the ridge, you view the destruction from the 1987 Teton Tornado—the highest altitude recorded of a tornado touchdown. It cut a swath up to three miles wide across a 20-mile strip, snapping trees like toothpicks and uprooting others. Trout fishing is available in the Buffalo Fork River, and the area offers big game hunting.

The campground—set in aspens and pines—circles on the end of a large, grassy meadow. Several of the campsites have views of the forest and mountains. This sunny, little-used campground is ultra-quiet and secluded, but you'll see other campers, if any are there.
Campsites, facilities: The campground has six RV or tent campsites. RVs are limited to 30

feet. Facilities include picnic tables, fire grates, vault toilet (wheelchair-accessible), bear boxes, garbage service, and stock facilities. Drinking water is not available. Bring your own, or fill up at Turpin Meadows 1.3 miles east. Leashed pets are permitted.
Reservations, fees: Reservations are not accepted. Campsites cost $10 per unit (RV, trailer, or tent). Cash or check. Open late May-September, weather permitting.
Directions: From Moran Junction, drive east on Highway 26/287 for 3.4 miles and turn north onto Buffalo Valley Road for 8.7 miles. Turn north onto the narrow dirt road with no pullouts and climb 0.7 mile to the campground. Note: On Buffalo Valley Road, the only sign notes Box Creek Trailhead with no mention of the campground. An alternative route to the campground road departs Highway 26/287 at milepost 13, heading north on the gravel Forest Road 30050 for 4.2 miles to the bridge over the Buffalo Fork River and then one mile on pavement.
GPS Coordinates: N 43° 51.617' W 110° 17.680'
Contact: Bridger-Teton National Forest, Buffalo Ranger District, Hwy. 26/287, Moran, WY 83013, 307/543-2386, www.fs.usda.gov/btnf.

47 TURPIN MEADOW

Scenic rating: 8
near Teton Wilderness in Bridger-Teton National Forest

Turpin Meadow Campground, at 7,300 feet, sits across the Buffalo Fork River from Turpin Meadow Guest Ranch in a high valley facing the Teton Mountains. From the river, the road, and the trailhead, you can see Mount Moran and the Tetons in the distance, but not from the campground. The river is a popular trout fishery, but be aware of private property if you head downstream. Paths lead from the campground to the river, which can be wade-fished. A popular trailhead, often packed with horse trailers, sits northeast of the campground, a jump-off point into the Teton Wilderness. The Clear Creek Trail makes an 18-mile loop with the Box Creek Trail, and the Buffalo Fork Trail follows the river west to the confluence of its north and south forks, where the trail divides to climb to the Continental Divide National Scenic Trail.

The gravel campground road weaves through a young lodgepole and fir forest surrounded by a lodgepole fence and huge sagebrush meadows. The first part of the loop features sunny campsites across from the outfitter camping area; the campsites at the end of the loop are more shaded—especially site 12. Big tent spaces are available. Mountain bluebirds frequent the campground.

Campsites, facilities: The campground has 18 RV or tent campsites. Sites can fit midsized RVs only. Facilities include picnic tables, fire rings with grills, vault toilet (wheelchair-accessible), drinking water, garbage service, bear boxes, and stock facilities. Leashed pets are permitted.

Reservations, fees: Reservations are not accepted. Campsites cost $10. Cash or check. Open late May-September; however, if weather permits, the campground stays open through fall without services.

Directions: From Moran Junction, drive east on Highway 26/287 for 3.4 miles and turn north onto Buffalo Valley Road for 9.7 miles. Before the bridge over Buffalo Fork River, swing east onto the gravel road for 0.1 mile and veer right for 0.2 mile and turn right into the campground. An alternative route to the bridge departs Highway 26/287 at milepost 13, heading north on gravel Forest Road 30050 for 4.2 miles.

GPS Coordinates: N 43° 51.335' W 110° 15.947'

Contact: Bridger-Teton National Forest, Buffalo Ranger District, Hwy. 26/287, Moran, WY 83013, 307/543-2386, www.fs.usda.gov/btnf.

48 COLTER BAY

Scenic rating: 10
on Jackson Lake in Grand Teton National Park

Colter Bay, at 6,793 feet on Jackson Lake, sits north of islands and inlets that provide boating, windsurfing, paddleboarding, waterskiing, canoeing, kayaking, swimming, and fishing sheltered from the big lake winds. Jet Skis are not allowed, and all boats require permits, available at the visitors center. The campground is part of the large Colter Bay Village, which contains a visitors center, restaurants, gas, grocery, and marina with a cement boat ramp, boat slips, trailer parking, docks, guided fishing, lake tours, and boat rentals (canoes, kayaks, and motorboats). The lake holds a variety of species for sport anglers. The picnic area has a designated swimming beach. The revamped visitors center contains a new Indian arts exhibit. Hikers can walk a maze of gentle trails to short destinations such as Swan Lake, Heron Pond, and the Lakeshore Trail, the latter yielding spectacular views of Mt. Moran and the Tetons. Longer loops tour Hermitage Point. Trailheads to Two Ocean and Emma Matilda Lakes are also within five miles. Mountain bikers can ride the short path along the breakwater along the bay or get stunning mountain views from the Two Ocean Lake Road. Horseback riding is available just south at Jackson Lake Lodge.

Divided into an RV hookup section and non-hookup loops, this giant lodgepole forest campground sits on a lodgepole bluff above Jackson Lake, its size more akin to a housing development than a campground. In the non-hookup loops, pullover sites line up close together, but many have fire pits and picnic tables tucked in forest nooks with visibility of only a neighbor or two. Only a handful of campsites in either section get views of the lake or the Teton Mountains. Although it crowds in summer, you can find

© BECKY LOMAX

Rental canoes, kayaks, and motorboats are available at Colter Bay on Jackson Lake.

breathing room in the off-season and quiet at night.

Campsites, facilities: The campground has 112 pull-throughs for large RVs with hookups for water, sewer, and electricity; 350 RV or tent campsites with no hookups, nine walk-in tent sites, shared hiker-biker campsites, and 11 group campsites. Facilities include picnic tables, fire pits with grills (non-hookup sites only), flush toilets, drinking water, disposal station, garbage service, bear boxes, and amphitheater for evening programs. Coin-op showers and launderette are available at Colter Bay Village. No tents, fires, or gas grills are permitted in the RV hookup campsites. Non-hookup loops include some generator-free zones. Leashed pets are permitted. Wheelchair-accessible facilities include toilets and campsites.

Reservations, fees: Reservations are accepted only for the RV hookup and group campsites (Grand Teton Lodge Company, 800/28-9988, 307/543-3100, www.gtlc.com). RV hookups cost $60. Non-hookup sites cost $21. Shared hiker and biker campsites cost $8 per person. Cash, check, or credit card. Open late May-late September.

Directions: From Jackson Lake Junction, drive 5.5 miles north, or from the south entrance to Yellowstone National Park, drive 18.5 miles south. Turn south into Colter Bay and drive 0.6 mile. Turn right into the campground. GPS Coordinates: N 43° 54.533' W 110° 38.493'

Contact: Grand Teton National Park, P.O. Drawer 170, Moose, WY 83102, 307/739-3300, www.nps.gov/grte/.

49 JACKSON LAKE

🚶 🏊 🚣 🛶 🎣 🐕 ⛺

Scenic rating: 10

on Jackson Lake in Grand Teton National Park

One of the largest high-altitude lakes in the United States at 6,772 feet, Jackson Lake is 15 miles long, 7 miles wide, and 438 feet deep. The lake tucks into the base of the jagged Teton Mountain Range with shoreline boat-in or hike-in campsites to get away from the crowds. The glacial lake trout waters are cold (only mid-50°F in August) and strong afternoon winds are common. Sailboats, windsurfers, and motorboats are permitted (No Jet Skis). Four boat launches rim the lake's east shore: Leeks Marina, Colter Bay Marina, Signal Mountain, and Spalding Bay. (Note: Budget cuts closed Spalding Bay in 2013. Call for status.) Hiking is available only from the Hermitage Point group campsite. Motorboat, canoe, and kayak rentals are available at Leeks Marina, Signal Mountain, and Colter Bay. Permits are required for boats; buy them at visitors centers.

Lake campsites are prized for their scenery, quiet, and solitude. Most campsites rim the lakeshore, set back into the trees for protection. Five campsites are on islands. Sites vary with sunrise or sunset views. Highly-prized ones face the Tetons.

Campsites, facilities: Jackson Lake has 10 individual tent campsites and five group tent campsites. Six people are allowed per campsite, except for group campsites, which can hold 12. Facilities include fire rings, bear boxes, and pit toilets, and a few campsites have tent platforms. No drinking water is available; bring your own, or treat lake water. Pets are not allowed in Jackson Lake campsites, except at Spalding Bay.

Reservations, fees: Reservation requests are accepted January 5-May 15. Applications are available online with a $25 nonrefundable fee. Then, 24 hours before your trip, obtain the required free overnight camping permits at the Craig Thomas and Colter Bay Visitor Centers or Jenny Lake Ranger Station. Boats must also have permits ($20 per week or $40 per season for motorized; $10 per week or $20 per season for nonmotorized). Purchase boat permits at Moose and Colter Bay Visitor Centers. Open June-October.

Directions: From Jackson Lake Junction, drive Highway 89/191/287 north to reach Colter Bay Marina in 5.5 miles or Leeks Marina in 6.3 miles. From Jackson Lake Junction, drive three miles south on Teton Park Road to reach Signal Mountain Marina. To reach Spalding Bay (a primitive launch for only single-axle trailers), drive north from North Jenny Lake Junction for 1.3 miles on Teton Park Road and turn northwest for 2.1 miles on dirt Spalding Bay Road.

GPS Coordinates for launch sites:
Leeks Marina: N 43° 55.797' W 110° 38.394'
Colter Bay Marina: N 43° 54.130' W 110° 38.611'
Signal Mountain Marina: N 43° 50.316' W 110° 36.976'
Spalding Bay: N 43° 49.446' W 110° 40.532'

Contact: Grand Teton National Park, P.O. Drawer 170, Moose, WY 83102, 307/739-3300, www.nps.gov/grte/.

50 SIGNAL MOUNTAIN

Scenic rating: 10
on Jackson Lake in Grand Teton National Park

BEST (

Signal Mountain Campground, at 6,802 feet, may command one of the best panoramic views of the jagged teeth of the Teton Mountains from its perch on the west shore of Jackson Lake. North of the campground, Signal Mountain Lodge houses a restaurant, convenience store, gas station, and marina with sailboat tours, guided fishing, and boat rentals (canoes, kayaks, and motorboats). Launching facilities sit south of the campground: cement boat ramp, dock, and trailer parking. The lake is popular for swimming, boating (no Jet Skis), fishing, waterskiing, kayaking, and canoeing, although be prepared for cold water and daily afternoon winds. Permits are required for all boats, available at park visitors centers. The steep 1.5-mile South Landing Trail connects the campground with the beach and boat launch. Driving tours along Teton Park Road often produce sightings of bugling elk in fall. The campground is named for the low mountain to the east. You can drive, bike, or hike to its summit for expansive views of the lake and Tetons. A 15-mile gravel road also parallels the Snake River eastward to Cottonwood—another option for wildlife-watching expeditions or mountain biking.

The campground loops around a hillside, where some of the campsites yield outstanding views of the lake and the Teton Mountains. A mix of fir and spruce provides some shade, but most of the campsites are sunny in midday. The campsites are small, with low brush creating partial privacy along with the trees. The narrow campground road and narrow parking pads can pose challenges for RV drivers unskilled in squeezing into tight spots. Loop 3 is generator-free. Because of its location and scenery, plan on arriving before noon to claim a campsite.

Campsites, facilities: The campground has 81 RV or tent campsites, four tent-only campsites, and one full hookup RV site (sewer, water, and electricity). RVs are limited to 30 feet. Facilities include picnic tables, fire rings with grills, flush toilets, drinking water, garbage service, amphitheater for evening programs, tent pads (30 sites), and disposal station. Only one vehicle is permitted per site. Leashed pets are permitted. A wheelchair-accessible toilet and campsite are available.

Reservations, fees: Reservations are not accepted. Campsites cost $21. RV site costs $55. Shared hiker and biker campsites cost $5. Cash or check. Open early May-early October.

Directions: From Jackson Lake Junction, drive south on Teton Park Road for three miles, or from Jenny Lake Visitor Center drive nine miles north. Turn west into Signal Mountain, continuing straight past the road heading right to the lodge to reach the campground. GPS Coordinates: N 43° 50.488' W 110° 36.809'

Contact: Grand Teton National Park, P.O. Drawer 170, Moose, WY 83102, 307/739-3300, www.nps.gov/grte/.

51 LEIGH LAKE

Scenic rating: 10

between Jenny Lake and Jackson Lake in Grand Teton National Park

Leigh Lake, a small 250-acre lake tucked at 6,877 feet below the giant toothy Teton Mountains, is a popular kayak and canoe destination for camping. Only human-powered boats are permitted on the lake, making it a quiet place to enjoy nature. Paddle trips to Leigh Lake start at String Lake, a three-mile-long small, shallow lake. A narrow, rocky, shallow stream requiring a 600-foot portage links the two lakes. Trails loop around String Lake and along Leigh Lake's east shore. Two islands—Mystic and Boulder—sit in Leigh Lake, good destinations for exploration. The Tetons are known for strong afternoon winds; plan paddling schedules accordingly. All boats, including kayaks and canoes, require permits, available at the visitors centers and the Jenny Lake backcountry office.

These coveted campsites are set back into the forest on the east and west shores of Leigh Lake. They are prized for their quiet, solitude, wildlife-watching, and scenery. Those on the eastern shore can capture dramatic mountain reflections and sunsets on the water. Those on the western shore do not have trail access, thus guaranteeing more privacy.

Campsites, facilities: Leigh Lake has seven individual tent campsites, plus one group tent site. Six people maximum are allowed per permit, except at group sites, which can hold 12. Boaters may stay in a designated site for two consecutive nights. Facilities include fire pits, bear boxes, and pit toilets, and some sites have tent platforms. No drinking water is available; treat lake water. Pack out your trash. Pets are not allowed.

Reservations, fees: Reservation requests are accepted January 5-May 15. Applications are available online with a $25 nonrefundable fee. Then, 24 hours before your trip, obtain the required free overnight camping permits at the Craig Thomas and Colter Bay Visitor Centers or Jenny Lake Ranger Station. Open June-October.

Directions: From Teton Lake Road, turn west at North Jenny Lake Junction and drive 1.5 miles. Turn right at the sign for String Lake Trailhead. Drive 0.2 mile northwest, opting for the parking area on the left or the one where the road ends. Both require 170-foot portages to the shore. GPS Coordinates: N 43° 47.173' W 110° 43.817'

Contact: Grand Teton National Park, P.O. Drawer 170, Moose, WY 83102, 307/739-3300, www.nps.gov/grte/.

© BECKY LOMAX

From Jenny Lake, hikers loop through the Paintbrush-Cascade Canyons below the Grand Teton.

52 JENNY LAKE

Scenic rating: 10

on Jenny Lake in Grand Teton National Park

BEST (

At 6,789 feet, Jenny Lake claims front-row seating below the immense Teton Mountains with exceptional scenery. A ranger station and general store serve as the hub for hikers, bikers, mountain climbers, and boaters. Hikers will want to stay for days. Trails lead to short destinations: Hidden Falls, Inspiration Point, Leigh Lake, and Jenny Lake Loop. The 18-mile Paintbrush-Cascade Loop Trail draws those looking for dramatic high-elevation backcountry and access to rock climbing. A shuttle boat speeds canyon hikers across the lake. Other trailheads sit just south of Jenny Lake, accessed via Teton Park Road. While the lake offers fishing, you may line up along the shore with hordes of anglers. A tour boat circles the lake, and paddlers can rent canoes or kayaks. A gravel boat launch is available for human-powered watercraft or motorboats with 10 horsepower or less. Boating permits are required, available at the backcountry office. The campground offers wildlife-watching, often with male elk rounding up harems in fall. A paved bike trail runs from Jenny Lake to the Craig Thomas Discover Education Center and Jackson. The scenic Jenny Lake Drive also has a paved bike lane.

Jenny Lake—the most popular campground in the park—fills by 9am each day. Its campsites, strung through the loose hilly pine forest and glacial boulders—are roomy. Some are partly shaded, but the best sit in open meadows claiming big views of the Tetons. Campsites are not private, but the trade-off in views is worth it. Trails run from the campground to the visitors center, lake, and boat dock. After day visitors retreat, the area quiets at night. Listen in September for elk bugling.

Campsites, facilities: The campground has 50 tent campsites including several walk-in sites. Pop ups, trailers, truck campers, and generators are prohibited. Vehicles must be smaller than 8 feet wide and 14 feet long. Two tents, one vehicle or two motorcycles, and six people are the maximum allowed per site. Facilities include picnic tables, fire rings with grills, bear boxes, vault toilets, drinking water, shared hiker and biker campsites, and garbage service. Leashed pets are permitted. Wheelchair-accessible facilities include toilets and campsites.

Reservations, fees: Reservations are not accepted. Campsites cost $21. Shared hiker and biker campsites cost $8. Cash or check. Open mid-May-late September.

Directions: On Teton Park Road, drive toward Jenny Lake Visitor Center. Turn west, entering the visitors center complex, for 0.1 mile and turn right at the campground sign for 0.1 mile. GPS Coordinates: N 43° 45.220' W 110° 43.261'

Contact: Grand Teton National Park, P.O. Drawer 170, Moose, WY 83102, 307/739-3300, www.nps.gov/grte/.

At Jackson Hole Mountain Resort, visitors and hikers can take a tram up to the top of Rendezvous Mountain in the Tetons.

53 JACKSON HOLE

Scenic rating: 8

in Jackson Hole

Sitting below the towering Teton Mountains, Jackson Hole Campground has convenience. Five miles north, hikers and sightseers can ride the iconic Jackson Hole Mountain Resort tram to the top of 10,450-foot Rendezvous Mountain for impressive views of the Jackson Hole valley and Grand Teton Mountain. Trails come back down the mountain or head into Grand Teton National Park. Lift-accessed mountain biking is also available at the resort. Across the highway from the campground, the Jackson Hole Community Pathway for runners, walkers, and cyclists connects with Teton Village, Moose, and Jackson.

Grassy campsites squeeze under mature cottonwoods and conifers for shade, but more open campsites grab prime views of the Teton Mountains. Larger RVs will feel cramped with low branches and narrow slots. Small tent sites tuck in between RV sites. Renovations in 2012 improved the gravel campground road and washrooms.

Campsites, facilities: This campground has 63 RV campsites, including eight tent campsites. RVs are limited to 40 feet. Hookups are available for water, sewer, and electricity up to 50 amps. Facilities include picnic tables, rock fire rings, flush toilets, showers, drinking water, launderette, camp store, wireless Internet, and disposal station. Leashed pets are permitted.

Reservations, fees: Reservations are accepted. RV sites cost $70-100. Tents cost $40-50. Rates cover four people; each extra person costs $8; kids under six stay for free. Add on sales tax. Cash, check, or credit card. Open May-mid-October.

Directions: From the junction of Highway 22 and Highway 390, drive north on Highway 390 (Moose Wilson Road) for 1.5 miles and turn right at the Fireside Resort sign. Or from Teton Village, drive 5.1 miles south and turn left.

GPS Coordinates: N 43° 31.222' W 110° 50.360'

Contact: Jackson Hole Campground, 2780 North Moose Wilson Road, Wilson, WY 83014, 307/732-2267, www.jacksonholecampground.com.

54 GROS VENTRE

Scenic rating: 8

on the Gros Ventre River in the south end of Grand Teton National Park

Gros Ventre Campground, at 6,568 feet, is not only the largest campground in Grand Teton National Park, but the closest national park campground to Jackson, about 12 miles south. The campground sits opposite the river from the National Elk Refuge, which attracts the largest collection of migrating elk each winter. Gros Ventre Road, a backroad cycling route, provides scenic opportunities for wildlife-watching for bison and elk. The campground's location is convenient for floating or fishing the lower stretches of the Snake River for 14 miles from Moose Landing to Wilson, which requires advanced boating skills. The Gros Ventre River, which flows past the campground, unfortunately often becomes a barren riverbed mid-July-September because of water diverted for irrigation.

The campground, which sits along the Gros Ventre River but with Black Butte blocking most of the Teton Mountains, sprawls its seven large loops on a flat sagebrush plateau beneath cottonwood trees for some shade. Paths lead to the river. Because of its road configurations and campsite parking pads, this campground is the best one in the national park for large trailers and RVs; it is also the last to fill up every day and often doesn't fill to capacity. Located several miles from the highway, the

campground is quiet, secluded, and a respite from busy downtown Jackson or the more popular tourist areas of the park. With no understory, campsites lack privacy.

Campsites, facilities: The campground has 350 individual RV and tent campsites and five large group sites. Two tents, two vehicles, and six people are the maximum allowed per site. The campsites can fit large RVs. Facilities include picnic tables, fire rings with grills, flush toilets, a disposal station, drinking water, an amphitheater for interpretive programs, and garbage service. Leashed pets are permitted. Wheelchair-accessible facilities include toilets and campsites.

Reservations, fees: Reservations are accepted only for group campsites (Grand Teton Lodge Company, 307/543-3100 or 800/628-9988). Campsites cost $21. Cash, check, or credit card. Open early May-early October.

Directions: From Gros Ventre Junction on Highway 89/191, turn northeast onto Gros Ventre Road for 4.6 miles. Turn south for 0.3 mile into the campground.

GPS Coordinates: N 43° 36.979' W 110° 39.979'

Contact: Grand Teton National Park, P.O. Drawer 170, Moose, WY 83102, 307/739-3300, www.nps.gov/grte/.

55 ATHERTON CREEK

Scenic rating: 8

in the Gros Ventre Mountains in Bridger-Teton National Forest

Atherton Creek Campground, elevation 7,000 feet, draws a varied boating crowd because of its location on the north shore of Lower Slide Lake in the colorful red- and orange-streaked Gros Ventre Mountains. Canoeists explore the shoreline, which has silvered trunks buried by water when the lake was formed by a 1925 landslide. Anglers fish for brook, lake, and cutthroat trout. Water-skiers weave a white trail across calm, blue water. When daily winds crop up, windsurfers hit the waves. The Gros Ventre Slide Geological Area still shows the track of the landslide, and an interpretive trail tells the story of the lake's creation. Mountain biking is an option on Gros Ventre Road, with bucolic views west of the Teton Mountains. A boat dock and ramp are available. May-July the Lower Gros Ventre River offers kayakers Class III-IV white water.

The sunny quiet hillside campground gleans a little shade from aspens, spruces, firs, and small willow bushes strung around its interconnected loops, which have back-in gravel parking pads. Sagebrush and wild roses complete the understory for campsites that range from shady and private to sunny and open. Sites 16 and 17 sit on the water, while sites 18 and 20 overlook the water; many of the other campsites have no view of the lake, but some have views of surrounding forest slopes. In the breeze, the aspen leaves clatter with a soothing background sound, but prepare for strong afternoon winds.

Campsites, facilities: The campground has 20 RV or tent campsites. Sites can fit midsized RVs only. Facilities include picnic tables, fire rings with grills, vault toilets (wheelchair-accessible), drinking water, garbage service, bear boxes, tent platforms, and campground hosts. Leashed pets are permitted.

Reservations, fees: Reservations are not accepted. Campsites cost $12. Cash or check. Open late May-September.

Directions: From Moose Junction, drive north 1.2 miles and turn east onto Antelope Flats Road for 3.2 miles. Turn south onto Lower Gros Ventre Road for 2.5 miles. Turn east onto Gros Ventre Road for 5.5 miles of bumpy paved road to the campground entrance on the right.

GPS Coordinates: N 43° 38.269' W 110° 31.333'

Contact: Bridger-Teton National Forest, Jackson Ranger District, 25 Rosencrans Ln., Jackson, WY 83001, 307/739-5400, www.fs.usda.gov/btnf.

56 RED HILLS AND CRYSTAL CREEK

Scenic rating: 8

in the Gros Ventre Mountains in Bridger-Teton National Forest

Sitting at 7,000 feet in the Gros Ventre Mountains of Bridger-Teton National Forest, Red Hill and Crystal Creek are a pair of small, older, adjacent campgrounds that allow exploration of the range facing the Teton Mountains. Red Hills is named for the red-orange sagebrush hills that create such a dramatic contrast in color. Crystal Creek Campground sits at the confluence of Crystal Creek with the Gros Ventre River. Both offer native cutthroat trout fishing, mountain biking on forest roads and nearby trails, and hiking. Trails run south along Crystal Creek into the Gros Ventre Wilderness, but only hikers may travel into the wilderness for climbing its 10,000-foot peaks, an important wildlife enclave for bighorn sheep, elk, and bears. Raft, kayaks, and canoes put in at the Warden Bridge to float eight miles of Class II-III rapids to Lower Slide Lake.

Both campgrounds squeeze in between the road and the river in a forest of spruces and firs. Willows line the riverbank. In Red Hills, sites 1, 2, 4, and 5 claim river frontage, with views of the red-orange hills surrounded by sagebrush. In Crystal Creek, sites 3 and 4 overlook the river, with big views of the richly colored countryside. The quiet, older campgrounds are popular with locals but rarely crowded.

Campsites, facilities: The campgrounds have 11 RV or tent campsites—five at Red Hills and six at Crystal Creek. Sites and the narrow campground roads can fit midsized RVs only. Red Hills has no turnaround. Facilities include picnic tables, fire rings with grills or rock fire rings, pit and vault toilets, drinking water, and bear boxes. Leashed pets are permitted.

Reservations, fees: Reservations are not

accepted. Campsites cost $10. Cash or check. Open late May-September, but Crystal Creek stays open into fall if weather permits.

Directions: From Moose Junction, drive north 1.2 miles and turn east onto Antelope Flats Road for 3.2 miles. Turn south onto Lower Gros Ventre Road for 2.5 miles. Turn east onto Gros Ventre Road for 10 miles of bumpy paved and dirt road. The campground entrances are on the left 0.4 mile apart.

Red Hills GPS Coordinates: N 43° 36.691' W 110° 26.266'

Crystal Creek GPS Coordinates: N 43° 36.643' W 110° 25.865'

Contact: Bridger-Teton National Forest, Jackson Ranger District, 25 Rosencrans Ln., Jackson, WY 83001, 307/739-5400, www.fs.usda.gov/btnf.

57 CURTIS CANYON

Scenic rating: 9

in the Gros Ventre Mountains in Bridger-Teton National Forest

Located at the north end of the Gros Ventre Mountains, the area around Curtis Canyon Campground has million-dollar views! At 7,000 feet on the east side of Jackson Hole, the area overlooks the Jackson Hole valley, National Elk Refuge, and the Teton Mountains. Across the road from the campground sits an overlook, a good place to walk in the evening to watch the sun set over the Tetons. The Curtis Canyon Road and spur forest roads attract mountain bikers and OHV riders. This is the closest Forest Service campground to the town of Jackson.

One prime campsite has the million-dollar view, like the overlook. The others cluster under a small forest of Douglas firs. Beneath the tree canopy, only tree trunks separate the grassy sites, letting you see the neighbors.

Campsites, facilities: The campground has 10 RV or tent campsites, plus two tent-only

sites. A few parking pads can fit RVs up 40 feet, but small RVs will fit the narrow campground road, access road, overhanging trees, and parking pad width and angles better. Two pull-through sites are available. Facilities include picnic tables, fire rings with grills, vault toilets, drinking water, garbage service, firewood for sale, and bear boxes. Leashed pets are permitted.

Reservations, fees: Reservations are not accepted. Campsites cost $12 for one unit (RV, trailer, or tent). Cash or check. Open late May-September.

Directions: In Jackson, take Broadway east to its terminus at Nelson Drive and the National Elk Refuge Road. Turn north onto the gravel refuge road for 4.6 miles. Turn right onto Curtis Canyon Road for 2.6 miles to climb to the campground entrance on the right. Curtis Canyon Road is narrow, rocky, and has one sharp hairpin.

GPS Coordinates: N 43° 30.788' W 110° 39.672'

Contact: Bridger-Teton National Forest, Jackson Ranger District, 25 Rosencrans Ln., Jackson, WY 83001, 307/739-5400, www.fs.usda.gov/btnf.

58 VIRGINIAN RV PARK

Scenic rating: 6

in Jackson

The Virginian RV Park is the only campground in downtown Jackson, making it a campground of convenience about one mile from the downtown area with shopping, galleries, restaurants, park with antler arches, and famous cowboy western saloons. A free shuttle across the street runs to downtown Jackson. The campground is part of the Virginian Lodge, a motel complex with a restaurant, saloon, liquor store, hair salon, and heated outdoor pool and hot tub. Hiking and mountain biking trails weave around Snow

King Mountain, which looms to the south of town. The ski area at Snow King transforms in summer with the thrill of zipping down alpine slides and horseback riding.

The sunny parking lot-style campground sits behind the Virginian Lodge surrounded by commercial properties. Narrow small plots of grass separate the sites, which are about 20 feet wide. A handful of small trees offer minimal shade.

Campsites, facilities: This campground has 103 RV campsites. RVs are limited to 40 feet. The campground has 64 pull-throughs and 39 back-in slots with gravel parking pads and road. Hookups are available for water, sewer, cable TV, and electricity up to 50 amps. Facilities include picnic tables, flush toilets, showers, drinking water, launderette, and wireless Internet. Campers can use the swimming pool and hot tub at the lodge. Leashed pets are permitted.

Reservations, fees: Reservations are accepted. Campsites cost $65-70. A 6 percent sales tax is added. Cash, check, or credit card. Open May-mid-October.

Directions: From the junction of highways 22/189/89, drive east on West Broadway for three blocks and turn right.

GPS Coordinates: N 43° 28.358' W 110° 46.679'

Contact: Virginian RV Park, 750 West Broadway, Jackson Hole, WY 83001, 307/733-7189 or 800/321-6982, http://virginianlodge.com.

59 SNAKE RIVER PARK KOA

Scenic rating: 7
on the Snake River near Jackson

The Snake River Park KOA, elevation 5,090 feet, is a combination campground and whitewater rafting outfitter on the Snake River between Hoback Junction and Jackson. Those camping at the park can get 10 percent off white-water rafting trips or saddle and paddle trips. The corral is across the street from the campground. The campground is 20 minutes from the entrance to Grand Teton National Park and 15 minutes from Jackson. Fishing is available on the Snake River from the campground.

Tucked into a deep narrow canyon, the campground squeezes between the busy two-lane highway rumbling with commercial haul trucks and the Snake River. Tent campsites sit along Horse Creek and the river with partial shade and views. The sunny RV campsites are lined up in parking-lot fashion with mowed lawns between sites. Stairs lead from the campground to the sandy riverbank.

Campsites, facilities: This campground has 47 RV back-in campsites and 10 tent campsites. RVs are limited to 36 feet. Hookups are available for water, sewer, and electricity up to 50 amps. Facilities include picnic tables, fire rings with grills, flush toilets, showers, drinking water, a coin-op launderette, a game room, firewood for sale, playground, pet walk, convenience store, and wireless Internet. Leashed pets are permitted.

Reservations, fees: Reservations are accepted. RV hookups costs $81-89. Tents cost $41-45. Rates run less during spring and fall. Rates cover four people; each extra person costs $8; kids under six stay for free. A 6 percent sales tax is added. Cash, check, or credit card. Open mid-April-November.

Directions: On Highway 26/89/197/191, drive 12 miles south of Jackson or 1.5 miles north of Hoback Junction. Turn west into campground.

GPS Coordinates: N 43° 20.450' W 110° 43.400'

Contact: Jackson South/Snake River KOA, 9705 S. Hwy. 89, Jackson, WY 83001, 307/733-7078 or 800/562-1878, www.srpkoa.com.

NORTHERN YELLOWSTONE GATEWAYS

© BECKY LOMAX

The Gallatin, Madison, Yellowstone, and Clarks Fork

of the Yellowstone River valleys provide the four main corridors to reach Yellowstone National Park's northern gateways of West Yellowstone, Gardiner, and Cooke City. Most of the campgrounds along these three rivers are easily accessible via pavement with only a few dirt-road driving miles. The Gallatin River draws the most crowds, due to its proximity to Bozeman. These campgrounds also lure campers for outstanding hiking, climbing, rafting, and mountain biking in Gallatin National Forest. Campgrounds are much more frequent on the Madison than on the Yellowstone River, which flows through more private land in Paradise Valley. The Beartooth Highway climbs over a two-mile-high pass en route to Yellowstone; six developed campgrounds sit within a few miles of one another, accessible for the three months it is snow-free.

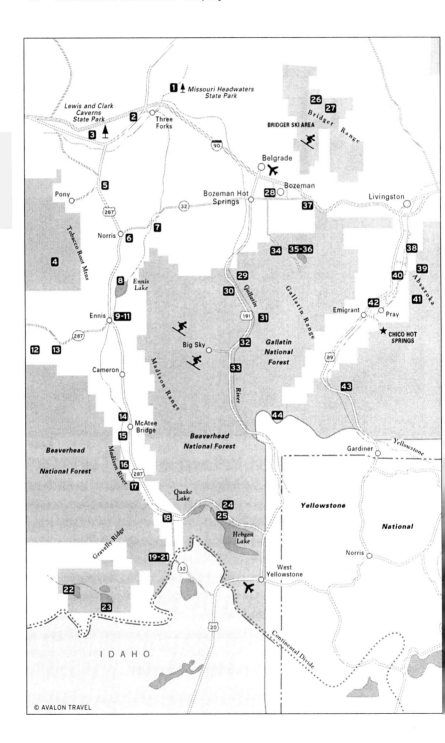

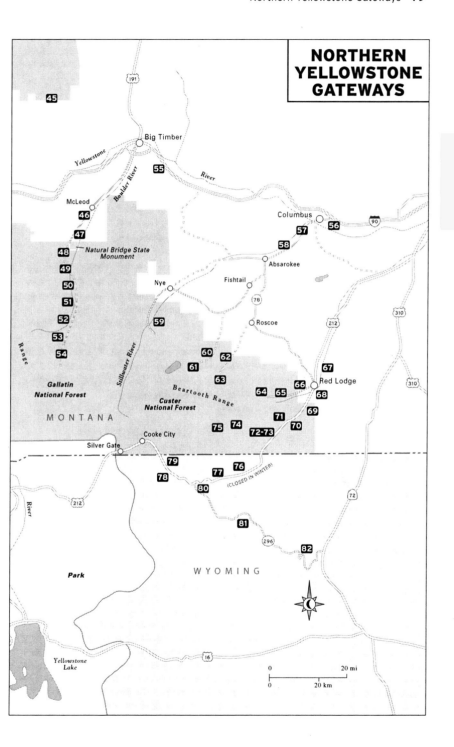

NORTHERN YELLOWSTONE GATEWAYS

191

45

Big Timber

Yellowstone

55

River

Boulder River

McLeod

46

47

48 Natural Bridge State Monument

49

50

51

52

53

54

Columbus

57   56

58

90

Absarokee

Fishtail

78

Nye

Roscoe

310

212

59

Stillwater River

60   62

61

63

67

64   65   66   Red Lodge

68

310

Range

Gallatin National Forest

Beartooth Range

71   69

Custer National Forest

75   74   72-73   70

M O N T A N A

Cooke City

Silver Gate

79

78   77   76

80   (CLOSED IN WINTER)

212

River

72

81

296

82

Park

W Y O M I N G

Yellowstone Lake

16

0   20 mi

0   20 km

1 MISSOURI HEADWATERS STATE PARK

🏃 🚴 ♒ 🛶 🚐 ⛴ 🎣 ♿ 🚍 ⛺

Scenic rating: 7

on the Missouri River near Three Forks

BEST (

Located at the confluence of the Gallatin, Madison, and Jefferson Rivers, Missouri Headwaters State Park marks the beginning of the Mighty Mo's 2,565-mile journey. At 4,045 feet, the 506-acre state park provides outstanding interpretive sites about Native American use of the area, Lewis and Clark's passage, and the river ecosystems. For anyone who lives along the Missouri, families with school-age kids, or history buffs, this is a "must do" educational stop. Four miles of hiking trails (some permit dogs) tour the park. A concrete ramp launches boaters, rafters, kayakers, and anglers to float the first eight miles of the nation's longest river. Along with the three rivers that form the Missouri, the big waters harbor trout. A paved six-mile bike trail connects with the town of Three Forks. The park provides superb habitat for watching wildlife: moose, raptors, songbirds, and waterfowl.

The small campground sits adjacent to the Madison River, but the thick jungle of willows, cattails, and brush block campsite views of the river. Short trails connect to it. The grassy campground packs sites close together; those at the front are wide open, but sites at the back garner a little privacy. A few large cottonwoods and willows lend morning shade, but most sites bake with hot afternoon sun, especially midsummer. Owls hoot at night, and catbirds fill the marsh with mimicry during the day.

Campsites, facilities: The campground has 17 RV or tent campsites. RVs are limited to 35 feet. Facilities include picnic tables on cement pads, fire rings with grills, vault toilets, drinking water, campfire programs, rental tipi, and campground hosts. Pack out your trash. Leashed pets are permitted. Wheelchair-accessible facilities include a toilet and campsite.

Reservations, fees: Reservations are accepted online or by phone (855/922-6768). Campsites cost $15 for Montana residents (seniors and disabled get half price) and $23 for nonresidents Memorial Day weekend-Labor Day, or campsites cost $12 for Montana residents and $20 for nonresidents September and May. Tipi rental costs $22-50. Nonresidents with a Non-Resident Entrance Pass ($25) get a $5 discount on camping fees. Cash, check, or credit card. The park is open year-round, but camping is available only May-September.

Directions: From I-90 at Three Forks, take Exit 278 and head on Highway 205 toward Trident for 1.8 miles. Turn north onto Highway 286 and drive 1.6 miles to the park's information plaza on the right. Pay for campsites here; the campground entrance is on the opposite side of the road.

GPS Coordinates: N 45° 55.214' W 111° 29.927'

Contact: Montana Fish, Wildlife, and Parks, Missouri Headwaters State Park, 1400 S. 19th St., Bozeman, MT 59718, 406/994-4042, http://stateparks.mt.gov.

2 CAMP THREE FORKS

🏃 🚴 ♒ 🛶 🚐 ⛴ 🎣 🐾 🚍 ⛺

Scenic rating: 6

west of Three Forks

Camp Three Forks is named for the nearby confluence of the Jefferson, Madison, and Gallatin Rivers, which together form the Missouri River. The Drouillard fishing access site is within a five-minute drive, providing access to the Jefferson River for fly-fishing, rafting, kayaking, and floating. Within four miles, Three Forks has a golf course, groceries, gas, the paved six-mile Headwaters Trail system for hikers and bikers, and ponds for canoeing, kayaking, and children's fishing. The campground also sits less than seven miles from Missouri Headwaters State Park. The Wheat Montana store and deli—the place to buy Montana flour—is 1.3 miles to the north. The campground conveniently lies at the junction of I-90 and the Madison and Jefferson River Valleys.

Flanked by flower beds, the landscaped campground has loops of gravel roads with gravel parking pads. A variety of leafy trees lend partial shade. This ex-KOA campground has sites close together, and truck noise from the highway floats in at night. Some of the campsites have southeast-facing views of the Gallatin Mountains.

Campsites, facilities: The campground has 65 pull-through RV sites and 21 tent campsites. RVs are limited to 63 feet. Facilities include picnic tables, fire rings, vault toilets, drinking water, garbage service, launderette, playground, wireless Internet, swimming pool, and firewood for sale. Leashed pets are permitted.

Reservations, fees: Reservations are accepted. Hookups cost $26-38. Tent sites cost $24. Cash or check. Open late May-mid-September.

Directions: From I-90 west of Three Forks, take Exit 274 and drive south on Highway 287 for 1.1 miles. Turn right onto KOA Road for 0.1 mile and turn left into the campground. GPS Coordinates: N 45° 54.174' W111° 36.134'

Contact: Camp Three Forks, 15 KOA Rd., Three Forks, MT 59752, 406/285-3611 or 866/523-1773, campthreeforks.com.

3 LEWIS AND CLARK CAVERNS STATE PARK

Scenic rating: 7

on the Jefferson River

BEST (

On the Jefferson River, Lewis and Clark Caverns State Park offers a tour through the limestone caves with fantastical stalactites, columns, dripstones, ribbons, and cave popcorn. Guided two-hour tours ($5-10) of the caverns are available May-September. You'll descend

The Lewis and Clark Caverns hold otherworldly limestone formations.

© BECKY LOMAX

600 steps and see utter darkness when the guide flips off the lights. The caverns are 1,400 vertical feet above the campground on a road not suitable for trailers. It's a 3.2-mile drive from the campground. Across the highway, an access site allows for shore or wade fishing on the Jefferson River. Nine miles of hiking trails, including a 0.25-mile nature trail, tour the 2,920-acre park. Mountain bikes are allowed on some of these. The park also provides good wildlife-watching.

The campground, which sits at river level in the dramatic canyon, is good for tenters, with oodles of flat spaces. The grassy campground, which turns brown by the end of summer, offers no privacy, and only a couple of trees provide partial shade to a few sites. With the highway and the railroad tracks in the canyon, the campground is noisy at night. Watch for rattlesnakes.

Campsites, facilities: The campground has 40 RV or tent campsites. RVs are limited to 60 feet long. Facilities include picnic tables, fire rings with grills, flush toilets

YELLOWSTONE GATEWAY RIVERS

Yellowstone National Park feeds some of the nation's most well-known blue-ribbon trout streams—waters that rush northward, forming its northern gateways. In Montana, these rivers wended their way into the history books, literature, and movies. From the Lewis and Clark expedition to the movie *A River Runs Through It*, the iconic image of wading thigh-deep in a river while casting a fly on its surface has sunk deep into the psyche of every angler.

For those who camp, the dream of lunker trout can become a reality in this region of rivers. Many of Yellowstone's northern gateway trout streams sit so far from towns brimming with hotels that tents and RVs become the way to travel if you want to savor days on the river. Campgrounds are much more frequent than lodges.

The northern Yellowstone gateway rivers flow south to north, lining up in parallel valleys with roads running alongside. You'll be lucky to find yourself alone in midsummer fly-fishing on a stretch of the famous **Madison, Gallatin,** or **Yellowstone Rivers.** The 140 miles of the Madison River may be the most famous Montana blue-ribbon trout stream, hopping with rainbow and brown trout, but its canyon and sagebrush banks are largely public. In addition, the Madison, Jefferson, and Gallatin Rivers feed the Mighty Mo, the **Missouri River.** The longest river in the U.S. has its birthplace in **Missouri Headwaters State Park.**

U.S. Forest Service and Bureau of Land Management campgrounds make up the largest camping options on the rivers. But

(wheelchair-accessible), electrical hookups, showers, drinking water, garbage service, amphitheater programs, disposal station, playground, and campground host. Leashed pets are permitted.

Reservations, fees: Reservations are accepted online or by phone (855/922-6768). Campsites cost $15 for Montana residents (seniors and disabled get half price) and $23 for nonresidents Memorial Day weekend-Labor Day, or $12 for Montana residents and $20 for nonresidents September-May. Campsites with electrical hookups cost $17-28, depending on season and residency. Nonresidents with a Non-Resident Entrance Pass ($25) get a $5 discount on camping fees. Cash, check, or credit card. Open year-round.

Directions: From I-90 east of Whitehall, take Exit 256. On the south side of the freeway, drive east on Highway 2 for 7.3 miles. From I-90 near Three Forks, take Exit 274 and go south on Highway 2/287 for 11.2 miles. Stay on Highway 2 as it splits off from 287 and head west for five miles. The signed park entrance is on the north side of the road.

Drive 0.2 mile up and turn left to enter the campground.

GPS Coordinates: N 45° 49.422' W 111° 51.324'

Contact: Montana Fish, Wildlife, and Parks, Lewis and Clark Caverns, P.O. Box 489, Whitehall, MT 59759, 406/287-3541, http://stateparks.mt.gov.

4 BRANHAM LAKES

Scenic rating: 9

in the Tobacco Root Mountains in Beaverhead-Deerlodge National Forest

At 8,800 feet in the Tobacco Root Mountains, Branham Lakes offer an idyllic pair of high subalpine lakes cradled in a basin below the 10,367-foot Mount Bradley. The tiny lakes make great swimming holes on hot days, but be prepared for chilly water. Trout fishing is best from a float tube, and a primitive boat ramp allows for launching small hand-carried watercraft such as in a testament to the popularity of fishing, rafting, floating, and kayaking, the state of Montana operates a horde of small, primitive campgrounds at fishing access sites. The rare RV park sidles up to the riverbank with hookups.

To escape the crowds of the three big-name rivers, head to the gaggle of smaller streams that plunge from the high peaks of the Absaroka-Beartooth Mountains. The **Stillwater, Big Timber, Rosebud,** and **Rock Creek Rivers** each offer something different for campers, hikers, mountain bikers, anglers, and rafters. However, routes into Montana's highest mountains along these rivers are mostly via long, dirt roads with wall-to-wall washboards and potholes sometimes large enough to swallow truck wheels. The smaller, more-primitive campgrounds along these rivers

fill with tenters and only small to mid-size RVs due to the difficulty of the access.

These smaller rivers plummet from glaciers in the Absaroka-Beartooth Wilderness. As Rock Creek tumbles eastward, its valley also forms the eastern ascent from Red Lodge for the Beartooth Highway. The Beartooth Highway—touted by Charles Kuralt as "America's most beautiful highway"—lives up to its nickname and outclasses other Yellowstone gateways with its high alpine plateaus framed by snowcapped peaks. Outside of its six developed campgrounds, you can find solitude in the ream of primitive dispersed campsites along **Rock Creek.**

Although Montana's gateways to Yellowstone are all rivers bouncing with trout, the state's highest mountains also provide unparalleled hiking and mountain biking. Camping is the way to see them best.

rowboats and canoes. A 1.5-mile, steep hiking trail departs from the campground for the ridge at 9,700 feet in high in alpine mountain goat terrain with panoramic views.

The campground loop snuggles under trees adjacent to the upper lake. The two sites at the north end of the loop sit nearest the lake. Utter quiet, privacy, and scenery abound with this campground. Be prepared for mosquitoes in July!

Campsites, facilities: The campground has six RV or tent campsites that can accommodate small RVs. Facilities include picnic tables, fire rings, and vault toilets (wheelchair-accessible). Drinking water is not available; bring your own or treat lake water. Pack out your trash. Leashed pets are permitted.

Reservations, fees: Reservations are not accepted. Camping is free. Open mid-May-September.

Directions: From Sheridan on Montana Highway 287, drive east on Mill Creek Road for 13 miles until it ends in the campground loop. The road becomes dirt, narrow, rough, slow-going, and not recommended for trailers, but it

is accessible by two-wheel-drive vehicles. Call to check on road conditions before driving. GPS Coordinates: N 45° 30.962' W 111° 59.469'

Contact: Beaverhead-Deerlodge National Forest, Madison Ranger District, 5 Forest Service Rd., Ennis, MT 59729, 406/682-4253, www.fs.usda.gov/bdnf.

⑤ HARRISON LAKE

Scenic rating: 6

on Willow Creek Reservoir

Harrison Lake, elevation 4,741 feet, is a primitive fishing access site run by the state. Its real name is Willow Creek Reservoir, but it carries the Harrison name after the nearby town. The 713-acre lake contains brown and westslope cutthroat trout and is stocked regularly with rainbow trout. True to its name, the lake is surrounded by willow brush, making the best fishing via boat. The access road to get to the campground is rough, rutted, and bumpy. It turns to gumbo when wet and is dusty when dry. A concrete boat ramp and a primitive boat ramp aid launching onto the lake in two different locations of the campground. The lake is a locals' hangout for waterskiing, boating, canoeing, and fishing.

The primitive campground spreads out in three different locations around a large peninsula with low mountain views in the distance. The weedy sites are rough, uneven, and dusty or muddy. Most of the sites are open, sunny, and visited by black flies. The campground sees more use on weekends and holidays, while weekdays have sparser visitation. After boats pull off the lake in the evening, the area is exceptionally quiet, with only a songbird or two in the early morning.

Campsites, facilities: The campground has 12 RV or tent campsites that can accommodate midsize RVs. Facilities include picnic tables, fire rings with grills, and vault toilets (wheelchair-accessible). Leashed pets are permitted.

Reservations, fees: Reservations are not accepted. Campsites cost $7 with a Montana fishing license and $12 without a Montana fishing license. Cash or check. Open year-round.

Directions: From Highway 287 in Harrison, turn east onto Harrison Lake Road for four dirt-road miles.

GPS Coordinates: N 45° 41.982' W 111° 42.582'

Contact: Montana Fish, Wildlife, and Parks, Region 3, 1400 S. 19th Ave., Bozeman, MT 59718, 406/994-4042, http://fwp.mt.gov.

6 NORRIS HOT SPRINGS

Scenic rating: 6

near Norris

BEST (

Norris Hot Springs, elevation 4,834 feet, is a true Montana relic with a cult-type following. The 30- by 40-foot wooden hot pool fills with hot mineral water every morning. Temperatures vary seasonally between 100°F and 106°F. The hot springs are open year-round, Wednesdays through Sundays, but closed two days per week for cleaning and letting the wood dry. Live music comes to the hot springs on Friday through Sunday nights. The All Local Foods Grill serves up organic, locally sourced Montana meats and fresh veggies, some grown in the hot springs greenhouse. An onsite saloon serves up Montana microbrews along with wine.

The small sunny campground lines up RV sites close together in a row, but separates the sites with privacy fences. The tent sites, located furthest from the hot springs pool, sit in a shared grassy area. Views from the campsites span the surrounding low arid hills and the highway. No shade trees are in the campground.

Campsites, facilities: The campground has nine RV sites and three tent campsites. RVs are limited to midsized rigs. Hookups include water, sewer, and electricity. Facilities include flush toilets, showers, wireless Internet, and discounts on unlimited soaking in the hot springs ($3 per day). Leashed pets are permitted. No generators are allowed.

Reservations, fees: Reservations are not accepted. Campsites cost $30 for hookups and $20 for tents. Cash or check. Open May-September.

Directions: From Highway 287 in Norris, turn east onto Highway 84 for 0.25-miles to the entrance on the right.

GPS Coordinates: N 45° 34.460' W 111° 41.074'

Contact: Norris Hot Springs, 1400 S. 19th Ave., Bozeman, MT 59718, 406/685-3303, www.norrishotsprings.com.

7 RED MOUNTAIN

Scenic rating: 8

on the Madison River

BEST (

On the banks of the lower Madison River,

Red Mountain Campground sits at the bottom of Bear Trap Canyon, a narrow slice through 1,500-foot-tall red cliffs on the Madison River. Upriver in the Lee Metcalf Wilderness, waters plunge through the canyon with the Class IV Kitchen Sink rapid. Paralleling the rapids, the nine-mile Bear Trap Canyon National Recreation Trail departs from Warm Springs Recreation Area, which also serves as the take-out for rafting the canyon about two miles south of the campground. A new boat launch now sits across the bridge from the campground, offering another option for launching or taking out. The river harbors 18-inch rainbow and brown trout, but the wade fishing is best before mid-July when the water warms up. It is also close to Norris Hot Springs, Montana's only wooden hot springs pool, eight miles west.

Recent additions have enlarged the camping opportunities here. Red Mountain, the original campground, rims with a few junipers and willow brush that survived the recent fire. Although surrounding slopes contain the burnt remnants of sparse trees, green grass and wildflowers have returned. The new Trapper Springs loop, located across the highway from Red Mountain, is rougher with mostly sagebrush. Two spur roads on both sides of the river (Beartrap and County Roads) lead to more primitive sites that vary with grass and willow brush, but line up along the riverfront. Sun is pervasive and hot in August. Given the lack of trees, none of the sites offer privacy. Even though you'll hear some trucking noise from the adjacent highway at night, catbirds will wake you in the morning. Watch for rattlesnakes.

Campsites, facilities: The zone has four camping areas for RVs or tents: Red Mountain has 17 sites, Trapper Springs has 15 sites, Beartrap Road has 7 sites, and County Road has 8 sites. Many can accommodate large RVs. Facilities at Red Mountain and Trapper Springs include picnic tables, fire rings with grills, vault toilets, drinking water, firewood for sale, and campground hosts. Facilities at the Beartrap and County Road sites include picnic tables and fire rings. Pack out your trash. Leashed pets are permitted. Wheelchair-accessible toilets are available.

Reservations, fees: Reservations are not accepted. Campsites in the Red Mountain loops or Trapper Springs loop cost $8. An extra vehicle costs $5. Campsites on the Beartrap or County Roads cost $5 per vehicle. Cash or check. Open May-November.

Directions: From Highway 287 at Norris, drive 8.1 miles to the campground. The entrance is on the north side of the road after crossing the Madison River.

GPS Coordinates: N 45° 36.666' W 111° 34.144'

Contact: Bureau of Land Management, Dillon Field Office, 1005 Selway Dr., Dillon, MT 59725, 406/683-8000, www.blm.gov.

8 MEADOW LAKE

Scenic rating: 8

on Ennis Lake

At 4,815 feet in elevation, Ennis Lake sits in the middle of the Madison River Valley surrounded by the Madison and Tobacco Root mountain ranges. The lake—a fishery known for its brown and rainbow trout—is also a haven for waterskiing, sailing, canoeing, and boating. Kobayashi Bay, with its buoyed swimming area and boat ramp, sits one mile east. From the campground, you can launch hand-carried boats, but no ramp is available. Because of the lake's shallowness, it warms in summer but kicks up with whitecaps in afternoon winds. The lake's outlet launches the Madison River through Bear Trap Canyon through a 1,500-foot-deep gorge and the Class IV Kitchen Sink rapid.

The sunny, treeless primitive campground—a fishing access run by the state—spreads out along the shore of the lake near the inlet for the mosquito-breeding haven Meadow Creek. Five of the campsites back in on gravel parking pads to waterfront with a brushy shoreline. Views look south to the Madison Range, which on a calm day reflects in the water. Ennis Lake Road garners substantial traffic during the summer from those heading to raft in the canyon or visit Kobayashi Bay, but the traffic dwindles at night.

Campsites, facilities: The campground has nine RV or tent campsites. RVs are limited to 25 feet. Facilities include picnic tables, fire rings with grills, and vault toilets. No water is available; bring your own or treat lake water. Leashed pets are permitted. Wheelchair-accessible facilities include toilet and campsite.

Reservations, fees: Reservations are not accepted. Camping is free. Open year-round.

Directions: From Highway 287 six miles north of Ennis, turn east at milepost 55 onto North Ennis Lake Road and drive 1.4 miles to the fishing access sign and campground on the right.

GPS Coordinates: N 45° 26.596' W 111° 42.414'

Contact: Montana Fish, Wildlife, and Parks, Region 3, 1400 S. 19th Ave., Bozeman, MT 59718, 406/994-4042, http://fwp.mt.gov.

9 ENNIS RV VILLAGE

Scenic rating: 7

in Ennis

One mile north of Ennis, this campground is convenient for shopping in the town's art galleries and western stores as well as for eating out in its restaurants. The town is best known for its Fourth of July parade and rodeo as well as fly-fishing. A small park in town has a kids-only fishing pond to get little ones started. Ennis Lake, good for swimming, fishing, boating, and water-skiing, sits five miles to the north, and the Kobayashi day-use area for swimming is less than seven miles north. Madison River

fishing access sites are within two miles, and white-water rafting companies are available for guided trips through Bear Trap Canyon and its Class IV Kitchen Sink rapid. Madison Meadows Golf Course is also in Ennis, and the surrounding Gallatin and Beaverhead-Deerlodge National Forests offer hiking and mountain-biking trails.

The campground lines up its RV campsites in parking-lot fashion along small patches of lawn in the sunny Madison River Valley. Views from the campground span the Madison Mountains to the east and the Tobacco Root Mountains to the northwest. In June, they are still covered by snow; in August, they are bare. You can hear some trucks along Highway 287 at night.

Campsites, facilities: The campground has 90 RV and 11 tent campsites. RVs are limited to 80 feet. Facilities include picnic tables, pedestal grills, flush toilets (wheelchair-accessible), showers, drinking water, garbage service, disposal station, wireless Internet, convenience store, launderette, and hookups for sewer, water, and electricity up to 50 amps. Leashed pets are permitted.

Reservations, fees: Reservations are not accepted. Hookups cost $27-38. Tent sites and dry camping for small RVs costs $19-25. Rates are based on two people per site. Additional campers are charged $2 each. Children under 12 years old camp for free. Use of the disposal station costs $6. The 7 percent Montana bed tax will be added on. Cash, check, or credit card. Open mid-April-mid-November.

Directions: Drive 1.2 miles north of Ennis on Highway 287. Turn east and drive 300 feet to the campground entrance, which is straight ahead.

GPS Coordinates: N 45° 22.053' W 111° 43.700'

Contact: Ennis RV Village, 15 Geyser Street, Ennis, MT 59729, 406/682-5272 or 866/682-5272, www.ennisrv.com.

10 VALLEY GARDEN

Scenic rating: 7

on the Madison River

Valley Garden, elevation 4,885 feet, is a state-run fishing access site on the Madison River. It is a popular location, as the town of Ennis, with its restaurants, shops, art galleries, and fishing outfitters, is less than a 10-minute drive away. The campground has a primitive gravel boat ramp where you can launch onto the river to float or paddle down to Ennis Lake. The Madison River gains worldwide fame for its blue-ribbon trout fishing, which is catch-and-release only for rainbow trout.

A narrow, potholed dirt road accesses the campground, where an osprey nest sits on a platform above the pay station. Views from the campsites span the Tobacco Root Mountains to the northwest and the Madison Mountains to the east. Two sunny loops through the tall grass offer flat spaces mowed out for tents. Four sites overlook the river; other sites can access the river through the brushy willows. The sites are spaced out for privacy, but the openness means you can see other campers. The myriad songbirds and the river fill the air with sound. The tall grass is green into July but fades to gold by August.

Campsites, facilities: The campground has nine RV or tent campsites. RVs are limited to 25 feet. Facilities include picnic tables, fire rings with grills, boat ramp, and vault toilets (wheelchair-accessible). Drinking water is not available; bring your own or treat river water. Leashed pets are permitted.

Reservations, fees: Reservations are not accepted. Camping costs $12 without a Montana fishing license or $7 with a fishing license. Open year-round.

Directions: From Ennis, drive south on Highway 287 about 1.5 miles to milepost 48. Turn north just after crossing Jeffers Creek and drive 1.9 miles. Turn left at the fishing access sign and drive over the cattle grate to reach the campground.

GPS Coordinates: N 45° 21.895' W 111° 42.319'

Contact: Montana Fish, Wildlife, and Parks, Region 3, 1400 S. 19th Ave., Bozeman, MT 59718, 406/994-4042, http://fwp.mt.gov.

11 ENNIS

Scenic rating: 4

on the Madison River

At 4,938 feet, Ennis is a state-run fishing access site on the Madison River. It is a popular location, as you can walk five minutes into the town of Ennis, which offers restaurants, shops, art galleries, and fishing outfitters. A primitive gravel boat ramp allows a place to launch onto the river to float down to Valley Garden or Ennis Lake, but you can also go catch-and-release wade-fishing for trout. The river harbors brown, rainbow, brook, Yellowstone cutthroat trout, and mountain whitefish. Bicyclists also use this campground while cycling Highway 287. A kid's fishing pond sits across the bridge in a community park.

A narrow, potholed dirt road accesses the campground's one big loop, which seems more like a maze because of the high brush. Campsites tuck into the brush under several large willow trees that provide partial shade and privacy from the 15-foot-high willow jungle, but a few are in sight of other campers. The three campsites on the river are open with views across the river to houses. The campsites, which are a mix of grass, dirt, and gravel, collect a combination of sounds, from the highway to songbirds. Locate the mowed path to the hand pump for drinking water by site 13. Some years the campground closes in late May and early June with high water flooding.

Campsites, facilities: The campground has 17 RV or tent campsites. RVs are limited to 25 feet. Facilities include picnic tables, rock fire rings, a boat ramp, drinking water, and vault toilets. Leashed pets are permitted.

Reservations, fees: Reservations are not accepted. Camping costs $12 without a Montana fishing license or $7 with a fishing license. Open May-November.

Directions: From Ennis, drive south on Highway 287 about 0.1 mile. Turn right at the fishing access sign as soon as you cross the Madison River.

GPS Coordinates: N 45° 20.665' W 111° 43.449'

Contact: Montana Fish, Wildlife, and Parks, Region 3, 1400 S. 19th Ave., Bozeman, MT 59718, 406/994-4042, http://fwp.mt.gov.

out your trash. Leashed pets are permitted. Two wheelchair-accessible toilets are available.

Reservations, fees: Reservations are not accepted. Camping is free. Open year-round.

Directions: From State Highway 287 west of Virginia City (not to be confused with Highway 287), take Judy Lane west for 0.5 mile. (The road sits just south of Alder.) Turn south onto the paved Upper Ruby Road (Forest Road 357) and drive eight miles south to the campground entrance on the right.

GPS Coordinates: N 45° 13.589' W 112° 7.124'

Contact: Bureau of Land Management, Dillon Field Office, 1005 Selway Dr., Dillon, MT 59725, 406/683-8000, www.blm.gov.

12 RUBY RESERVOIR

Scenic rating: 6

on the Madison River

Located at 5,409 feet, the Ruby Reservoir is a 2.5-mile-long lake set between the Ruby and Greenhorn Mountains. Because it was created to supply irrigation water for agriculture, water levels drop significantly in late summer. In early summer, the lake attracts anglers, boaters, and paddlers. Rainbow trout are stocked in the reservoir, and hand-carried watercraft can easily be launched from multiple locations. Rock hounds can find garnets along the shore.

Located on an arid dusty bench on the southeast shore of Ruby Reservoir, the campground offers very primitive camping in unmaintained sites. The area garners full sun and wind. A handful of campsites sidle up to a few trees for protection. More campsites are available along pullouts between the campground and Ruby Dam.

Campsites, facilities: The campground has seven primitive RV or tent campsites that can accommodate large RVs. Facilities include fire pits in some locations and vault toilets. Drinking water is not available; bring your own. Pack

13 VIRGINIA CITY RV PARK

Scenic rating: 4

in Virginia City

Surrounded by arid juniper and sagebrush hills, the campground is within a 10-minute walk to Virginia City's main street, where the town has preserved more than 100 historical buildings from its 1860s gold rush days, when it was the largest town in the inland Northwest. Shopping, restaurants, living history and frontier museums, galleries, and live theaters operate out of the ghost town buildings connected by boardwalks at this National Historic Landmark. You can also take rides in a 1910 refurbished steam locomotive, a stagecoach, or a 1941 fire engine. Kids can fish in the Virginia City ponds. Horseback riding and garnet or gold panning are also possibilities. Nevada City, a second ghost town, is 1.5 miles west of Virginia City.

The small, cramped campground is sunny and hot with only a few trees that shade a couple of sites. Most campers are here to see the ghost towns rather than spend time in their campsites, though, as this is the only campground within 13 miles of Virginia City. Some of the campsites overlook the graveyard, and full-time residents also live in the park. Even though sites can accommodate longer RVs on the paved parking pads, spaces between sites are dry and dusty.

Campsites, facilities: The campground has 50 RV campsites and four tent campsites. RVs are limited to 52 feet. Facilities include picnic tables, pedestal grills, flush toilets, showers, drinking water, garbage service, disposal station, wireless Internet, and hookups for sewer, water, and electricity up to 30 amps. Leashed pets are permitted.

Reservations, fees: Reservations are highly recommended. Hookups cost $33-39. Tent sites cost $25. Rates are based on four people per site. Additional campers are charged $3 each. Children under four years old camp for free. Extra vehicles are $5. A 10 percent tax will be added. Cash or credit card. Open mid-May-late September.

Directions: On State Route 287 (not to be confused with Highway 287), from Ennis drive southwest for 13.1 miles, or from Virginia City drive 0.5 mile east. Turn south for 0.1 mile to enter the campground.

GPS Coordinates: N 45° 17.670' W 111° 55.660'

Contact: Virginia City RV Park, P.O. Box 235, Virginia City, MT 59755, 406/843-5493 or 888/833-5493, www.virginiacityrvpark. com.

14 RUBY CREEK

Scenic rating: 8
on the Madison River

Located at 5,500 feet on the west bank of the Madison River south of Ennis, Ruby Creek Campground attracts mostly anglers looking to hook trout. Sometimes, this upper Madison catch-and-release-only area fills with anglers at every river bend. The campground also backs against the Wall Creek Wildlife Management Area, a wintering range for elk but also home to pronghorn antelope, moose, deer, black bears, and raptors. Designated roads, open May-November, allow touring for wildlife-watching, hiking, or hunting. The boat launch sits south of the campground, accessed quicker by walking than driving. By vehicle, drive out of the campground, turn left, and wrap 0.4 mile around to the boat launch, from which you can float or paddle the river north to McAtee Bridge.

Surrounded by sagebrush bench lands, the campground sits on an arid, bunchgrass prairie with large rocky outcroppings to the west and the Madison Mountains looming to the east. Unfortunately, you can also see a few houses up on the plateau, but the highway disappears—along with its noise—behind the plateau. Two gravel loops swing through the sunny campground, one on each side of Ruby Creek. The campground houses only a handful of 20-foot-high willows—not enough for shade or windbreaks. Both loops have four sites adjacent to the river. Three sites have pull-over parking, which can accommodate those with trailers.

Campsites, facilities: The campground has 22 RV or tent campsites that can accommodate midsized RVs. Facilities include picnic tables, fire rings with grills, vault toilets (wheelchair-accessible), drinking water, and campground hosts. Pack out your trash. Leashed pets are permitted.

Reservations, fees: Reservations are not accepted. Campsites cost $8. An extra vehicle costs $5. Only three vehicles are allowed per site. Cash or check. Open year-round; fees collected May-November.

Directions: From Highway 287 south of Ennis, turn west at the campground sign at milepost 30.9 onto a wide gravel road and cross the Madison River. Turn left just past the McAtee Bridge fishing access site and drive 2.6 miles south to the campground entrance on the left.

GPS Coordinates: N 45° 3.593' W 111° 39.929'

Contact: Bureau of Land Management, Dillon Field Office, 1005 Selway Dr., Dillon, MT

59725, 406/683-8000, www.blm.gov/mt/st/en.html.

15 PALISADES (MADISON RIVER)
🚣 🏕 ⛴ 🚻 ♿ 🚐 ⛺

Scenic rating: 7

on the Madison River

BEST (

On the east bank of the Madison River at 5,662 feet, Palisades Campground is named for the several-mile-long cliff band that runs along the hillside on the opposite side of the river. The cliffs light up in the morning sun. The paved boat ramp for launching rafts, drift boats, canoes, and kayaks onto the Madison River is in the Palisades picnic area, 0.9 mile south of the campground. You can float from here 8.5 miles to McAtee Bridge. Catch-and-release anglers can go wade fishing in the river, which has a blue-ribbon reputation for its brown and rainbow trout. This area of the river can sometimes fill with anglers in every stretch.

Surrounded by sagebrush bench lands, the campground's sites are on a wide-open, arid, treeless bunchgrass prairie with views of the Madison Mountains. Unfortunately, those views also include a few homes up on the bluff, but the highway is hidden behind. Half of the sites sit on the river. You can see pronghorn antelope and deer from the campground as well as wake up to songbirds. All of the sites are sunny gravel back-ins with neighboring campers in sight.

Campsites, facilities: The campground has 10 RV or tent campsites that can accommodate midsized RVs. Facilities include picnic tables, fire rings with grills, vault toilets (wheelchair-accessible), drinking water, and campground hosts. Pack out your trash. Leashed pets are permitted.

Reservations, fees: Reservations are not accepted. Campsites cost $8. An extra vehicle costs $5. Three vehicles are permitted per site.

Cash or check. Open year-round; fees are collected May-December.

Directions: From Highway 287 south of Ennis, turn west at milepost 22.9 onto the gravel road. Drive a bumpy 0.4 mile to a junction and veer right for the campground, which you'll reach 0.6 mile later.

GPS Coordinates: N 44° 59.775' W 111° 39.562'

Contact: Bureau of Land Management, Dillon Field Office, 1005 Selway Dr., Dillon, MT 59725, 406/683-8000, www.blm.gov/mt/st/en.html.

16 WEST FORK CABINS AND RV
🚣 🏕 ⛴ 🚻 🐴 🚐 ⛺

Scenic rating: 7

on the Madison River

Located at 5,880 feet along the Madison River, West Fork Cabins Camp offers fishing adjacent to the campground in the catch-and-release section of the Madison River. This upper section of the Madison River often is packed in summer with wading anglers at every bend in the river—it has a blue-ribbon reputation for wild trout. The company also offers guided fishing and float trips, plus rents rafts with trailers and personal kick boats. The campground is surrounded by Beaverhead-Deerlodge National Forest and the Madison Mountains. Horses are also available for riding.

The campground has two loops surrounding a grassy lawn. While some trees surround the campground, they are not in locations to provide shade. But those looking for satellite reception will have a clear shot at the sky. The campsites are all visible from each other, but each has its own cement patio. You can hear the highway across the river in the campground.

Campsites, facilities: The campground has 24 RV campsites that can accommodate large RVs, and 20 tent sites. Facilities include picnic tables, flush toilets, showers, drinking water, garbage service, launderette, tackle shop, and hookups for sewer, water, and electricity. Leashed pets are permitted.

Reservations, fees: Reservations are accepted. Hookups cost $30. Tent spaces cost $15. A 7 percent Montana bed tax is added. Cash, check, or credit card. Open April-November.

Directions: From Ennis, drive 35 miles south on Highway 287. (From West Yellowstone, the drive is also 35 miles.) Exit Highway 287 to the west and cross the Madison River, turning left onto Sundance Bench Road. GPS Coordinates: N 44° 53.246' W 111° 34.831'

Contact: West Fork Cabins and RV, 24 Sundance Bench Rd., Cameron, MT 59720, 406/682-4802 or 866/343-8267, http://wfork.com.

🔢17 WEST FORK MADISON

🛶🚤🎣🏕🦽🚐⛺

Scenic rating: 7

on the Madison River in Beaverhead-Deerlodge National Forest

At 5,950 feet, the campground squeezes in between the West Fork of the Madison River and the main stem of the Madison River. The Madison River—one of Montana's blue ribbon trout fisheries—attracts anglers, who wade fish or use drift boats. Canoes also float the river. River access sites for launching are located north and south of the campground.

This reconstructed campground now sits in two separated loops on open sagebrush terrain overlooking the river and homes on the other side. Sites are sunny with little privacy. With the road between the loops and the Madison River, the north loop sits on a gentle hillside above the river while the south loop parallels the river.

Campsites, facilities: The campground has 27 RV or tent campsites that can accommodate midsized RVs. Facilities include picnic tables,

fire rings with grills, drinking water, vault toilets (wheelchair-accessible), and campground hosts. Pack out your trash. Leashed pets are permitted.

Reservations, fees: Reservations are not accepted. Campsites cost $10. Open year-round, but services are available only May-September.

Directions: From Highway 287 at milepost 15.9, exit west and cross the Madison River. Turn left onto Sundance Bench Road for 0.4 mile to the campground entrance on the right. The second loops sits 0.3 mile further south. GPS Coordinates: N 44° 52.916' W 111° 34.598'

Contact: Beaverhead-Deerlodge National Forest, Madison Ranger District, 5 Forest Service Rd., Ennis, MT 59729, 406/682-4253, www.fs.usda.gov/bdnf.

🔢18 RAYNOLD'S PASS

🛶🚤🎣🏕🚐⛺

Scenic rating: 6

on the Madison River

At 6,140 feet, Raynold's Pass Campground is a state-run fishing access site on the Madison River, the main attraction. The Madison River is known for its wild trout fishery—particularly brown, rainbow, and Yellowstone cutthroat trout. This is a catch-and-release only section. You can go wade fishing in the river or launch a drift boat, kayak, canoe, or raft from the revamped gravel boat ramp. From here, you can float three river miles west to Three Dollar Bridge or continue for a 10-mile float to Lyons Bridge. A geological site of the 1959 earthquake slide that killed 28 people and dammed up the Madison River, the Earthquake Lake Visitor Center (open daily Memorial Day-mid-September) sits 3.2 miles to the east.

The arid, dusty campground loop sits in the open sagebrush and dry grass prairie with views of the Madison Mountains. No trees are available for shade or windbreaks, and the sites lack privacy because of the openness and the small loop. The proximity to the two highways adds noise from large trucks, even at night.

Campsites, facilities: The campground has six RV or tent campsites. RVs are limited to 25 feet. Facilities include picnic tables, rock fire rings, boat ramp, and vault toilets (wheelchair-accessible). Drinking water is not available; bring your own or treat river water. Leashed pets are permitted.

Reservations, fees: Reservations are not accepted. Camping is free. Open year-round.

Directions: From Ennis, drive south on Highway 287 to the junction with Highway 87. Turn south onto Highway 87 and drive 0.4 mile. Turn right into the fishing access site. GPS Coordinates: N 44° 49.622' W 111° 29.214'

Contact: Montana Fish, Wildlife, and Parks, Region 3, 1400 S. 19th Ave., Bozeman, MT 59718, 406/994-4042, http://fwp.mt.gov.

19 WADE LAKE

Scenic rating: 8

in the Gravelly Mountains in Beaverhead-Deerlodge National Forest

BEST (

At 6,200 feet steep mountains, skinny Wade Lake sinks into a deep forest trough. The lake is popular, especially with kids, for its sandy beach and turquoise water in the shallows. Lake water warms a bit by August. Anglers have caught record-breaking brown trout, and you can often see bald eagles and ospreys fishing, plus river otters. Canoes and kayaks are available to rent from the adjacent Wade Lake Resort. Only nonmotorized watercraft are permitted. The surrounding forested slopes contain hiking trails, one of which is a nature trail that climbs one mile to the Hilltop Campground.

The quiet, shady campground stacks on a steep hillside above the boat ramp and swimming area with steep access trails. Sites 3-6 have outstanding water views but also garner campground traffic on the way to the boat launch. Several sites in the upper loop have peek-a-boo views plummeting down to the lake. The upper loop sites offer more privacy because people aren't tromping by all day. Douglas firs shade most of the campground, and hollyhocks, pink sticky geraniums, and wild roses grow in sunny spots.

Campsites, facilities: The campground has 30 RV or tent campsites. RVs are limited to 32 feet. Facilities include picnic tables, fire rings with grills, vault toilets (wheelchair-accessible), drinking water, and campground hosts. Leashed pets are permitted.

Reservations, fees: Reservations are not accepted. Campsites cost $12. Open mid-May-September.

Directions: From Highway 287 south of Ennis, turn off south at milepost 9.6 at the Cliff and Wade Lake sign onto Wade Lake Road (Forest Road 241). Drive over the Madison River and pass the Three Dollar Bridge fishing access site. Be prepared for a long, bumpy drive with large rocks in the road. At 3.4 miles, turn right at the fork and climb steeply over the ridge for 1.7 miles. Watch for cattle on the road. At the signed fork in the road, turn right and drive 0.7 mile to the campground entrance. GPS Coordinates: N 44° 48.400' W 111° 33.971'

Contact: Beaverhead-Deerlodge National Forest, Madison Ranger District, 5 Forest Service Rd., Ennis, MT 59729, 406/682-4253, www.fs.usda.gov/bdnf.

20 HILLTOP

Scenic rating: 7

in the Gravelly Mountains in Beaverhead-Deerlodge National Forest

At 6,800 feet up a short, steep mountain, Hilltop is aptly named, for it sits on the spine of a ridge in between Wade and Cliff Lakes. A one-mile trail drops from the campground to Wade Lake, where you can swim, fish, and rent canoes or kayaks from Wade Lake Resort. The climb back up the hill requires more than 500 feet of ascent.

Hilltop is an older campground with smaller, back-in dirt parking pads, overhanging branches on the campground road, and trees that make for narrow turns. But it also has sites with spacious flat tent spaces. Douglas firs and lodgepole pines filter the sunlight and lend partial shade. More open campsites are rimmed with cow parsnip and lupine. Sites 11-14 and 16-18 overlook the canyon and opposite cliff wall, with a rail fence marking the end lip of the cliff. A few campsites offer peek-a-boo views of the Madison Mountains. Its remote location makes the campground quiet. Also, it is less crowded than Wade or Cliff Lake; you can often gain privacy just because of vacant neighboring campsites.

Campsites, facilities: The campground has 18 RV or tent campsites that can accommodate RVs up to 22 feet. Facilities include picnic tables, fire rings with grills, vault toilets (wheelchair-accessible), drinking water, and campground host. Leashed pets are permitted.

Reservations, fees: Reservations are not accepted. Campsites cost $12. Open mid-May-September.

Directions: From Highway 287 south of Ennis, turn off south at milepost 9.6 at the Cliff and Wade Lake sign onto Wade Lake Road (Forest Road 241). Drive over the Madison River and pass the Three Dollar Bridge fishing access site. Be prepared for a long, bumpy drive with large rocks in the road. At 3.4 miles, turn right at the fork and climb steeply over the ridge down for 1.7 miles. Watch for cattle on the road. At the signed fork in the road, turn left for 0.1 mile and turn right to climb steeply for 0.8 mile to the campground.

GPS Coordinates: N 44° 47.769' W 111° 33.682'

Contact: Beaverhead-Deerlodge National Forest, Madison Ranger District, 5 Forest Service Rd., Ennis, MT 59729, 406/682-4253, www.fs.usda.gov/bdnf.

21 CLIFF POINT

🥾 🏊 🛶 🚣 🎣 🏕 ♿ 🚐 ⛺

Scenic rating: 8

in the Gravelly Mountains in Beaverhead-Deerlodge National Forest

BEST (

At 6,335 feet on the shore of Cliff Lake, the tiny Cliff Point Campground clusters around a small peninsula with popular campsites. Surrounded by steep forested slopes, the narrow lake is actually twice as big as Wade Lake, but more serene. The one-mile Fault Trail (#430) departs from the campground, touring through the canyon and connecting with the Wade Lake nature trail. As at Wade Lake, Cliff Lake's shallow bays shine turquoise because of the sandy bottom. Only nonmotorized boating is permitted, making it a quiet place for canoeing or kayaking. The lake's clear waters produce rainbow trout and cutthroat trout, and you can often watch bald eagles fish, plus see beaver.

These campsites are coveted for their locations on the point. Sites 3 and 4 claim the prime spots with big lake views and waterfront. Most of the sites have flat spaces for big tents. Small in size and filled with pink sticky geraniums and a few large Douglas fir trees for partial shade, this campground is one where you will see the neighbors, but you'll also get to wake up to the call of loons.

Campsites, facilities: The campground has six RV or tent campsites. RVs are limited to 16 feet. Facilities include picnic tables, fire rings with grills, vault toilets (wheelchair-accessible), drinking water, bear boxes, and garbage service. Leashed pets are permitted.

Reservations, fees: Reservations are not accepted. Campsites cost $12. Open mid-May-September.

Directions: From Highway 287 south of Ennis, turn off south at milepost 9.6 at the Cliff and Wade Lake sign onto Wade Lake

Road (Forest Road 241). Drive over the Madison River and pass the Three Dollar Bridge fishing access site. Be prepared for a long, bumpy drive with large rocks in the road. At 3.4 miles, turn right at the fork and climb steeply over the ridge down for 1.7 miles. Watch for cattle on the road. At the signed fork in the road, turn left for 0.4 mile to the boat ramp and continue another 0.6 mile to the campground. The road narrows to a single lane with curvy, blind corners.

GPS Coordinates: N 44° 47.600' W 111° 33.703'

Contact: Beaverhead-Deerlodge National Forest, Madison Ranger District, 5 Forest Service Rd., Ennis, MT 59729, 406/682-4253, www.fs.usda.gov/bdnf.

22 RIVER MARSH

Scenic rating: 6

in Red Rock Lakes National Wildlife Refuge

At the outlet of Lower Red Rock Lake's west shore, this campground sits in the 45,000-acre Red Rock Lakes National Wildlife Refuge—an essential nesting area for trumpeter swans, with more than 2,000 using the lakes during the fall migration. The refuge is also an outstanding wildlife-watching area with 232 species of birds. The lakes are open for nonmechanized boats (except sailing) from mid-July to freeze out, and you can paddle between the two lakes. Fishing is permitted on Odell Creek east of the lower lake. Mountain bikers ride the refuge roads to Red Rock Pass, and around the lower lake the Idlewild and Odell trails lead to wildlife-watching areas from the refuge headquarters area about five miles from the campground. The refuge also permits antelope, elk, deer, and waterfowl hunting. Reaching the refuge requires miles of rough dirt road driving without any services; call the refuge to check road conditions, and gas up.

The primitive sunny campground sits in mixed prairie grass and sagebrush. With no trees, the campsites claim big views of the Centennial Mountains and the Continental Divide, but the marsh area produces voluminous summer mosquitoes, which abate as long as the wind blows. Very few people camp here, almost guaranteeing privacy, and you'll wake up to the sounds of birds.

Campsites, facilities: The primitive campground has four RV or tent campsites that can accommodate small RVs. Facilities include fire pits and pit toilets. Water is available at refuge headquarters in Lakeview between the two lakes. Pack out your trash. Leashed pets are permitted.

Reservations, fees: Reservations are not accepted. Camping is free. Open year-round, although snow can close the roads and cover the campgrounds.

Directions: From Monida on I-15, take Exit 0 and drive north on the gravel Southside Centennial Road (MT Hwy. 509) for 24.8 miles. Turn north and drive 2.6 miles; then turn right. From Highway 87/287 in Idaho at the north end of Henry's Lake, you can also drive over Red Rock Pass to reach the campground in 29 miles.

GPS Coordinates: N 44° 38.790' W 111° 52.806'

Contact: Red Rocks Lake National Wildlife Refuge, 27820 Southside Centennial Rd., Lima, MT 59739, 406/276-3536, www.fws.gov/redrocks/.

23 UPPER RED ROCK LAKE

Scenic rating: 8

in Red Rock Lakes National Wildlife Refuge

BEST (

On the south shore of Upper Red Rock Lake, the campground sits in the middle of the 45,000-acre Red Rock Lakes National Wildlife Refuge. The refuge is an essential nesting area for trumpeter swans, with more than 2,000 using the lakes during the fall migration. The lakes are open for nonmechanized boats (except sailing) from mid-July to freeze out, and you can paddle between the two lakes. Fishing is permitted in Red Rock and Elk Springs Creeks, plus three ponds east of the upper lake. Mountain bikers ride the refuge roads to Red Rock Pass, and two hiking trails connect to wildlife-watching areas around the lower lake. The refuge also permits antelope, elk, deer, and waterfowl hunting. Reaching the refuge requires miles of rough dirt-road driving without any services; call the refuge to check road conditions, and gas up.

Of the two campgrounds in the refuge, Upper Red Rock Lake is visited more, but more often than not, you'll have the place to yourself. It fills with summer mosquitoes but offers views of the upper lake and Centennial Mountains, and sits on a lush hillside with aspens, chokecherries, willows, nettles, and sticky pink geraniums. Most of the sites garner full sun; a few tuck under the aspens for partial shade. At night, you won't hear a sound until the sandhill cranes call in the morning.

Campsites, facilities: The primitive campground has seven RV or tent campsites that can accommodate small RVs. Facilities include picnic tables, fire pits, pit toilets, and drinking water from a spring. Pack out your trash. Leashed pets are permitted. A gravel-path wheelchair-accessible toilet and campsite are available.

Reservations, fees: Reservations are not accepted. Camping is free. Open year-round, although snow can close the roads and cover the campgrounds.

Directions: From Monida on I-15, take Exit 0 and drive north on gravel Southside Centennial Road (MT Hwy. 509) for 31.8 miles. The campground is on the north side of the road. From Highway 87/287 in Idaho at the north end of Henry's Lake, you can also drive over Red Rock Pass to reach the campground in 22 miles.

GPS Coordinates: N 44° 35.590' W 111° 43.736'

Contact: Red Rocks Lake National Wildlife Refuge, 27820 Southside Centennial Rd., Lima, MT 59739, 406/276-3536, www.fws.gov/redrocks/.

24 CABIN CREEK

Scenic rating: 7

in the Madison Mountains in Gallatin National Forest

Cabin Creek Campground sits at 6,400 feet in the Madison Range. The Earthquake Scarp Interpretive Area is adjacent to the campground. At the beginning of the Cabin Creek Scarp Trailhead, you'll pass a fault scarp, a 20-foot-high dirt bank where the ground dropped down and the earth rose up, trapping some campers during the 1959 earthquake. The trailhead for the Cabin Creek Scarp-Red Canyon complex of trails is across the creek from the campground. Many of the trails are open to hikers, mountain bikers, motorcycles, and ATVs. To the west, Quake Lake's boat launch is 2.3 miles away, followed by the Earthquake Center Visitor Area eight miles away. Fishing and boating are available on Quake Lake.

The campground rests alongside the busy highway. Sites are very close together, and many have views of the road. A canopy of Douglas firs shades the campground, but with only low ground cover and cow parsnips, you can see the entire campground from almost every site. Double-wide dirt parking pads allow for two vehicles or a trailer separated from its vehicle. Four sites line up along Cabin Creek.

Campsites, facilities: The campground has 15 RV or tent campsites. RVs are limited to 30 feet. Facilities include picnic tables, fire rings with grills, vault toilets, drinking water, bear boxes, garbage service, firewood for sale, and campground host. Leashed pets are permitted. Wheelchair-accessible facilities include toilet and one campsite.

Reservations, fees: Reservations are

accepted (877/444-6777, www.recreation. gov). Campsites cost $14. An extra vehicle costs $6. Cash, check, or credit card. Open mid-May–mid-September.

Directions: On Highway 287 east of Quake Lake Visitor Center and west of Hebgen Lake, turn north off the highway at milepost 8.6 into the campground.

GPS Coordinates: N 44° 52.273' W 111° 20.691'

Contact: Gallatin National Forest, Hebgen Lake Ranger Station, 330 Gallatin Rd., West Yellowstone, MT 59758, 406/823-6961, www. fs.usda.gov/gallatin.

25 BEAVER CREEK

🥾 🚴 🛶 🛟 🛶 🏇 ♿ 🚐 ⛺

Scenic rating: 9

in the Madison Mountains in Gallatin National Forest

BEST (

Located on the slopes of a small mountain at 6,600 feet at the foot of Quake Lake, Beaver Creek is the closest campground to the Earthquake Lake Visitor Center (open daily Memorial Day–mid-September) 4.6 miles to the west. The center marks the site of a 1959 earthquake landslide that killed 28 people and dammed the Madison River, forming Quake Lake. Short walks lead to Memorial Rock and overlooks of the landslide path. Expert kayakers run the 1.5 miles of Class IV-V river from Quake Lake's outlet. From the campground, two short hiking trails descend to the six-mile-long Quake Lake, and a boat launch 0.5 mile to the west allows access for boating, canoeing, and fishing for brown and rainbow trout. Mountain bikers, hikers, and ATVers can use many of the Cabin Creek trails 1.7 miles to the east.

Situated in three loops on meadow hilltops, the campground blooms prolifically in July with paintbrush, lupines, and harebells. Loose groves of aspens and thin lodgepoles provide partial shade; other sites draw full sun. Three sites on A loop flank the beaver ponds,

The dead trees in Quake Lake are a testament to the landslide that formed the lake.

© BECKY LOMAX

where lily pads bloom with yellow flowers. Sites spread out for privacy, and thanks to the open forest, you get views of the surrounding peaks or Quake Lake but also can see other campers. The quiet campground rings with the sounds of songbirds or the light chatter of aspen leaves clacking in the breeze.

Campsites, facilities: The campground has 64 RV or tent campsites. RVs are limited to 50 feet. Facilities include picnic tables, fire rings with grills, vault toilets, drinking water, garbage service, firewood for sale, and campground hosts. Leashed pets are permitted. Wheelchair-accessible facilities include toilets and two campsites.

Reservations, fees: Reservations are accepted (877/444-6777, www.recreation.gov). Campsites cost $14. An extra vehicle costs $6. Cash, check, or credit card. Open early June-mid-September.

Directions: On Highway 287, east of Quake Lake Visitor Center and west of Hebgen Lake, turn south off the highway at milepost 7 onto the paved narrow road. Climb 0.6 mile to the campground entrance junction, with loop A to the left and loops B and C to the right. GPS Coordinates: N 44° 51.390' W 111° 22.384'

Contact: Gallatin National Forest, Hebgen Lake Ranger Station, 330 Gallatin Rd., West Yellowstone, MT 59758, 406/823-6961, www.fs.usda.gov/gallatin.

26 FAIRY LAKE

👥 🚲 ⛵ 🛶 🏊 🎣 🏕 ♿ 🚐 ⛰

Scenic rating: 9

in the Bridger Mountains in Gallatin National Forest

Plan to arrive early at this popular campground at 7,640 feet in the Bridger Mountains. Tucked below the rugged 9,665-foot ramparts of Sacagawea Peak, the campground sits near picturesque Fairy Lake—a

place to swim on a hot day, but at this elevation and with late snowmelt, be ready for frigid water. A 2.5-mile trail (#534) climbs the peak—the highest in the Bridger Range—for spectacular views and encounters with mountain goats. A 0.1-mile path leads to Fairy Lake, which you can circumnavigate in less than an hour. The lake trail is short enough that you can carry a canoe or inflatable raft, although the lake is only 0.2-mile long. A mountain biking option, the Shafthouse Trail (#540) runs along Fairy Lake and traverses the northeast side of the Bridger Mountains below the crest. Anglers can fish the lake and Fairy Creek.

Reconstruction in 2012 improved this campground dramatically. Some trees were removed, opening up the thick forest to more sunlight, and the campground road, parking spurs, campsites, and facilities were rebuilt. Considering the campground's popularity, plan to arrive by early afternoon to claim a site.

Campsites, facilities: The campground has nine RV or tent campsites. Parking spurs can accommodate RVs to 32 feet; however, they are not recommended on the access road. Facilities include picnic tables, fire rings with grills, vault toilets (wheelchair-accessible), and drinking water. Pack out your trash. Leashed pets are permitted.

Reservations, fees: Reservations are not accepted. Camping is free. Open July-mid-September.

Directions: From Bozeman, travel north on Bridger Canyon Road (Hwy. 86) for 22.5 miles. Turn left onto the steep, gravel Fairy Lake Road for five miles, continuing straight past Cache Creek Road. The road is not recommended for RVs or trailers. Call for access road status. GPS Coordinates: N 45° 54.409' W 110° 57.635'

Contact: Gallatin National Forest, Bozeman Ranger District, 3710 Fallon St., Bozeman, MT 59718, 406/522-2520, www.fs.usda.gov/gallatin.

27 BATTLE RIDGE

Scenic rating: 8

in the Bridger Mountains in Gallatin National Forest

At 6,391 feet, Battle Ridge Campground cowers on the valley floor below the Bridger Mountains, where their height casts an early twilight on the camp. The campground attracts off-road motorists, mountain bikers, and hikers who want to explore the Bridger Range, and it is the only designated campground available in early summer. For hiking, visitors pulling trailers can leave the RV to drive up the rough road to Fairy Lake Recreation Area, located 5.5 miles west. Intermediate-skilled mountain bikers will want to ride the 26-mile Bangtail Ridge singletrack (31 miles for full loop without shuttling) for views of the Bridger and Crazy Mountains. South of the campground, Bohart Ranch opens their cross-country ski trails in summer for mountain biking.

Broad meadows that are lush green in June, but dry brown in August weave around the pine forest that shades some campsites sprinkled on a gentle slope above the road. Many of the campsites have views of the Bridger Mountains to the west. After dark, the road tends to see minimal traffic, quieting the area.

Campsites, facilities: The campground has 13 RV or tent campsites. RVs are limited to 30 feet. Facilities include picnic tables, fire rings, pit toilets, and drinking water. Leashed pets are permitted.

Reservations, fees: Reservations are not accepted. Camping is free. Open mid-May-mid-September.

Directions: From Bozeman, travel north on Bridger Canyon Road (Hwy. 86) for 22 miles. Turn right to the campground entrance.

GPS Coordinates: N 45° 52.922' W 110° 52.800'

Contact: Gallatin National Forest, Bozeman Ranger District, 3710 Fallon St., Bozeman, MT 59718, 406/522-2520, www.fs.usda.gov/gallatin.

28 BOZEMAN KOA

Scenic rating: 6

in the Gallatin Valley

BEST (

At 4,741 feet, about 10 minutes south of I-90, the Bozeman KOA has two creeks running through the campground, which offer fishing. But its big attraction is the neighboring Bozeman Hot Springs and Spa (open daily, 406/586-6492, www.bozemanhotsprings.com). It has nine pools between 59°F and 106°F for dips ranging from icy to steaming. Cascading waterfalls plunge into two pools, and a large pool accommodates lap swimming. One pool is outdoors. Dry and wet saunas, a fitness facility, and spa services are available. The campground sits 0.5 mile from 27 holes of golf and 20 minutes from the Museum of the Rockies. Its location at the head of the Gallatin Valley makes an easy 40-minute drive to Yellowstone National Park.

The campground sits on a busy highway—the main road heading down the Gallatin River Valley to Yellowstone National Park. Vehicle traffic is nonstop in summer and during rush hours. The KOA has partially shaded campsites on mowed lawn with sites very close together. The KOA's swimming pool, hot tub, and splash park closed in 2013; call for updates.

Campsites, facilities: The campground has 126 campsites: Hookups at 86 sites, 27 non-hookup sites for smaller RVs or tents, plus 13 overflow sites with water and electrical hookups or no hookups. RVs are limited to 90 feet. Hookups are available for water, sewer, and electricity up to 50 amps. Facilities include flush toilets, showers, picnic tables, fire rings with grills, garbage service, cable TV, wireless Internet, playground, disposal station, pet walk, mini-golf, camp store, firewood for sale, electrical hookups at tent sites, and camping kitchen. Leashed pets are permitted.

Reservations, fees: Reservations are accepted. Hookups cost $40-51. Tent sites cost $30-34. Rates cover two people. Extra campers are charged $5-6. Children 14 and under stay free. Add on 7 percent tax. Cash, check, or credit card. Open mid-April-October.

Directions: On the west side of Bozeman at Belgrade on I-90, take Exit 298 and turn south on Jackrabbit Lane (Hwy. 85) for 7.7 miles. The road becomes Highway 191. Turn right on Lower Rainbow Road for one-half block to the campground entrance on the right. GPS Coordinates: N 45° 39.584' W 111° 11.360'

Contact: Bozeman KOA, 81123 Gallatin Rd. (Hwy. 191), Bozeman, MT 59718, 406/587-3030 or 800/562-3036, www.koa.com.

29 SPIRE ROCK

Scenic rating: 7

in the Gallatin Mountains in Gallatin National Forest

Spire Rock Campground nestles at 5,500 feet in a narrow canyon just south of Storm Castle Mountain in Gallatin National Forest. The canyon is home to several trailheads for hikers and mountain bikers. You can summit the 7,165-foot Storm Castle Mountain or 8,202-foot Garnet Mountain Lookout for views of the Spanish Peaks or head to Rat Lake. Just south of Storm Castle in the Gallatin Canyon, the Scorched Earth area offers sport climbing ranging in grade from 5.8 to 5.13. To the north in the canyon, rock climbers will find traditional routes on Gallatin Towers. The forested canyon yields a color drama in the evening with the limestone outcroppings lighting up.

Along a very skinny dirt road, the campground sprawls for one mile up the canyon with the campsites clumped together in twos and threes with 0.1 mile or so in between clusters. That creates a feeling of camping in a tiny campground with only a couple campsites. Many of the campsites sit along the creek, with large, flat tent spaces. Lush undergrowth of thimbleberries, wild roses, and vine maples lends privacy between sites, many of which are partially shaded by Douglas firs. The only sound you'll hear is the creek.

Campsites, facilities: The campground has 19 RV or tent campsites. RVs are limited to 50 feet. Facilities include picnic tables, fire rings with grills, pit toilets (wheelchair-accessible), bear boxes, garbage service, and firewood for sale. Drinking water is not available; bring your own or treat creek water. Leashed pets are permitted.

Reservations, fees: Reservations are accepted (877/444-6777, www.recreation.gov). Campsites cost $10. An extra vehicle costs $6. Cash, check, or credit card. Open mid-May-late September.

Directions: West of Bozeman, travel south on Highway 191 to milepost 65.2. Turn east and cross the river. Turn immediately south onto the dirt road and drive past the heli-base. The gravel road narrows along the river, with an abrupt drop-off and potholes for 1.6 miles, and then turns east for one mile, passing the trailhead for Storm Castle Mountain before reaching the campground. Turn right into the campground. GPS Coordinates: N 45° 26.477' W 111° 12.398'

Contact: Gallatin National Forest, Bozeman Ranger District, 3710 Fallon St., Bozeman, MT 59718, 406/522-2520, www.fs.usda.gov/gallatin.

30 GREEK CREEK

Scenic rating: 7

in Gallatin Canyon in Gallatin National Forest

Located at 5,800 feet in elevation, Greek Creek

Campground splits on both sides of the highway cutting through the Gallatin Canyon in Gallatin National Forest. The loops on the west side flank the river; those on the east side tuck into the forest up against a mountainside. For guided raft trips on the Class II-III river, Montana Whitewater Rafting Company is six miles north. Kayaker, rafters, and anglers going after brown and rainbow trout use the river. The Lava Lake Trailhead is 3.2 miles north at Cascade Creek. The trail, for hikers only past the wilderness boundary, climbs into the Spanish Peaks of the Lee Metcalf Wilderness, reaching the lake in 3.5 miles after a 1,600-foot elevation gain. The trail is one of the most popular in the area, so you won't find solitude here—especially on weekends. Bicyclists riding to Yellowstone use this campground.

In the narrow canyon, the campground squeezes around the highway, making the sound of passing vehicles ubiquitous in the campground. Not even the river can drown out the larger trucks. Unfortunately, some campsites have views of the road, too. The Douglas fir forest admits filtered sunlight to the mountainside loops, which are more private, separated from each other by low brush, wild roses, and tall grass. The river loops, which are roomier with larger flat spaces for tents, are more open. On the left river loop, sites 14 and 15 overlook the river. The hot midsummer sun leaves the canyon early, cooling off the campground.

Campsites, facilities: The campground has 14 RV or tent campsites. RVs are limited to 60 feet. Facilities include picnic tables, fire rings with grills, vault toilets, drinking water, bear boxes, garbage service, and firewood for sale. Leashed pets are permitted. Wheelchair-accessible toilets and seven sites are available.

Reservations, fees: Reservations are accepted (877/444-6777, www.recreation.gov). Campsites cost $13. An extra vehicle costs $8. Cash or check. Open mid-May-late September.

Directions: West of Bozeman, travel south on Highway 191 to milepost 58.2. The campground splits on both sides of the highway, so turn right or left, depending on whether you want a site near the river or not.

GPS Coordinates: N 45° 22.818' W 111° 10.945'

Contact: Gallatin National Forest, Bozeman Ranger District, 3710 Fallon St., Suite C, Bozeman, MT 59718, 406/522-2520, www.fs.usda.gov/gallatin.

31 SWAN CREEK

Scenic rating: 7

in the Gallatin Mountains in Gallatin National Forest

At 5,800 feet, Swan Creek Campground sits in a quiet side canyon east of Gallatin Canyon in Gallatin National Forest. The forested, steep-walled canyon pinches the narrow access road with overhanging branches, precluding many larger RVs from access. At the end of Swan Creek Canyon, a steep trail, #186, leads about 12 miles to Hyalite Peak. It is open to hikers, mountain bikers, and motorcycles. More hiking and mountain-biking trails are available from the Moose Creek area about 1.5 miles south on the highway. The nearby Gallatin River provides rafting, kayaking, and fishing.

Swan Creek Campground's two loops offers respite from the busy Gallatin Canyon campgrounds right on the highway. All of the campsites, which have back-in gravel parking spurs, line Swan Creek, where the burbling water is the sound you'll hear, rather than traffic. Douglas firs, spruces, and lodgepole pines lend partial to heavy shade to the campsites, and sunnier spots bloom with paintbrush, pink fireweed, and white yarrow. Several campsites have large, flat gravel spaces for tents.

Campsites, facilities: The campground has 14 RV or tent campsites. RVs are limited to 45 feet. Facilities include picnic tables, fire rings with grills, pit and vault toilets, hand

Gallatin National Forest offers camping, hiking, and rafting.

pumps for drinking water, bear boxes, garbage service, and firewood for sale. Leashed pets are permitted. Wheelchair-accessible facilities include toilets and seven sites.

Reservations, fees: Reservations are accepted (877/444-6777, www.recreation.gov). Campsites cost $14. An extra vehicle costs $6. Cash, check, or credit card. Open mid-May-late September.

Directions: West of Bozeman, travel south on Highway 191 to milepost 57.4. Turn east onto Swan Creek Road (Forest Road 481), a single-lane road with turnouts (trailers should be able to back up), and drive 0.5 mile. Use caution on turning off from the curvy highway as locals drive fast. Both loops sit on the right side of the road about 0.6 mile apart. GPS Coordinates: N 45° 22.399' W 111° 9.287'

Contact: Gallatin National Forest, Bozeman Ranger District, 3710 Fallon St., Suite C, Bozeman, MT 59718, 406/522-2520, www.fs.usda.gov/gallatin.

32 MOOSE CREEK FLATS

Scenic rating: 7

in Gallatin Canyon in Gallatin National Forest

At 5,700 feet, Moose Creek Flats Campground squeezes into an open meadow between the Gallatin River and the highway. The Class II-III river is popular for white-water rafting, kayaking, and wade-fishing. The campground works as both a take-out and put-in. For hikers and mountain bikers, the Moose Creek Trail (#187) departs on a spur road across the highway, leading eventually to the Gallatin Crest and Windy Pass Cabin. Other nearby trails for hikers access the Spanish Peaks of the Lee Metcalf Wilderness. The campground is the closest one to the north of Big Sky Resort, which offers summer scenic chair rides, mountain biking, ziplining, and hiking.

A paved road with gravel back-in parking spurs and three pull-throughs weaves through the campground. Surrounded by a wide-open flat grassy meadow, all of the sunny campsites have views of the forested canyon walls as well as views of other campsites plus the highway, with its accompanying noise. A few Douglas firs are sprinkled along the river. Within the narrow Gallatin Canyon, the hot midsummer sun sinks out of sight earlier, which cools the campground. Sites 1-9 overlook the river.

Campsites, facilities: The campground has 13 RV or tent campsites. RVs are limited to 60 feet. One of the sites is for small groups. Facilities include picnic tables, fire rings with grills, vault toilets, drinking water, bear boxes, garbage service, and firewood for sale. Leashed pets are permitted. Toilets, four campsites, and a fishing access are wheelchair-accessible.

Reservations, fees: Reservations are accepted (877/444-6777, www.recreation.gov). Campsites cost $14. An extra vehicle costs $6. Cash, check, or credit card. Open mid-May-mid-September.

Directions: West of Bozeman, travel south on Highway 191 to milepost 56.3. Be cautious about turning into the campground as locals drive fast in the canyon. The campground sits on the west side of the highway.

GPS Coordinates: N 45° 21.363' W 111° 10.318'

Contact: Gallatin National Forest, Bozeman Ranger District, 3710 Fallon St., Suite C, Bozeman, MT 59718, 406/522-2520, www.fs.usda.gov/gallatin.

33 RED CLIFF

Scenic rating: 8
in Gallatin Canyon in Gallatin National Forest

At 6,250 feet, Red Cliff Campground is the only Forest Service campground in the upper Gallatin Canyon between Big Sky and Yellowstone National Park. The campground, which is named for the orange cliffs in the area, has places to carry rafts and kayaks to the Gallatin River for launching. The river houses rainbow, brown, brook, and Yellowstone cutthroat trout,

plus mountain whitefish and arctic grayling. At the end of the south loop, the 4.8-mile Elkhorn Trail (#165) is open to hiking and horse-packing only, in a significant wildlife area. The campground is the closest one to the south of Big Sky Resort, which offers summer scenic chair rides, mountain biking, ziplining, and hiking.

When you enter the campground on the gravel road, loops head off in both directions. The north loop contains the campsites without hookups; the south loop has those with electrical hookups. Although the campground is on the opposite side of the river from the highway, the water doesn't drown out the motor sounds. A young Douglas fir forest covers most of the campground, with both shady and partly sunny campsites available. The south loop ends in a meadow blooming with pink sticky geraniums, and five north loop sites have views of the treed canyon. Several riverside sites have large flat spaces for tents where the door can sit right on the bank.

Campsites, facilities: The campground has 65 RV or tent campsites. RVs are limited to 50 feet. One of the sites is for small groups. Electrical hookups are available at 27 sites. Facilities include picnic tables, fire rings with grills, vault toilets, drinking water, bear boxes, garbage service, campground hosts, and firewood for sale. Leashed pets are permitted. Wheelchair-accessible toilets, tables, and water are available.

Reservations, fees: Reservations are accepted (877/444-6777, www.recreation.gov). No-hookup campsites cost $14; electrical hookup campsites cost $16. An extra vehicle costs $6. Cash, check, or credit card. Open mid-May-late September.

Directions: West of Bozeman, travel south on Highway 191 to milepost 41.5. Be cautious about turning into the campground—locals drive fast in the canyon. Turn east off the highway and cross the Gallatin River.

GPS Coordinates: N 45° 10.603' W 111° 14.490'

Contact: Gallatin National Forest, Bozeman

Ranger District, 3710 Fallon St., Suite C, Bozeman, MT 59718, 406/522-2520, www.fs.usda.gov/gallatin.

34 LANGOHR

🏃 🚵 ⛵ 🎣 🏊 ⛴ 🏕 ♿ 🚐 ⛺

Scenic rating: 8
in Hyalite Canyon in Gallatin National Forest

At 6,100 feet in Hyalite Canyon, Langohr Campground sits on the site of the first ranger station for the national forest. A short interpretive trail crosses the creek in the campground, and Hyalite Canyon is packed with hiking and mountain-biking trails, but the most popular trails depart from the no-wake Hyalite Reservoir area five miles farther up the road. The Blackmore picnic area and boat launch sits at the northwest corner of the reservoir. Hyalite Creek, which flows through the campground, harbors rainbow and Yellowstone cutthroat trout. Class IV-V stretches of white water in the canyon north of the campground draw expert kayakers.

The campground has two paved loops with paved campsite spurs lining up along Hyalite Creek. Most of the campsites enjoy creek frontage. The campground sits in a wild garden of midsummer color with yarrow, sticky pink geraniums, cow parsnips, and bladder campions surrounded by a Douglas fir forest. The lush surroundings make up for the fact that you can see neighboring campers, despite the spread-out sites. After dark, a few late hikers still race back down the canyon to Bozeman on the adjacent road (which you can see above), but then only the sound of the stream remains. Most of the campsites have views of meadow hillsides and mixed forest slopes.

Campsites, facilities: The campground has 19 RV or tent campsites. RVs are limited to 32 feet. Facilities include picnic tables, fire rings with grills, vault toilets, drinking water, garbage service, bear boxes, firewood for sale, and campground host. Leashed pets are permitted.

Wheelchair-accessible facilities include toilets, a trail, and two campsites.

Reservations, fees: Reservations are accepted (877/444-6777, www.recreation.gov). Campsites cost $14. An extra vehicle costs $6. Cash, check, or credit card. Open mid-May-mid-September.

Directions: From downtown Bozeman, drive west on Highway 191 to Cottonwood Road. Turn south and drive 5.5 miles. Turn east onto South 19th Avenue and go one mile. Turn south onto Hyalite Canyon Road, which turns into Forest Road 62. Climb 5.9 miles to the campground entrance on the right.
GPS Coordinates: N 45° 31.970' W 111° 0.908'
Contact: Gallatin National Forest, Bozeman Ranger District, 3710 Fallon St., Suite C, Bozeman, MT 59718, 406/522-2520, www.fs.usda.gov/gallatin.

35 HOOD CREEK

🏃 🚵 ⛵ 🎣 🏊 ⛴ 🏕 ♿ 🚐 ⛺

Scenic rating: 10
in Hyalite Canyon in Gallatin National Forest

At 6,730 feet, Hood Creek Campground sits on Hyalite Reservoir's northeast shore in Gallatin National Forest, with views up the canyon to Hyalite Peak. The lake is a no-wake zone, best for canoes, kayaks, and small sailboats, which can be launched from the boat ramp in the campground; motorboats can launch from the Blackmore picnic area less than a mile away. For anglers, the lake harbors Yellowstone cutthroat trout, brook trout, and arctic grayling. Across the road from the campground, Mystic Lake Trail (#436) leads 5.5 miles up to the lake. The trail is open to hikers, mountain bikers, and motorbikes.

The quiet, idyllic campsites at Hood Creek are prized for their location right on the reservoir shore with big views of Hyalite Peak. The close proximity of the picnic tables and tent sites to the water is rare because of concerns over water quality. The reconstructed campground now features level campsites, new facilities, and a smoother gravel road. Large conifers lend shade to some campsites, while others campsites enjoy sunny meadows bursting with wildflowers.

Campsites, facilities: The campground has 25 RV or tent campsites and one group site. RVs are limited to 50 feet. Facilities include picnic tables, fire rings with grills, vault toilets, drinking water, bear boxes, garbage service, firewood for sale, tent pads, and campground host. Leashed pets are permitted. Wheelchair-accessible facilities include toilets and two campsites.

Reservations, fees: Reservations are highly recommended (877/444-6777, www.recreation.gov). Campsites cost $14. An extra vehicle costs $6. Cash, check, or credit card. Open mid-May-late September.

Directions: From downtown Bozeman, drive west on Highway 191 to Cottonwood Road. Turn south and drive 5.5 miles. Turn east onto South 19th Avenue and go one mile. Turn south onto Hyalite Canyon Road, which turns into Forest Road 62. Drive 10.5 miles to the campground entrance on the right. (You'll cross over Hyalite Dam.) GPS Coordinates: N 45° 29.101' W 110° 58.136'

Contact: Gallatin National Forest, Bozeman Ranger District, 3710 Fallon St., Suite C, Bozeman, MT 59718, 406/522-2520, www.fs.usda.gov/gallatin.

36 CHISHOLM

Scenic rating: 9

in Hyalite Canyon in Gallatin National Forest

Chisholm Campground, elevation 6,740 feet, sits on the west side of Hyalite Reservoir. But contrary to Hood Creek waterfront campsites, this campground offers only peek-a-boo water views through the trees and trails to the reservoir. However, its location lends easy access to several trails, including wheelchair-accessible trails. The paved 0.5-mile Palisades Falls trail, littered with 50-million-year-old basalt from volcanoes, departs one mile from the campground and leads to the 80-foot waterfall. Trail #434 leads 5.5 miles to Emerald and Heather Lakes, and #427 saunters past 11 waterfalls en route to Hyalite Lake and the 10,299-foot summit of Hyalite Peak. You can launch boats at the Blackmore picnic area about 1.5 miles away. The lake, which harbors Yellowstone cutthroat trout and arctic grayling, is a no-wake zone. With the campground's location on the reservoir's upper end, late summer can leave this end dry when water levels drop.

The campground has one loop with all back-in parking spurs. Sites are spread out for privacy; some have a thick forest of pines and firs between them, but others are more open, with neighboring campers in view. Most of the campsites sit under heavy shade or filtered sunlight. A creek runs along the northwest side of the campground, with three sites along it. Besides the creek, you'll hear only songbirds in the morning.

Campsites, facilities: The campground has 10 RV or tent campsites. RVs are limited to 60 feet. Facilities include picnic tables, fire rings with grills, vault toilets (wheelchair-accessible), drinking water, bear boxes, garbage service, firewood for sale, and campground hosts. Leashed pets are permitted.

Reservations, fees: Reservations are accepted (877/444-6777, www.recreation.gov). Campsites cost $14. An extra vehicle costs $6. Cash or, check, or credit card. Open mid-May-late September.

Directions: From downtown Bozeman, drive west on Highway 191 to Cottonwood Road. Turn south and drive 5.5 miles. Turn east onto South 19th Avenue and go one mile. Turn south onto Hyalite Canyon Road, which turns into Forest Road 62. Drive 11.7 miles to the campground entrance on the right. (You'll cross over Hyalite Dam.) GPS Coordinates: N 45° 28.491' W 110° 57.325'

Contact: Gallatin National Forest, Bozeman Ranger District, 3710 Fallon St., Suite C, Bozeman, MT 59718, 406/522-2520, www.fs.usda.gov/gallatin.

37 BEAR CANYON

Scenic rating: 6

east of Bozeman

Located five minutes from downtown Bozeman, Bear Canyon Campground is convenient for shopping, nightlife, galleries, and restaurants along the main street as well as concerts in the Emerson Center. Bozeman is also home to golf courses, the Bozeman Hot Springs, and the Museum of the Rockies, with its celebrated dinosaur exhibits. A five-minute drive on the freeway also puts you at the entrance to Bridger Canyon, where the Bridger Bowl Ski Area hosts the annual Raptor Festival in early October. The free event takes place during the largest golden eagle migration in the United States, and you can hike to the ridge for a better view of the birds flying overhead. Hiking and mountain-biking trails are also in Bridger Canyon.

Bear Canyon Campground sits on a bluff above the freeway, but despite the proximity, some of the sites are surprisingly quiet. The campground commands views of the valley and surrounding mountains. Campsites are close together lined up in parking-lot fashion with some shorter trees providing partial shade. The campground has both pull-through and back-in gravel sites for RVs.

Campsites, facilities: The campground has 80 RV sites that can fit large RVs and 14 tent sites. Hookups are available for water, sewer, and electricity up to 50 amps. Facilities include flush toilets, showers, picnic tables, garbage service, wireless Internet, outdoor swimming pool, playground, launderette, disposal station, and camp store. Leashed pets are permitted.

Reservations, fees: Reservations are accepted. Hookups cost $28-35. Tent sites cost $20. Rates are for two people and one vehicle (includes trailer). Additional campers are charged $5 per person. Children age three or younger stay free. An extra vehicle costs $2. For each pet, add $1. A 7 percent Montana bed tax will be added on. Cash or credit card. Open May-mid-October.

Directions: From Bozeman, drive east on I-90 about 3.5 miles. Take Exit 313 and drive to the southwest side of the freeway, turning left into the campground in 400 feet.

GPS Coordinates: N 45° 39.080' W 110° 56.780'

Contact: Bear Canyon Campground, 4000 Bozeman Trail Road, Bozeman, MT 59718, 406/587-1575 or 800/438-1575, www.bearcanyoncampground.com.

38 PARADISE VALLEY KOA

Scenic rating: 8

on the Yellowstone River

At 4,700 feet in the Paradise Valley, the KOA flanks the Yellowstone River with 500 feet of waterfront. Flowing between the Gallatin and Absaroka Mountains, the Yellowstone River is favored by anglers as an iconic blue-ribbon trout stream. Anglers fish from drift boats, canoes, and rafts in addition to wading. A wheelchair-accessible 1.5-mile trail to Pine Creek Falls departs less than three miles away, and Pine Creek Road offers pleasant bicycle touring.

Large cottonwood trees shade the grassy campground, but a few sunny sites in the open garner views of the rugged Absaroka Mountains. Located on the opposite side of the river from the highway, the campground is quiet. Sites pack close together, with back-in and pull-through parking. Summer features pancake breakfasts and ice cream socials.

Campsites, facilities: The campground has 52 RV campsites with a maximum length pull-through of 95 feet. Hookups include water, sewer, and electricity up to 50 amps. The campground also has 27 tent campsites, some with electricity. Facilities include picnic tables, fire rings, flush toilets, showers, outdoor swimming pools (late May-early October), launderette, drinking water, playground, dog walk, wireless Internet, camp store, firewood and propane for sale, and bicycle rentals. Leashed pets are permitted.

Reservations, fees: Reservations are accepted. Hookups cost $43-50. Tent sites cost $28-35. Rates cover two adults. Extra campers are charged $4. Kids under 12 years old stay free. A 7 percent Montana bed tax will be added on. Open May-early October.

Directions: From Livingston, drive 10 miles south on Highway 89 toward Yellowstone Park to around milepost 42.8. Turn east on Pine Creek Road and drive 1.25 miles across the river to the campground entrance on the left. GPS Coordinates: N 45° 30.718' W 110° 34.731'

Contact: Livingston/Paradise Valley KOA, 163 Pine Creek Rd., Livingston, MT 59047, 406/222-0992 or 800/562-2805, www.koa.com.

39 PINE CREEK

Scenic rating: 8

in the Absaroka Mountains in Gallatin National Forest

Pine Creek Recreation Area, located at 5,600 feet just up from the floor of Paradise Valley, tucks in the northwest foothills of the Absaroka Mountains. Anglers can fish in Pine Creek for rainbow trout and mountain whitefish. A 0.5-mile nature trail explores the creek, and the Pine Creek Trail has two worthy destinations: Pine Creek Falls roars one flat mile up the trail, spraying mist onto the bridge, and hikers can reach Pine Creek Lake in five uphill miles with switchbacks. The 32-acre idyllic

alpine lake cuddles in a cirque below massive rock walls and is stocked for fishing.

A loose forest of Douglas fir and spruce provides mixed sun and shade for the quiet campground. A lush understory between most of the sites lends a sense of privacy, but a few have neighbors in view. Trails lead to Pine Creek, which runs adjacent to Loop B.

Campsites, facilities: The campground has 23 RV or tent campsites, including one group site, and two tent-only sites (one is a walk-in). RVs are limited to 50 feet. Facilities include picnic tables, fire rings, vault toilets, drinking water (Memorial Day-Labor Day), garbage service, firewood for sale, and campground hosts. Leashed pets are permitted. Wheelchair-accessible facilities include toilets, nature trail, fishing dock, and 17 campsites.

Reservations, fees: Reservations are accepted (877/444-6777, www.recreation.gov). Campsites cost $14. An extra vehicle costs $6. Cash or, check, or credit card. Open mid-May-October.

Directions: From Livingston, drive nine miles south on Highway 89. Turn east onto Pine Creek Road for 2.4 miles, crossing the Yellowstone River. At State Route 540, turn right for 0.7 miles. Turn left onto Forest Road 202 for 2.75 miles of narrow, winding road to the Pine Creek Recreation Area. GPS Coordinates: N 45° 29.901' W 110° 31.415'

Contact: Gallatin National Forest, Yellowstone Ranger District/Livingston Office, 5242 Hwy. 89, Livingston, MT 59047, 406/222-1892, www.fs.usda.gov/gallatin.

40 MALLARD'S REST

Scenic rating: 6

on the Yellowstone River

At 4,731 feet south of Livingston, Mallard's Rest is a state-run fishing access on the Yellowstone River in Paradise Valley. A cement boat ramp with trailer parking is available for launching rafts, drift boats, canoes, and kayaks, and the river garners fame as a blue-ribbon trout fishery. Located between Loch Leven and Pine Creek fishing access sites, Mallard's Rest is one of nine fishing access sites with boat ramps in the 56 river miles of the Yellowstone River between Livingston and Gardiner.

With reconstructed campsites and road, the state revamped this campground that sits on a tall grass and juniper river bar—green in early summer, but gold by the end of July. Willow brush flanks part of the riverbank, and a handful of big willow trees offer partial shade to a few campsites. All of the sunny campsites have big views across the river of the Absaroka Mountains. Some traffic noise filters down into the campground.

Campsites, facilities: The campground has 12 RV or tent campsites that can accommodate RVs up to 30 feet. Facilities include picnic tables, fire rings with grills, drinking water, vault toilets (wheelchair-accessible), and concrete boat ramp. Leashed pets are permitted.

Reservations, fees: Reservations are not accepted. Campsites cost $7 with a Montana fishing license and $12 without a Montana fishing license. Cash or check. Open year-round.

Directions: From Livingston, drive south on Highway 89 for approximately nine miles to milepost 41.5. Turn east onto the 0.2-mile steep gravel road, which swings around a sharp hairpin down to the river level and the campground.
GPS Coordinates: N 45° 28.975' W 110° 37.235'

Contact: Montana Fish, Wildlife, and Parks, Region 3, 1400 S. 19th Ave., Bozeman, MT 59718, 406/994-4042, http://fwp.mt.gov.

41 SNOWBANK

Scenic rating: 8

in the Absaroka Mountains in Gallatin National Forest

Located at 5,750 feet at the western edge of the Absaroka-Beartooth Wilderness, Snowbank Campground is a place to go for solitude, fishing, and hiking. The only interruption to the quiet can be motors from off-road vehicles on some trails and roads outside the wilderness area. Mill Creek harbors several species of trout and mountain whitefish. Near the campground entrance, the 6.3-mile Wicked Ridge Trail (#78) for hikers or mountain bikers climbs past logging roads to some views, but better hiking trails into the wilderness launch within a few miles up further up the road. An easy two-mile trail (#58) leads to scenic Passage Falls.

A thick fir and spruce forest broken by grassy meadows lends a mix of shade and sun to the quiet campground. Between a lush understory of wild berry bushes screening sites and spacious distribution along the campground road, most campsites are private. You'll wake to the sounds of birds and the stream. Eight sites spread along the creek while two campsites sit on a hillside spur.

Campsites, facilities: The campground has 10 RV or tent campsites, including one group site. RVs are limited to 35 feet. Facilities include picnic tables, fire rings, vault toilets, drinking water (Memorial Day-Labor Day), garbage service, firewood for sale, and campground hosts. Leashed pets are permitted.

Reservations, fees: Reservations are accepted (877/444-6777, www.recreation.gov). Campsites cost $14. An extra vehicle costs $6. Cash or, check, or credit card. Open mid-May-October.

Directions: From Livingston, drive 15 miles south on Highway 89. Turn east onto Mill Creek Road for 12 miles, crossing the

Yellowstone River. Drive the gravel forest road to the campground entrance on the right.
GPS Coordinates: N 45° 17.281' W 110° 32.508'
Contact: Gallatin National Forest, Yellowstone Ranger District/Livingston Office, 5242 Hwy. 89, Livingston, MT 59047, 406/222-1892, www.fs.usda.gov/gallatin.

42 YELLOWSTONE'S EDGE RV PARK

Scenic rating: 6
on the Yellowstone River

At 4,850 feet, the Yellowstone's Edge RV Park sits on the west bank of the Yellowstone River south of Livingston in the Paradise Valley. From the campground, you can launch hand-carried canoes, kayaks, or rafts and fish for brown and rainbow trout from the river's bank. A state-run fishing access site with a boat ramp and a fishing guide service is five miles south at Emigrant. Scenic floats are also available on the river. Chico Hot Springs is seven miles south.

The campground sits on a sunny, flat bar with 3,000 feet of river frontage. More than one-third of the campsites line up along the river, but all sites have views of the surrounding Gallatin and Absaroka Mountains. At such a proximity to the highway, vehicle noise is prevalent. The campground has evening campfires for socializing. Both back-in and pull-through sites—some with concrete patios—line up very close together with mowed lawn in between.

Campsites, facilities: The campground has 80 RV campsites. RVs are limited to 90 feet. Hookups are available for sewer, water, and electricity up to 50 amps. Facilities include picnic tables, flush toilets, showers, garbage service, convenience store, wireless Internet, launderette, game room, horseshoe pits, and dog walk. Leashed pets are permitted. A wheelchair-accessible toilet and shower are available.

Reservations, fees: Reservations are recommended. Campsites cost $48-53. Rates are based on two people. Additional adults are charged $4.50; for additional children ages 4-17, add $2.50. A 7 percent Montana bed tax will be added on. Cash, check, or credit card. Open May-early October.

Directions: On Highway 89 between Livingston and Yellowstone National Park, find the campground on the east side of the road at milepost 35. It is 18 miles south of Livingston and 35 miles north of the park.
GPS Coordinates: N 45° 24.998' W 110° 41.077'
Contact: Yellowstone's Edge RV Park, 3502 Hwy. 89 S., Livingston, MT 59047, 406/333-4036 or 800/865-7322, www.mtrv.com.

43 CANYON

Scenic rating: 7
in Yankee Jim Canyon in Gallatin National Forest

At 5,073 feet, Canyon Campground nestles in Yankee Jim Canyon below Dome Mountain, 15 miles from the northwest entrance to Yellowstone National Park. The canyon is home to bighorn sheep, the famed cutthroat trout fishery of the Yellowstone River, and white-water rafting and kayaking. The campground sits across the highway from the river, which drops about 25 feet per mile in the five miles of Class III rapids through the canyon. You can launch rafts and kayaks at Joe Brown Creek and take out at Carbella on either side of the campground. Guided raft trips are available in Gardiner. History buffs and hikers can walk the Yankee Jim interpretive trail on the opposite side of the river, accessed at the Tom Miner Bridge.

© BECKY LOMAX

rafting on the Yellowstone River in Paradise Valley

The Joe Brown trailhead also sits east of the campground. The trail originally served as the access to Yellowstone and even earlier a Native American route. Because of the easy access, the campground works for cyclists touring Paradise Valley. Hunters use the camp in fall.

Sitting at the base of a massive talus slope, the campground is a cluster of open junipers, Douglas firs, and giant granitic boulders, some bigger than vehicles. Between the trees and boulders, some of the arid campsites are partly shaded; others are sunny. With the highway running adjacent to the campground, you can hear passing vehicles. Sites 3, 4, and 6 tuck back in mini-canyons in the boulders and trees, with minimal views of the road. Of the campground's two loops, the right one features more open sites; the left one has more private sites that offer better protection when winds howl through the canyon. Watch for rattlesnakes. Larger RVs may have difficulty squeezing on the narrow road through the boulders.

Campsites, facilities: The campground has 17 RV or tent campsites. RVs are limited to 48 feet. Facilities include picnic tables, fire rings with grills, vault toilets, and bear boxes. Drinking water is not available; bring your own. Pack out your trash. Leashed pets are permitted. Wheelchair-accessible toilets and tables are available.

Reservations, fees: Reservations are not accepted. Campsites cost $7. An extra vehicle costs $3. Cash or check. Open year-round.

Directions: From Livingston, travel south on Highway 89 to milepost 14.9. Turn north off the highway into the campground immediately after entering Gallatin National Forest. You can also reach the campground about 15 minutes northwest of Gardiner.

GPS Coordinates: N 45° 10.964' W 110° 53.285'

Contact: Gallatin National Forest, Gardiner Ranger District, 805 Scott Street, Gardiner, MT 59030, 406/848-7373, www.fs.usda.gov/gallatin.

44 TOM MINER

Scenic rating: 8

in the Gallatin Mountains in Gallatin National Forest

At 7,000 feet, Tom Miner Campground hides far off the beaten path at the tail end of a long dirt road in the Gallatin Mountains. From the back of the campground, a trail heads to the Petrified Forest, a geological wonder 35-55 million years old where trees were petrified in upright positions as well as horizontal. A 0.5-mile steep interpretive trail teaches visitors what to look for in the rock cliffs to identify specimens. Another trail leads through alpine meadows and pine forests in 2.5 miles to Buffalo Horn Pass or five miles to the impressive summit views from 10,296-foot Ramshorn Peak—both on the crest of the Gallatin Range.

The shady campground clusters under pines and aspens with wildflower meadows flanking the hillsides in July. Views look up the steep arid southern slope of the southeast Ramshorn ridge. The sheer distance from the highway guarantees quiet at night.

Campsites, facilities: The campground has 16 RV or tent campsites. RVs are limited to 42 feet. Facilities include picnic tables, fire rings, vault toilets (wheelchair-accessible), hand pump for drinking water, and bear boxes. Pack out your trash. Leashed pets are permitted.

Reservations, fees: Reservations are not accepted. Campsites cost $7. An extra vehicle costs $3. Cash or check. Open June-October.

Directions: From Gardiner, travel northwest on Highway 89 for 16 miles or from Livingston, go 37 miles south. Turn sharply off the west side of the highway to head south on Tom Miner Road for 12 miles, following signs at junctions to campground.

GPS Coordinates: N 45° 7.750' W 111° 3.781'

Contact: Gallatin National Forest, Gardiner Ranger District, 805 Scott Street, Gardiner, MT 59030, 406/848-7375, www.fs.usda.gov/gallatin.

45 HALFMOON

Scenic rating: 8

in the Crazy Mountains in Gallatin National Forest

Fifty million years ago, the Crazy Mountains rose to 11,000 feet from magma cutting through the muddy bottom of an inland sea, leaving an island of mountains shooting up from the prairie. Glaciers sculpted the rock into dramatic alpine basins, many containing lakes. Halfmoon Campground is the only designated vehicle-accessible campground in the Crazies, hence its popularity. You might even see skiers hiking in July to make turns down snowfields. From the campground, the Big Timber Creek Trail #119 (hikers and horses only) ascends into terrain inhabited by mountain goats, elk, and a patchwork of private landowners. Big Timber Creek Falls sits about 0.25 miles up the trail; look for an unmarked path on the left. The double gems of Twin Lakes sit three miles up the trail, with abundant mosquitoes and fishing. Spur trails lead to Granite and Blue Lakes, and a 2,000-foot ascent tops out on a pass at the divide with big views down the drainage.

Despite the popularity of the area, the remoteness of this campground guarantees after dark quiet and solitude—something you will earn on the long gravel access road. A mix of meadows and pine forest give campsites views of the Crazy Mountains. The campground loop sits adjacent to Big Timber Creek, with sites 1, 2, and 7 in audible distance. Two trails access the stream for fishing and wading.

Campsites, facilities: The campground has 12 RV or tent campsites. Some parking spurs can fit 60-foot RVs, but the Forest Service recommends RVs be 32 feet or shorter because of the access road. Facilities include picnic tables, fire rings, drinking water (Memorial Day-Labor Day), and vault toilets. Pack out your trash. Leashed pets are permitted.

Wheelchair-accessible facilities include toilets and six campsites.

Reservations, fees: Reservations are not accepted. Camping costs $5. Cash or check. Open year-round, but snowbound in winter.

Directions: From Big Timber, travel north on Highway 191 for 11.5 miles. Turn west onto the gravel Big Timber Canyon Road (Wormser Rd. on some maps) for two miles. Turn right onto Big Timber Canyon Road for 10 miles until its terminus at the campground.

GPS Coordinates: N 46° 2.508' W 110° 14.429'

Contact: Gallatin National Forest, Yellowstone Ranger District/Big Timber Office, 225 Big Timber Loop Road, Big Timber, MT 59011, 406/932-5155, www.fs.usda.gov/gallatin.

46 WEST BOULDER

Scenic rating: 8

in the Absaroka Mountains in Gallatin National Forest

At 5,550 feet in Gallatin National Forest, West Boulder Campground requires a long gravel and dirt road drive with rough curvy stretches in its final miles. As the only designated campground on the West Boulder River, it serves to access the canyon and 10,000-foot-high peaks of the Absaroka Mountains. The river provides a fly-fishing haven for wild trout, especially for hikers heading three miles up to the West Boulder Meadows where the river slows into giant pools. The Davis Creek Trail (#38) departs via a bridge across the river to climb for 10 miles to Deep Creek Divide for views of the Paradise Valley and Absaroka Mountains.

Surrounded by private ranches, the ultra-quiet campground offers choices of sunny campsites with big views of the canyon and mountains or campsites partially shaded by pines and aspens. Most campsites sit back from the river, but trails connect to the riverbank.

Sites spread out for privacy; the one at the end of the turnaround loop has the most spacious setting.

Campsites, facilities: The campground has 10 RV and tent campsites. Although a couple parking pads can fit rigs up to 60 feet, the Forest Service recommends an RV limit of 20 feet because of the access road. Facilities include picnic tables, fire rings, pit toilet, drinking water (Memorial Day-Labor Day), and bear boxes. Pack out your trash. Leashed pets are permitted.

Reservations, fees: Reservations are not accepted. Camping costs $5. Open year-round, but snowbound in winter.

Directions: From Big Timber, travel south on Highway 298 for 16 miles. After passing McLeod, turn right onto the gravel County Road 30 for 7.5 miles. Turn left onto the West Boulder Road for six miles to the campground entrance on the right.

GPS Coordinates: N 45° 32.826' W 110° 18.444'

Contact: Gallatin National Forest, Yellowstone Ranger District/Big Timber Office, 225 Big Timber Loop Road, Big Timber, MT 59011, 406/932-5155, www.fs.usda.gov/gallatin.

47 BOULDER FORKS

Scenic rating: 6

on the Boulder River

At 4,780 feet south of Big Timber, Boulder Forks is a state-run fishing access on the Upper Boulder River at the confluence of the west, main, and east forks. The Boulder is a tributary of the Yellowstone River, drawing its water from the high reaches of the Absaroka-Beartooth Wilderness to the south—Montana's tallest peaks. You can launch rafts and kayaks (boats you can carry) from the primitive ramp to float 4.5 miles north to the highway bridge in Class III white water. The blue-ribbon trout stream that anglers wade-fish houses brown trout and rainbow trout, plus mountain whitefish. Littered periodically with boulders, the river is aptly named.

On the perimeter of a sunny pasture with big views of the Absaroka Mountains, the campground spreads the campsites within sight of each other around a small loop. Mature cottonwood trees line the river, but unfortunately, they produce little shade for the south-facing campground. The only sounds you'll hear are the river, the songbirds, and the wind. This is a popular fishing access; the sites frequently fill.

Campsites, facilities: The campground has three primitive RV or tent campsites that can accommodate midsized RVs. Facilities include rock fire rings and a vault toilet. No water is available; bring your own or treat creek water. Pack out your trash. Leashed pets are permitted. The toilet is wheelchair-accessible.

Reservations, fees: Reservations are not accepted. Camping is free. Open year-round.

Directions: From Big Timber, drive south on McLeod Street, which turns into Highway 298. Go 16 miles to just past McLeod. At milepost 16.4, turn east onto the single-lane gravel road 0.3 mile and drive over the cattle grate. GPS Coordinates: N 45° 39.445' W 110° 6.566'

Contact: Montana Fish, Wildlife, and Parks, Region 5, 2300 Lake Elmo Dr., Billings, MT 59105, 406/247-2940, http://fwp.mt.gov.

48 FALLS CREEK

Scenic rating: 7

in the Absaroka Mountains in Gallatin National Forest

At 5,227 feet, Falls Creek sits on the Boulder River's west bank, surrounded by 10,000-foot-high peaks of the Absaroka Mountains. It is 4.9 miles south of Natural Bridge Falls, an interpretive site with a wheelchair-accessible trail where the river flows over a 100-foot

Bridges and trails tour Natural Bridge Interpretive Area along the Boulder River.

© BECKY LOMAX

drop in high water; in low water, it disappears into an underground channel. The 5.5-mile Green Mountain Trail (#14), a route with less elevation gain than many of the other trails in the area, also departs from the falls. Summer homes and small ranches populate some of the private land around the campground. The fast plummet of the Boulder River slows here to riffles alternating with deep pools, coughing up 20-inch trout to expert fly-fishers. Kayakers and rafters tackle some of the river's Class II-III boulder-strewn white water above Natural Bridge through early summer.

Each campsite has a large, flat tent space along the creek with aspens, pines, and Douglas firs lending partial shade to some of the sites. The sites are spread out and some tuck under trees for privacy, but you can see the neighboring campsites. The sunnier campsites also have views of the canyon and forest. The nearby road is busy in midsummer but quiets at night, so you only hear the river. No RV turnaround is available.

Campsites, facilities: The campground has eight tent campsites. Facilities include picnic tables, fire rings, vault toilet (wheelchair-accessible), drinking water (Memorial Day-Labor Day), and bear boxes. Pack out your trash. Leashed pets are permitted.

Reservations, fees: Reservations are not accepted. Camping is free. Open year-round, but snowbound in winter.

Directions: From Big Timber, travel south on Highway 298 for 25.6 miles to the Gallatin National Forest boundary, where the road (Forest Road 6639) turns to bumpy dirt and gravel. (Locals call it the Boulder Road.) Drive to milepost 5.1 past the forest boundary and turn left onto the narrow campground road. GPS Coordinates: N 45° 29.409' W 110° 13.149'

Contact: Gallatin National Forest, Yellowstone Ranger District/Big Timber Office, 225 Big Timber Loop Road, Big Timber, MT 59011, 406/932-5155, www.fs.usda.gov/gallatin.

49 BOULDER RIVER PRIMITIVE

🚶 🚴 🛶 🚐 🚣 🏕 ♿ 🚙 ⛺

Scenic rating: 8

in the Absaroka Mountains in Gallatin National Forest

Along the Boulder River, dispersed primitive campsites are sprinkled down the entire glaciated canyon length. These campsites, prized for their seclusion and privacy, sit between 5,350 and 6,700 feet in elevation on both the east and west banks of the river, flanked by the Absaroka Mountains and the Absaroka-Beartooth Wilderness. The river—a blue-ribbon trout stream—works best for wade fishing, but its boulders require care. From Fourmile to Boulder Falls, rafters and kayakers navigate the river's technical Class II-IV rapids. The floating season usually ends after early summer when water levels drop too low and expose too many boulders. Long hiking trails—requiring 3,000 feet or more of ascent—access the high summits in the wilderness. Mountain bikers and ATV riders tour the Boulder Road.

Most of the dispersed primitive campsites along the Boulder River sit right on the river. You'll find sites shaded under Douglas firs, in filtered sunlight in aspens, and in full sun in grassy fields with big open views of the mountains. Find most of the sites by a small sign with a tent icon; a few are unmarked. Scout their dirt roads and turnaround space before you drive in blind. Etiquette dictates one site per party. Respect private property along the river.

Campsites, facilities: More than 30 dispersed, primitive RV or tent campsites sit along the Boulder River. The Forest Service recommends only RVs up to 32 feet in length on the Boulder Road. Facilities include rock fire rings. Use pre-existing fire rings rather than constructing new ones. Treat river water before drinking. Follow Leave No Trace principles for human waste. Pack out your trash. Leashed pets are permitted.

Reservations, fees: Reservations are not accepted. Camping is free. Open year-round, but snowbound in winter.

Directions: From Big Timber, travel south on Highway 298 for 25.6 miles to the Gallatin National Forest boundary, where the road (Forest Road 6639) turns to bumpy dirt and gravel that alternates between rocky washboards and large potholes. (Locals call it the Boulder Road.) After Falls Creek Campground at 5.1 miles past the forest boundary, it's 20 miles farther to the end of the road at Box Canyon.

GPS Coordinates: N 45° 28.691' W 110° 12.469' (first primitive site)

Contact: Gallatin National Forest, Yellowstone Ranger District/Big Timber Office, 225 Big Timber Loop Road, Big Timber, MT 59011, 406/932-5155, www.fs.usda.gov/gallatin.

50 BIG BEAVER

Scenic rating: 7
in the Absaroka Mountains in Gallatin National Forest

At 5,336 feet, Big Beaver Campground sits on the east bank of the Boulder River surrounded by the 10,000-foot-high peaks of the West and East Boulder Plateaus in the Absaroka Mountains. The Absaroka-Beartooth Wilderness is across the river. One mile to the north, the Graham Creek Trail grinds up countless switchbacks to gain 4,500 feet in elevation and reach the flanks of Chrome Mountain in 11.8 miles. This stretch of rocky river services the expert trout angler who can wade-fish as well as Class II-III white-water rafters and kayakers through early summer. Floaters put in at Chippy Park, about two miles upstream.

The campground squeezes between the road and the river, with flat tent spaces 10 feet from the water. The partly shaded sites, tucked under Douglas firs, line up left and right of the entrance, with views of the canyon walls and talus slopes to the east, plus the road. This stretch of the river and road is quite populated, despite the road's deplorable condition, as a church camp borders the campground. The road kicks up dust all day long with traffic in midsummer, but quiets at night to where you'll just hear the sound of the river.

Campsites, facilities: The campground has five RV or tent campsites. The largest parking pad can accommodate an RV up to 42 feet, but the Forest Service warns the road is not suitable for vehicles longer than 32 feet. Facilities include picnic tables, fire rings, and vault toilet (wheelchair-accessible). No drinking water is available; bring your own or treat creek water. Pack out your trash. Leashed pets are permitted.

Reservations, fees: Reservations are not accepted. Camping is free. Open year-round, but snowbound in winter.

Directions: From Big Timber, travel south on Highway 298 for 25.6 miles to the Gallatin National Forest boundary, where the road (Forest Road 6639) turns to bumpy dirt and gravel that alternates between rocky washboards and large potholes. (Locals call it the Boulder Road.) Drive to milepost 7.3 past the forest boundary, crossing to the east side of the river, and turn right into the campground.

GPS Coordinates: N 45° 27.857' W 110° 11.910'

Contact: Gallatin National Forest, Yellowstone Ranger District/Big Timber Office, 225 Big Timber Loop Road, Big Timber, MT 59011, 406/932-5155, www.fs.usda.gov/gallatin.

51 ASPEN

Scenic rating: 7

in the Absaroka Mountains in Gallatin National Forest

At 5,386 feet, Aspen Campground sits on the Boulder River's east bank, tucked under the 10,000-foot-high summits of the Absaroka Mountains and the Absaroka-Beartooth Wilderness across the river. About 1.5 miles north, Graham Creek Trail grunts up 4,500 feet in elevation through innumerable switchbacks for 11.8 miles to Chrome Mountain. The boney Boulder River in this stretch services both the expert trout angler who can wade-fish as well as white-water rafters and kayakers with its Class II-III froth. Only through early summer, floaters launch at Chippy Park about 1.5 miles upstream. The campground is adjacent to an elk wintering range.

With campsites divided into two loops, the campground sits in a thick grove of aspens and willows blooming with wild roses and bee balm. Unlike the other Boulder campgrounds, most campsites do not flank the river but short trails cut through the brush to reach it. The partly sunny, private sites hear the sound of the river and some passing traffic, but the undergrowth blocks the view of the road. Several campsites grab views of the surrounding mountains.

Campsites, facilities: The campground has eight RV or tent campsites. RVs are limited to 42 feet, but the Forest Service recommends 32 feet or less on the road. Facilities include picnic tables, fire rings, drinking water (Memorial Day-Labor Day), bear boxes, and pit and vault toilets (wheelchair-accessible). Pack out your trash. Leashed pets are permitted.

Reservations, fees: Reservations are not accepted. Camping costs $5. Cash or check. Open year-round, but snowbound in winter.

Directions: From Big Timber, travel south on Highway 298 for 25.6 miles to the Gallatin National Forest boundary, where the road (Forest Road 6639) turns to bumpy dirt and gravel that alternates between rocky washboards and large potholes. (Locals call it the Boulder Road.) Drive to milepost 8 past the forest boundary, crossing to the east side of the river, and turn right down the skinny road into the campground.

GPS Coordinates: N 45° 27.386' W 110° 11.829'

Contact: Gallatin National Forest, Yellowstone Ranger District/Big Timber Office, 225 Big Timber Loop Road, Big Timber, MT 59011, 406/932-5155, www.fs.usda.gov/gallatin.

52 CHIPPY PARK

Scenic rating: 8

in the Absaroka Mountains in Gallatin National Forest

At 5,452 feet, Chippy Park Campground sits on the Boulder River's east bank, tucked under the 10,000-foot-high summits of the Absaroka Mountains. The Absaroka-Beartooth Wilderness flanks both sides of the river. About 2.5 miles south, Speculator Creek Trail climbs 4,500 feet in elevation for 7.3 miles to the West Boulder Plateau north of Boulder Mountain. Chippy Park serves as a starting point for rafters and kayakers to descend the river's Class II-III white water to Boulder Falls. The river from Speculator Creek to Chippy Park contains Class IV rapids. Both boulder-strewn sections are floatable only through early summer. The blue-ribbon trout stream is best fished by wading.

A forest of aspens and Douglas firs provides partial shade for the campground sunk in tall grass. The campsites, which all (except site 5) line up along the riverbank, offer some sunny locations with views of the surrounding mountains. Back-in sites that can accommodate RVs sit to the left; two walk-in tent sites are to the right. Site 3 has spaciousness; site 4 garners more privacy at the loop's end.

Campsites, facilities: The campground has seven RV or tent campsites. RV parking is limited to 42 feet, but the Forest Service advises that only vehicles under 32 feet drive the access road. Facilities include picnic tables, fire rings, drinking water (Memorial Day-Labor Day), bear boxes, and pit and vault toilets. Pack out your trash. Leashed pets are permitted. Wheelchair-accessible facilities include toilets and two campsites.

Reservations, fees: Reservations are not accepted. Camping costs $5. Cash or check. Open year-round, but snowbound in winter.

Directions: From Big Timber, travel south on Highway 298 for 25.6 miles to the Gallatin National Forest boundary, where the road (Forest Road 6639) turns to bumpy dirt and gravel that alternates between rocky washboards and large potholes. (Locals call it the Boulder Road.) Drive to milepost 9.5 past the forest boundary, crossing to the east side of the river, climbing a steep hill, and dropping to the campground road on the right.

GPS Coordinates: N 45° 26.234' W 110° 11.369'

Contact: Gallatin National Forest, Yellowstone Ranger District/Big Timber Office, 225 Big Timber Loop Road, Big Timber, MT 59011, 406/932-5155, www.fs.usda.gov/gallatin.

53 HELLS CANYON

Scenic rating: 8

in the Absaroka Mountains in Gallatin National Forest

At 6,100 feet, Hells Canyon Campground sits on the Boulder River's west side, flanked by the Absaroka-Beartooth Wilderness and 10,000-foot-high pinnacles of The Needles to the west. The constriction of the forested slopes doesn't allow you to see the summits of the Absaroka Mountains unless you slog up 4,500 feet in elevation. Trailheads are located about one mile to the north and south of the campground. The Hawley Creek Trail climbs six miles to Breakneck Plateau, and the Fourmile Creek Trail ascends 7.8 miles to Silver Lake. The mountain slopes constrict to form Hells Canyon, running with four miles of Class III-IV rapids between Fourmile to the south and Speculator Creek to the north, floatable only in early summer. The river is best fished by wading. Be prepared for tedious, slow-driving miles on the ragged Boulder Road.

Contrary to other area campgrounds, this site sits back from the river under the thick shade of conifers, with some campsites having snippets of views of the surrounding mountains. Sites seem spacious because of little underbrush. Owing to the rough road, traffic drops off considerably in this upper section, making this campground ultra-quiet and private.

Campsites, facilities: The campground has 11 RV or tent campsites. While parking can accommodate vehicles up to 48 feet, the Forest Service recommends that RVs limit length to 20 feet on the campground road. Facilities include picnic tables, fire rings, bear boxes, and pit toilets. Pack out your trash. Leashed pets are permitted.

Reservations, fees: Reservations are not accepted. Camping is free. Open year-round, but snowbound in winter.

Directions: From Big Timber, travel south on Highway 298 for 25.6 miles to the Gallatin National Forest boundary, where the road (Forest Road 6639) turns to bumpy dirt and gravel that alternates between rocky washboards and large potholes. (Locals call it the Boulder Road.) Drive to milepost 15.5 past the forest boundary, crossing the river twice, and turn left into the campground.

GPS Coordinates: N 45° 21.756' W 110° 12.935'

Contact: Gallatin National Forest,

Yellowstone Ranger District/Big Timber Office, 225 Big Timber Loop Road, Big Timber, MT 59011, 406/932-5155, www.fs.usda.gov/gallatin.

54 HICKS PARK

Scenic rating: 8

in the Absaroka Mountains in Gallatin National Forest

At 6,350 feet, Hicks Park Campground sits on the Boulder River's east side, flanked by the Absaroka-Beartooth Wilderness and 10,000-foot-high pinnacles of Carbonate Mountain and Hicks Peak. Requiring climbs of over 3,000 feet in elevation in less than eight miles, Upsidedown Creek Trail departs from the campground to switchback up to Horseshoe Lake, and Bridge Creek Trail climbs to Bridge Lake. Be prepared for long, slow-driving miles on the rough Boulder Road. Hicks Park, the last designated campground, makes a base camp for exploring the road's terminus at Box Canyon and continuing farther on the boulder-filled, curvy trail via mountain bike or ATV to the mining ghost town of Independence. The road ends on Independence Peak, with a short trail to Blue Lake set in an alpine cirque. The Boulder River is best when wade fishing.

Grassy campsites line up overlooking the river, with a loose forest of conifers lending partial shade. The open forest also permits views of the surrounding steep mountain slopes. The campsites are spread out for privacy, but you can see neighboring campers through the trees. With fewer people traveling the upper Boulder Road, the river is the pervasive sound.

Campsites, facilities: The campground has 16 RV or tent campsites. The largest parking pad can accommodate vehicles up to 51 feet, but the Forest Service recommends that RVs driving Boulder Road be no longer than 32 feet. Facilities include picnic tables, fire rings, bear boxes, drinking water (Memorial Day-Labor Day), and pit and vault toilets (wheelchair-accessible). Pack out your trash. Leashed pets are permitted.

Reservations, fees: Reservations are not accepted. Campsites cost $5. Cash or check. Open year-round, but snowbound in winter.

Directions: From Big Timber, travel south on Highway 298 for 25.6 miles to the Gallatin National Forest boundary, where the road (Forest Road 6639) turns to bumpy dirt and gravel that alternates between rocky washboards and large potholes. (Locals call it the Boulder Road.) Drive to milepost 21 past the forest boundary, crossing the river three times, and turn right into the campground.

GPS Coordinates: N 45° 18.014' W 110° 14.431'

Contact: Gallatin National Forest, Yellowstone Ranger District/Big Timber Office, 225 Big Timber Loop Road, Big Timber, MT 59011, 406/932-5155, www.fs.usda.gov/gallatin.

55 BIG TIMBER KOA

Scenic rating: 4

east of Big Timber

Big Timber KOA is convenient for those road-tripping along I-90. At 3,948 feet, it's about a five-minute drive from Greycliff Prairie Dog Town State Park (nonresidents $5 per vehicle, Montana residents free), an interpretive site where you can watch the black-tailed prairie dogs skitter about their natural habitat. The 9-hole Overland Golf Course also is five minutes away. Adjacent to the campground, Big Timber Waterslide Park has an outdoor pool and big slides for older kids and adults as well as small slides for children. The Yellowstone River parallels the freeway's north side, offering fishing and floating in rafts and kayaks.

Being right next to the freeway, you'll hear

trucking noise at night. The grassy campground offers partly shaded campsites under large trees or sunny campsites tucked close to each other in parking-lot fashion on gravel parking pads connected by a gravel road. For kids, the campground has a 68-foot-long jumping air pillow, playground, and swimming pool.

Campsites, facilities: The campground has 17 RV campsites with several that can accommodate big rigs up to 100 feet. Hookups include water, sewer, cable TV, and electricity up to 50 amps. The campground also includes eight tent sites. Facilities include picnic tables, pedestal grills, flush toilets, showers, launderette, drinking water, private hot tub room, game room, horseshoe pits, wireless Internet, café camp store, firewood for sale, and disposal station. Leashed pets are permitted.

Reservations, fees: Reservations are accepted. Hookups cost $42-48. Tent campsites cost $31. Rates are for two people. Extra adults are charged $5 each; for extra children, add $2.50 each. Cash, travelers checks, or credit card. Open mid-May-early September.

Directions: From I-90 nine miles east of Big Timber, take Exit 377. Drive to the south side of the freeway to Frontage Road (Hwy. 10) and turn west for 0.25 mile to the campground entrance on the right.

GPS Coordinates: N 45° 46.405' W 109° 47.984'

Contact: Big Timber KOA, 693 Hwy. 10 E., Big Timber MT 59011, 406/932-6569 or 800/562-5869, www.bigtimberkoa.com.

56 ITCH-KEP-PE PARK

Scenic rating: 5

on the Yellowstone River

Located at 3,350 feet, Itch-Kep-Pe Park, a city park, sits between the railroad tracks, downtown Columbus, and the Yellowstone River. You can walk or bicycle the half-mile to town for restaurants, shops, and bars—including the first bar to be licensed in Montana. With a boat ramp at the park's east end, the Yellowstone River offers fishing and floating in drift boats, rafts, kayaks, and canoes. Floaters and anglers also launch on the Stillwater River south of Columbus to float back to the park. The river diverts south of the campground around a few islands, making good places to swim before the water level drops too low. Children can bicycle the park roads, and free wood is sometimes delivered to the campground from a local timber company. The campground, which is popular because of its price, is maintained by the city and patrolled regularly by the city police.

The potholed campground road makes several loops under huge cottonwood trees that provide shade to cool the grassy campground. Although no campsites command water frontage, many sit within sight of the river, and the long shoreline allows plenty of space for campers to spread out to enjoy the water. Campsites are a mix of shade, partial shade, and sunny, depending on location. Some tuck back in between trees for privacy, but most of the campsites are open, with views of neighbors. You'll hear the river, railroad, and trucks on the highway at night. Some sites are pull-throughs, but most are back-ins on gravel spurs.

Campsites, facilities: The campground has 30 RV or tent campsites that can accommodate RVs up to 55 feet long. Facilities include picnic tables, fire rings, flush and pit toilets, drinking water, and a concrete boat ramp. Leashed pets are permitted.

Reservations, fees: Reservations are not accepted. Camping is free, but donations are appreciated. Open April-October.

Directions: From Columbus, drive south on Highway 78 for 0.5 mile. Before the bridge over the Yellowstone River, turn left to enter the campground.

GPS Coordinates: N 45° 37.735' W 109° 15.187'

Contact: City of Columbus, P.O. Box 549, Columbus, MT 59019, 406/322-5313.

57 SWINGING BRIDGE
🏊 🎣 � 🛥 🎿 🏕 ♿ 🚌 ⛰

Scenic rating: 5

on the Stillwater River

At 3,740 feet, Swinging Bridge is a state-run fishing access site on the east bank of the Stillwater River. The river divides around islands creating places to swim, but in high water the Swinging Bridge Rapid and the Beartooth Drop—both at the campground—require caution. The Stillwater runs past the campground with Class II-III rapids. Rafters and kayakers usually put-in farther upstream at Whitebird and float past Swinging Bridge Campground to Fireman's Point, two miles south of Columbus, or Itch-Kep-Pe Park, after the Stillwater pours into the Yellowstone River. As the water level drops throughout the summer, large rocky bars extend as beaches along the shore. The Stillwater contains brook, rainbow, and Yellowstone cutthroat trout.

The campground shows wear from overuse at some sites, three of which sit right on the river. Junipers, large cottonwoods, and willows lend partial shade to the campground, and several sites have room for small tents. The gravel campground road kicks up dust when vehicles drive through, but the area is quiet at night.

Campsites, facilities: The campground has four primitive RV or tent campsites that can accommodate small RVs. Facilities include rock fire rings, vault toilet, and a ramp for hand-carried watercrafts. Treat river water before use. Leashed pets are permitted. The toilet is wheelchair-accessible.

Reservations, fees: Reservations are not accepted. Camping is free. Open year-round.

Directions: From Columbus, drive 5.3 miles south on Highway 78. Turn west at milepost 40.6 onto the one-lane gravel road. The 0.7-mile road jogs right, then left through private property before reaching the campground. Be ready to back up if you meet oncoming vehicles. The road has only a couple of narrow turnouts.

GPS Coordinates: N 45° 35.104' W 109° 19.875'

Contact: Montana Fish, Wildlife, and Parks, Region 5, 2300 Lake Elmo Dr., Billings, MT 59105, 406/247-2940, http://fwp.mt.gov.

58 WHITEBIRD
🏊 🎣 � 🛥 🎿 🏕 ♿ 🚌 ⛰

Scenic rating: 5

on the Stillwater River

At 3,780 feet, Whitebird is a state-run fishing access site on the east bank of the Stillwater River. Here, the lower river curves through arid juniper hillsides, flanks with farms and small ranches, and runs past the campground with Class II-III rapids. Rafters, kayakers, and white-water canoeists usually put-in here to float past Swinging Bridge Campground to Fireman's Point, two miles south of Columbus, or to Itch-Kep-Pe Park, after the Stillwater pours into the Yellowstone River. As the water level drops throughout the summer, large rocky bars extend as beaches along the shore. The Stillwater contains brook, rainbow, and Yellowstone cutthroat trout. The site offers archery and shotgun hunting in season.

None of the campsites have river frontage. Back-in grassy campsites tuck under tall cottonwoods, with a mix of willows providing partial shade. The location is still close enough to the highway to hear a little truck traffic at night.

Campsites, facilities: The campground has seven primitive RV or tent campsites that can accommodate small RVs. Facilities include picnic tables, fire rings with grills, vault toilet, and a ramp for hand-carried watercrafts. Treat river water before use. Leashed pets are permitted. The toilet is wheelchair-accessible.

Reservations, fees: Reservations are not accepted. Campsites cost $7 with a Montana fishing license and $12 without a Montana fishing license. Cash or check. Open year-round.

Directions: From Columbus, drive about seven miles south on Highway 78. Turn west at milepost 39.8 onto the gravel Whitebird Creek Road, crossing the creek on a one-lane bridge. Drive 0.5 mile to the campground entrance. GPS Coordinates: N 45° 34.504' W 109° 20.192'

Contact: Montana Fish, Wildlife, and Parks, Region 5, 2300 Lake Elmo Dr., Billings, MT 59105, 406/247-2940, http://fwp.mt.gov.

59 WOODBINE

Scenic rating: 8

in the Beartooth Mountains in Custer National Forest

At 5,200 feet, Woodbine Campground is the only national forest campground on the Stillwater River. Sitting at the north edge of the Absaroka-Beartooth Wilderness, the campground provides access to very remote country that few people visit. Cathedral Peak and the Granite Range make up the 10,000-foot Absaroka and Beartooth peaks south of the campground. From the campground, the 0.75-mile Woodbine Falls Trail (#93) departs for viewing the waterfall. While horses (hitch rails and loading ramps available) and backpackers use the entire 25-mile-long Stillwater Trail (#29), day hikers climb it 3.1 miles to the marshy Sioux Charley Lake. Small Yellowstone cutthroat trout inhabit Woodbine Creek, and the swift-flowing Stillwater River that you cross when entering the campground harbors small rainbow and brook trout.

Plan to arrive early at this popular campground where many of the campsites command views of the Beartooth Mountains. The two loops of the campground flank a mixed meadow and forest hillside where you have a choice of sunny or partly shaded sites. Despite the miles of dirt road driving, the campground road and parking aprons are paved, and your long drive is rewarded with natural sounds of the wind or the creek.

Campsites, facilities: The campground has 44 RV or tent campsites. RVs are limited to 32 feet. Facilities include picnic tables, fire rings with grills, vault toilets, drinking water, bear boxes, garbage service, and campground hosts. Leashed pets are permitted. Wheelchair-accessible facilities include toilets and campsites.

Reservations, fees: Reservations are accepted (877/444-6777, www.recreation.gov). Campsites cost $16. An extra vehicle costs $9. Cash or check. Open late May-mid-September.

Directions: From Absarokee, drive west on County Road 420 (locals call it the Stillwater River Road) for 20.4 miles and left for one mile as the road swings south to Nye. The road is paved to Nye but potholed. Turn right onto County Road 419 and drive 7.8 miles southwest on the gravel road. The road becomes Forest Road 4200 at the boundary to the national forest. At the signed junction, turn east for 0.2 mile to reach the campground entrance. GPS Coordinates: N 45° 21.189' W 109° 53.872'

Contact: Custer National Forest, Beartooth Ranger District, 6811 Hwy. 212 S., Red Lodge, MT 406/446-2103, www.fs.usda.gov/custer.

60 PINE GROVE

Scenic rating: 8

in the Beartooth Mountains in Custer National Forest

Located at 5,895 feet, Pine Grove is one of two Forest Service campgrounds in the West Rosebud Creek valley on the northeast corner of the Absaroka-Beartooth Wilderness. The river attracts expert kayakers for its three miles of Class III-V white water from Emerald Lake to the campground. Anglers go after brook, brown, rainbow, and Yellowstone cutthroat trout as well as mountain whitefish. Five miles south at the road's terminus at the power plant, trails depart for Mystic Lake (3.1 miles) and Island Lake (5 miles). For huge views, you can also climb scads of switchbacks up to the edge of Froze to Death Plateau (6.6 miles), on the flanks of the 11,765-foot Froze to Death Mountain. These three hikes are in the wilderness area.

Sitting at the base of a long, deep, glacier-carved valley, the quiet campground flanks both sides of the river in a forested setting. Sites are partly shaded, but some garner outstanding views of the surrounding Beartooth Mountains. Pull-through sites are in the section across the river.

Campsites, facilities: The campground has 27 RV or tent campsites that can accommodate RVs up to 30 feet. Another 19 campsites are for tents only. Facilities include picnic tables, fire rings with grills, vault toilets (wheelchair-accessible), drinking water, bear boxes, garbage service, and campground hosts. Leashed pets are permitted.

Reservations, fees: Reservations are not accepted. Campsites cost $9. Extra vehicles cost $5. Cash or check. Open late May–early September.

Directions: From Highway 78 south of Absarokee, take Highway 419 southwest to Fishtail. At a T intersection 0.5 mile south of Fishtail, turn left onto West Rosebud Road (Hwy. 425) for 6.5 miles to where the road turns to bumpy washboard and potholed gravel. Continue 8.8 miles farther to the campground, which sits about 1.2 miles south of the Custer National Forest boundary. The campground has four entrances on the east side of the road, the first leading to the tent campsites and the last connecting across the river with sites best for RVs. GPS Coordinates: N 45° 16.551' W 109° 38.732'

Contact: Custer National Forest, Beartooth Ranger District, 6811 Hwy. 212 S., Red Lodge, MT 406/446-2103, www.fs.usda.gov/custer.

61 EMERALD LAKE

Scenic rating: 10

in the Beartooth Mountains in Custer National Forest

At 6,180 feet, Emerald Lake nestles in West Rosebud Creek valley below the immense Beartooth Mountains. Despite its name, the campground does not flank the lake's shore, but instead parallels the West Rosebud River between Emerald and West Rosebud Lakes. From Emerald Lake to Pine Grove Campground, the river attracts expert kayakers for its three miles of Class III-V white water. Flat-water paddlers and anglers also tour small Emerald Lake (no motors allowed), which you can also reach via a five-minute walk from the campground. The river harbors brook, brown, rainbow, and Yellowstone cutthroat trout as well as mountain whitefish. One mile south, the road terminates at the power plant, where trails depart into Absaroka-Beartooth Wilderness. Scenic hikes include Mystic Lake (3.1 miles), Island Lake (5 miles), and Froze to Death Plateau (6.6 miles), which are also accesses for rock climbing and mountaineering.

The quiet campground splits into two roads, both with gravel back-in parking. The left spur has no RV turnaround, but the right one does. Set on the edge of a heavily forested slope, the campsites vary between partly shaded to more open, garnering superb views of the snowy Beartooth Mountains in early summer.

Campsites, facilities: The campground has 19 RV or tent campsites that can accommodate RVs up to 30 feet. Another 12 campsites are for tents only. Facilities include picnic tables, fire rings with grills, vault toilets (wheelchair-accessible), drinking water, bear boxes, garbage service, and campground hosts. Leashed pets are permitted.

Reservations, fees: Reservations are not accepted. Campsites cost $9. Extra vehicles cost $5. Cash or check. Open late May-November, but services end in early September.

Directions: From Highway 78 south of Absarokee, take Highway 419 southwest to Fishtail. At a T intersection 0.5 mile south of Fishtail, turn left onto West Rosebud Road (Hwy. 425) for 6.5 miles to where the road turns to gravel. Continue 13 miles farther, entering Custer National Forest about halfway, where the road turns to bumpy washboards and potholes. After passing Emerald Lake, turn east into the campground.

GPS Coordinates: N 45° 15.225' W 109° 41.936'

Contact: Custer National Forest, Beartooth Ranger District, 6811 Hwy. 212 S., Red Lodge, MT 406/446-2103, www.fs.usda.gov/custer.

62 JIMMY JOE

Scenic rating: 9

in the Beartooth Mountains in Custer National Forest

At 5,600 feet, Jimmy Joe Campground tucks into the northeast corner of the high Beartooth Mountains along East Rosebud Creek. Summer homes and small farms dot the prairie valley en route to the campground, which is flanked on both canyon walls by the Absaroka-Beartooth Wilderness. Anglers can wade-fish the stream for brown, rainbow, and Yellowstone cutthroat trout. Trailheads for hiking are located four miles farther south around East Rosebud Lake. Trail #17—the nearest one—ascends Phantom Creek up to Froze to Death Plateau, one of two access routes to climbing 12,799-foot Granite Peak, Montana's highest mountain. A stiff 3.5-mile day hike gains 3,900 feet to the saddle between Prairieview Mountain and Froze to Death Mountain.

Set at the bottom of the scooped-out glacier valley, the campground commands big views of the surrounding Beartooth Mountains. A forest fire in 1995 swept through the area, which now blooms with cow parsnips, fireweed, and red paintbrush amid the new-growth lodgepole pines. A few surviving lodgepoles and cottonwoods partially shade a handful of the campsites, but full sun hits most of them. Eight of

Jimmy Joe Campground in the Beartooth Mountains

© BECKY LOMAX

the campsites flank the river. The wind and the river are the only sounds you'll hear at night. Hand pumps have been installed for drinking water, but were not functional in 2013.

Campsites, facilities: The campground has 10 RV or tent campsites. RVs are limited to 30 feet. Facilities include picnic tables, fire rings with grills, and vault toilets. Drinking water is not available; bring your own or plan to treat river water. Pack out your trash. Leashed pets are permitted.

Reservations, fees: Reservations are not accepted. Camping is free. Open late May–early September.

Directions: From Highway 78 at Roscoe south of Absarokee, take East Rosebud Road south for 2.6 miles, where the rough pavement ends and the dusty, potholed, rutted dirt road begins. Go 1.2 miles farther and turn right, staying on East Rosebud Road for 6.5 miles to the campground entrance on the right. The campground is 10.3 miles south of Roscoe. GPS Coordinates: N 45° 13.921' W 109° 36.187'

Contact: Custer National Forest, Beartooth Ranger District, 6811 Hwy. 212 S., Red Lodge, MT 406/446-2103, www.fs.usda.gov/custer.

63 EAST ROSEBUD

Scenic rating: 10

in the Beartooth Mountains in Custer National Forest

BEST (

At 6,400 feet, East Rosebud Campground sits above East Rosebud Lake in the Beartooth Mountains, where rugged cliffs and scooped-out cirques demonstrate the power of glaciers on the landscape. Unfortunately, private property and summer homes surround the lake, but the community provides a primitive boat launch and parking area (relock the gate after entering) for canoes, kayaks, and rafts. The lake is stocked regularly with rainbow trout. Two trails departing from the

campground enter the Absaroka-Beartooth Wilderness. One climbs 5.9 steep miles to Sylvan Lake at the timberline. The other tours the lake's southeast rim on a more gentle 5.8-mile ascent to Elk Lake, the first in a long string of backpacking lakes along East Rosebud Creek.

The one campground loop—a narrow, steep, rocky road—circles a hillside on the mixed fir and pine forest fringe. Most of the back-in sites tuck under trees for protection from the sun and wind; the others sit in the sunny north-facing meadows, with big views of the lake and surrounding mountains. Buckwheat, bee balm, and harebells bloom in the meadows. The quiet campground packs its small sites close enough that you'll see neighbors; some in the trees are more private.

Campsites, facilities: The campground has 14 RV or tent campsites. RVs are limited to 20 feet. Another 12 campsites are for tents only. Facilities include picnic tables, fire rings with grills, vault toilets (wheelchair-accessible), drinking water, bear boxes, and garbage service. Leashed pets are permitted.

Reservations, fees: Reservations are not accepted. Campsites cost $9. A second vehicle costs $5. Cash or check. Open late May–early September.

Directions: From Highway 78 at Roscoe south of Absarokee, take the East Rosebud Road south for 2.6 miles, where the rough pavement ends and the dusty, bumpy, potholed, dirt road begins. Go 1.2 miles farther and turn right, staying on East Rosebud Road for 9.9 miles to a junction. Veer left for 0.6 mile over the single-lane bridge and left at the next junction, too. The campground entrance is on the left just past the campground exit. GPS Coordinates: N 45° 11.923' W 109° 38.087'

Contact: Custer National Forest, Beartooth Ranger District, 6811 Hwy. 212 S., Red Lodge, MT 406/446-2103, www.fs.usda.gov/custer.

64 CASCADE

🏃 🚴 🛶 🎣 ♿ 🚐 ⛺

Scenic rating: 8

in the Beartooth Mountains in Custer National Forest

At 7,550 feet, Cascade Campground sits on West Fork Rock Creek, known for its trout fishing, wedged in a high mountain valley on the eastern rim of the Beartooth Mountains. Within 1.5 miles west of the campground, trails depart into the Absaroka-Beartooth Wilderness. Climb 4.6 miles up to Timberline Lake, a glacial cirque below the 12,500-foot Timberline Peak. A 4.3-mile trail grunts up to the Red Lodge Creek Plateau, where the views fly endlessly out onto the prairie. A shorter, gentler trail of less than two miles leads to Calamity Falls and Sentinel Falls. Backpackers continue farther to loop over the 11,037-foot Sundance Pass, also a mountaineering access for several peaks. Mountain bikers go for the 15-mile loop trail on the Silver Run Plateau.

Although a 2008 fire burned the west tip of the quiet campground, the fast re-emerging vegetation blooms with wildflowers and young lodgepole pines. The campground has two loops, and most sites still tuck under the partial shade of green lodgepole pines. On the smaller left loop, site 30 is a very private site at the end with a large, flat tent space. Twelve sites overlook the creek. Sites 11, 13, and 14 have been cleared hazardous trees, which opened up the views to the rocky peaks of the East Rosebud Plateau.

Campsites, facilities: The campground has 30 RV or tent campsites. RVs are limited to 30 feet. Facilities include picnic tables, fire rings with grills, vault toilets, drinking water, garbage service, firewood for sale, bear boxes, and campground hosts. Leashed pets are permitted. A wheelchair-accessible toilet and two campsites are available.

Reservations, fees: Reservations are accepted (877/444-6777, www.recreation.gov). Campsites cost $10. An extra vehicle costs $8.

Cash, check, or credit card. Open late May-early September.

Directions: From Red Lodge on Highway 212 at the sign for the ski area, drive west on Ski Run Road for 2.8 miles and turn left onto West Fork Rock Creek Road (Forest Road 2071). Drive 7.7 miles to the campground entrance on the left. The last 3.3-mile stretch is on a single-lane potholed road with turnouts. GPS Coordinates: N 45° 10.378' W 109° 27.052'

Contact: Custer National Forest, Beartooth Ranger District, 6811 Hwy. 212 S., Red Lodge, MT 406/446-2103, www.fs.usda.gov/custer.

65 BASIN

🏃 🚴 🛶 🏊 🎣 ♿ 🚐 ⛺

Scenic rating: 7

in the Beartooth Mountains in Custer National Forest

At 6,900 feet, Basin Campground sits on West Fork Rock Creek, a brook trout fishery, in a high mountain valley in the eastern Beartooth Mountains. Three national recreation trails depart nearby for hikers and mountain bikers. Across the road, the 3.8-mile Basin Lakes Trail climbs to a small glacial cirque. One mile east of the campground, the Silver Run Trail provides a 7.7-mile loop, and a 15-minute nature trail circles Wild Bill Lake. Wild Bill Lake also has wheelchair-accessible ramps and docks for fishing, and you can paddle the small lake, too. Basin is the most popular campground in the West Fork drainage because the access and campground road are paved. Plan to arrive early in the day to claim a campsite or make reservations.

The quiet campground sprinkles its campsites under the partial shade of a lodgepole forest. Unfortunately, because there's no undergrowth, you can see other campers or cars passing on the road. Pine needles and cones cover the forest floor of the campsites, which have plenty of big, level spaces for tents. Sites

3, 5, 7, 9, and 10 overlook the creek. Some sites are more open, with views onto hillsides burned in the 2008 fire. All of the gravel parking aprons are back-ins, but several are double-wide.

Campsites, facilities: The campground has 30 RV or tent campsites. RVs are limited to 30 feet. Facilities include picnic tables, fire rings with grills, vault toilets, drinking water, garbage service, bear boxes, firewood for sale, and campground hosts. Leashed pets are permitted. Wheelchair-accessible facilities include toilets and three campsites.

Reservations, fees: Reservations are accepted (877/444-6777, www.recreation.gov). Campsites cost $15. An extra vehicle costs $8. Cash, check, or credit card. Open mid May-September.

Directions: From Red Lodge on Highway 212 at the sign for the ski area, drive west on Ski Run Road for 2.8 miles and turn left onto West Fork Rock Creek Road (Forest Road 2071). Drive 4.4 miles to the campground entrance on the right.
GPS Coordinates: N 45° 9.618' W 109° 23.232'

Contact: Custer National Forest, Beartooth Ranger District, 6811 Hwy. 212 S., Red Lodge, MT 406/446-2103, www.fs.usda.gov/custer.

66 PALISADES (CUSTER NATIONAL FOREST)

Scenic rating: 6

in the Beartooth Mountains in Custer National Forest

At 6,350 feet, Palisades Campground is named for the swath of limestone spires that poke up from a forested ridge on the eastern lip of the Beartooth Mountains. The campground tucks into the Willow Creek drainage tumbling from Red Lodge Ski Area. For hikers and mountain bikers, the Willow Creek Trail (#105) departs from the top of the campground to follow the

creek upstream to the ski area. Bikers can continue to loop back on the road from the ski area. The Forest Service is planning to build a new 2.5-mile trail from the campground to Fox Lane.

The campground tucks into a draw along the creek that's forested with cottonwoods, aspens, and Douglas firs as well as lush meadows of sticky geraniums, fireweed, and tall grass. Half of the campsites sit along the creek, with the lowest one and the highest one having the most privacy and biggest tent spaces. Two sunny, open sites across the road from each other have views of the Palisades. The campground is also far enough from town to provide quiet, but close enough to run back in for supplies.

Campsites, facilities: The campground has six RV or tent campsites. RVs are limited to 22 feet. Facilities include picnic tables, fire rings with grills, and vault toilet. Pack out your trash. Leashed pets are permitted.

Reservations, fees: Reservations are not accepted. Camping is free. Open late May-early September.

Directions: From Red Lodge on Highway 212, at the sign for the ski area, drive west on Ski Run Road for one mile and veer right onto the rough but paved Palisades Campground Road for 1.2 miles to the top of the hill. Turn right and then left on the road, which narrows and gets rougher with big potholes, before reaching the campground in 0.6 mile.
GPS Coordinates: N 45° 10.294' W 109° 18.547'

Contact: Custer National Forest, Beartooth Ranger District, 6811 Hwy. 212 S., Red Lodge, MT 406/446-2103, www.fs.usda.gov/custer.

67 RED LODGE KOA

Scenic rating: 5

near Red Lodge

At 5,148 feet, the Red Lodge KOA is a

five-minute drive north of downtown Red Lodge, with its restaurants, art galleries, shops, and funky western bars. The Red Lodge Mountain Golf Course sits about 10 minutes south of the campground, and the town is home to several fishing and rafting outfitters. Red Lodge is also the eastern portal to the Beartooth Highway, worth the scenic drive. At the campground, a small children's fishing pond and banana bike rentals are also available.

The grassy campground, ringed by cottonwoods and aspens, offers mostly sunny campsites that pack in tight to each other. Partly shaded tent sites, which are a bit wider than the RV sites, ring the perimeter farthest from the highway. The campground's location right on the highway means you'll hear commercial trucks at night, and vehicle traffic starts up in the early morning. The campground permits after-hours self-registration.

Campsites, facilities: The campground has 68 RV campsites and 19 tent campsites. RVs are limited to 90 feet. Hookups include water, sewer, and electricity up to 50 amps. Facilities include picnic tables, rock fire rings, pedestal grills, flush toilets, showers, launderette, drinking water, playground, swimming pool (late May-early September), dog walk, wireless Internet, camp store, firewood for sale, and disposal station. Leashed pets are permitted.

Reservations, fees: Reservations are accepted. Hookups cost $34-40. Tent sites cost $26-34. Rates cover two adults. Additional adults are charged $4 each; for kids ages 7-17, add $3. Children under six years old stay free. Add on 7 percent Montana bed tax. Cash, check, or credit card. Open early May-September.

Directions: From Red Lodge, drive four miles north on Highway 212 to the campground entrance on the east side of the road.

GPS Coordinates: N 45° 15.407' W 109° 13.698'

Contact: Red Lodge KOA, 7464 Hwy. 212, Red Lodge, MT 59068, 406/446-2364 or 800/562-7540, www.koa.com.

68 PERRY'S RV PARK AND CAMPGROUND

Scenic rating: 6

in Red Lodge

At 5,840 feet, Perry's RV Park and Campground is a three-minute drive or a 10-minute walk from downtown Red Lodge, with its restaurants, art galleries, shops, and funky western bars. The Red Lodge Mountain Golf Course sits about seven minutes north of the campground, and the town is home to several fishing and rafting outfitters. Red Lodge is also the eastern portal to the Beartooth Highway, worth the scenic drive. Fishing is available for brook and brown trout on Rock Creek, which flanks the back of the campground.

The campground has two gravel loops. A large, open, sunny parking-lot-type area houses bigger RVs and borders the highway. Other campsites, including the tent sites, tuck back under cottonwood trees, which offer partial shade. Several campsites line up on the bank of Rock Creek. Campsites are close together, and the highway noise is audible at night. The campground does not permit after-hours self-registration.

Campsites, facilities: The campground has 30 RV campsites and 13 tent sites. RVs are limited to 45 feet. Hookups include water and electricity. Facilities include picnic tables, flush toilets, showers, drinking water, camp store, and disposal station. Leashed pets are permitted.

Reservations, fees: Reservations are accepted. Hookups cost $35. Tent sites cost $20. Rates cover two people. Additional campers are charged $10 each. Add on 7 percent Montana bed tax. Cash or check only. Open late May-September.

Directions: From Red Lodge, drive two miles south on Highway 212. Find the campground entrance on the east side of the road.

GPS Coordinates: N 45° 9.082' W 109° 16.383'

Contact: Perry's RV Park and Campground, 6664 S. Hwy. 212, Red Lodge, MT 59068, 406/446-2722, www.perrysrv.us.

69 SHERIDAN

Scenic rating: 7

in the Beartooth Mountains in Custer National Forest

At 6,282 feet, Sheridan Campground is one of two Forest Service campgrounds at the eastern portal to the Beartooth Highway. Set in a narrow canyon on Rock Creek where you can fish for trout, the two campgrounds provide quick access to Red Lodge for supplies and a good jumping-off point for exploring the scenic highway. Departing 1.1 miles south of the campground, Corral Creek Trail (#9) climbs over 3,000 feet in 4.1 miles up to Line Creek Plateau, for views of the snowcapped Beartooth Mountains. You can also turn the route into a 12.7-mile loop with a waltz along the scenic plateau for views of Wyoming and the prairie before dropping down Maurice Creek. The loop ends about one mile north of the campground. Starting the loop at Maurice Creek lets you face the peaks as you hike. For expert kayakers and rafters, Rock Creek provides Class III-IV white water. Families can mountain bike the road between Sheridan and Ratine campgrounds.

In a forest of cottonwoods, aspens, and Douglas fir, the campground offers a mix of partly shaded (sites 4-8) or sunny campsites with views of mountain slopes (sites 1-3) that are also open to those driving in on the gravel campground road. Lyall's angelica, wild roses, and harebells bloom in the small meadows surrounding some of the sites. Light highway noise can be heard above the burbling creek, but it diminishes at night. Four campsites flank Rock Creek, with short paths through brush to the water.

Campsites, facilities: The campground has nine RV or tent campsites. RVs are limited to 30 feet. Facilities include picnic tables, fire rings with grills, vault toilets, drinking water, garbage service, and firewood for sale. The campground hosts stay one mile west at Rattin. Leashed pets are permitted. A toilet and one campsite are wheelchair-accessible.

Reservations, fees: Reservations are accepted (877/444-6777, www.recreation.gov). Campsites cost $14. An extra vehicle costs $8. Cash or check. Open late May-early September.

Directions: From Red Lodge, drive 7.5 miles southwest on Highway 212 to milepost 61.8. Turn east onto the narrow, potholed, dirt East Side Road and cross the single-lane bridge. The campground entrance is on the left side of the road in 1.3 miles.

GPS Coordinates: N 45° 6.013 W 109° 18.491'

Contact: Custer National Forest, Beartooth Ranger District, 6811 Hwy. 212 S., Red Lodge, MT 406/446-2103, www.fs.usda.gov/custer.

70 RATINE

Scenic rating: 7

in the Beartooth Mountains in Custer National Forest

At 6,380 feet, Ratine Campground is one of two Forest Service campgrounds at the eastern portal to the Beartooth Highway. In a narrow canyon on Rock Creek where you can fish for trout, the campgrounds provide quick access to Red Lodge for supplies and a good jumping-off point for exploring the scenic highway. Departing 0.1 mile south of the campground, Corral Creek Trail (#9) climbs over 3,000 feet in 4.1 miles up to Line Creek Plateau for views of the snowcapped Beartooth Mountains. You can also turn the route into a 12.7-mile loop with an open walk along the crest of the scenic plateau for views of Wyoming and the prairie before dropping down Maurice Creek, which ends about two miles north of the campground. Starting the loop at Maurice Creek lets you face the peaks as you hike. For expert kayakers and rafters, Rock Creek provides Class III-IV white water. Families can mountain bike the road between Sheridan and Ratine campgrounds.

In a forest of cottonwoods, aspens, pines, and Douglas fir, the campground flanks Rock Creek but doesn't have views of the water. You can hear it, though, along with vehicles on the highway, but the traffic dies down at night. Short paths cut through the brush to the creek. Some of the campsites have partial views of the mountains plus a bit of shade. Foliage limits visibility of other campsites to just a neighbor or two. The skinny, dusty campground road has no turnaround loop at the end.

Campsites, facilities: The campground has six RV or tent campsites. RVs are limited to 30 feet. Facilities include picnic tables, fire rings with grills, vault toilets (wheelchair-accessible), drinking water, garbage service, firewood for sale, and campground hosts. Leashed pets are permitted.

Reservations, fees: Reservations are accepted (877/444-6777, www.recreation.gov). Campsites cost $14. An extra vehicle costs $8. Cash or check. Open mid-May-late September.

Directions: From Red Lodge, drive 7.5 miles southwest on Highway 212 to milepost 61.8. Turn east onto the narrow, potholed, dirt East Side Road and cross the single-lane bridge. The campground entrance is on the left side of the road in 0.3 mile.

GPS Coordinates: N 45° 5.245' W 109° 19.498'

Contact: Custer National Forest, Beartooth Ranger District, 6811 Hwy. 212 S., Red Lodge, MT 406/446-2103, www.fs.usda.gov/custer.

71 PARKSIDE

Scenic rating: 9

in the Beartooth Mountains in Custer National Forest

At 7,150 feet, Parkside is one of three campgrounds clustered within 0.6 mile on Rock Creek Road at the eastern base of the Beartooth Highway, where the scenic highway begins its five-switchback climb to the Beartooth Plateau. From Vista Point at 9,100 feet, you can spot the campground on the valley floor. Cyclists on the Beartooth Highway opt to stay at Parkside to start the 4,000-foot climb up to Beartooth Pass first thing in the morning before the sun hits the switchbacks. The campground also sits adjacent to the Wyoming Creek Trailhead, a two-mile-long, hiking-only Parkside National Recreation Trail that links up four campgrounds along Rock Creek and tiny Greenough Lake. For anglers, Rock Creek harbors rainbow, brook, and Yellowstone cutthroat trout. Because of the campground's popularity in midsummer and on holidays, reservations are highly recommended.

Parkside Campground straddles Rock Creek on a paved road with a single-lane bridge. On the creek's west side, paved back-in parking pads line up sites closer together and visible from each other in the pine forest, which has an open understory with some peek-a-boo views of the peak. Sites 1, 2, 4, and 7-10 overlook Rock Creek. The loop on the creek's east side offers more private, shaded campsites under Douglas firs, aspens, and cottonwoods, with sites 17-19 overlooking the creek. Despite the proximity to the highway, the campground is quiet at night.

Campsites, facilities: The campground has 28 RV or tent campsites. RVs are limited to 40 feet. Facilities include picnic tables, fire rings with grills, vault toilets, drinking water, garbage service, firewood for sale, bear boxes, and campground hosts. Leashed pets are permitted. A toilet and two campsites are wheelchair-accessible.

Reservations, fees: Reservations are accepted (877/444-6777, www.recreation.gov). Campsites cost $15. An extra vehicle costs $8. Cash or check. Open mid-May-September.

Directions: From Red Lodge, drive 11.5 miles southwest on Highway 212 to milepost 57.2.

Turn right onto the paved Rock Creek Road for 0.3 mile to the campground entrance on the right.

GPS Coordinates: N 45° 3.633' W 109° 24.285'

Contact: Custer National Forest, Beartooth Ranger District, 6811 Hwy. 212 S., Red Lodge, MT 406/446-2103, www.fs.usda.gov/custer.

72 GREENOUGH LAKE

Scenic rating: 9

in the Beartooth Mountains in Custer National Forest

At 7,200 feet, Greenough Lake is one of three campgrounds clustered within 0.6 mile of each other on the Rock Creek Road at the eastern base of the Beartooth Highway with a scenic five-switchback climb to the alpine Beartooth Plateau. The campground, on Rock Creek's east bank, lies at the base of a glacier-carved valley flanked by the above-tree-line rocky plateaus of the Beartooth Mountains. At the north end of the campground, the two-mile hiking-only Parkside National Recreation Trail, which links up four campgrounds along Rock Creek, leads 0.25 mile to tiny Greenough Lake, a shallow mosquito pond that is stocked with rainbow trout. Campers often use mountain bikes and ATVs to tour two dirt roads—the continuation of Rock Creek Road and Forest Road 2004, which climbs to Hellroaring Plateau.

With paved internal roads, parking pads, and proximity to the Beartooth Highway, Greenough Lake is a popular campground that requires reservations to get a site on weekends and holidays. Despite the nearness of the highway, the campground is quiet at night, with only the sound of the creek. Sites 1, 2, 3, 5, 7, 9, and 10 overlook Rock Creek and some of the Limber Pine campsites across the creek. A mixed forest of aspens, pines, and short willows lends partial shade and partial privacy to

the campsites, some with views to mountain slopes. Site 13 houses a giant glacial erratic, a boulder dropped by receding ice.

Campsites, facilities: The campground has 18 RV or tent campsites. RVs are limited to 45 feet. Facilities include picnic tables, fire rings with grills, vault toilets, drinking water, garbage service, firewood for sale, and bear boxes. The campground hosts stay at adjacent Parkside Campground. Leashed pets are permitted. A wheelchair-accessible toilet and two campsites are available.

Reservations, fees: Reservations are accepted (877/444-6777, www.recreation.gov). Campsites cost $15. An extra vehicle costs $8. Cash or check. Open mid-May-September.

Directions: From Red Lodge, drive 11.5 miles southwest on Highway 212 to milepost 57.2. Turn right onto paved Rock Creek Road for 0.8 mile to the campground entrance on the left.

GPS Coordinates: N 45° 3.375' W 109° 24.738'

Contact: Custer National Forest, Beartooth Ranger District, 6811 Hwy. 212 S., Red Lodge, MT, 406/446-2103, www.fs.usda.gov/custer.

73 LIMBER PINE

Scenic rating: 9

in the Beartooth Mountains in Custer National Forest

At 7,200 feet, Limber Pine is one of three campgrounds clustered within 0.6 mile on the Rock Creek Road at the eastern base of the Beartooth Highway below the five scenic switchbacks that climb to the Beartooth Plateau. Flanked by the immense above-tree-line meadow plateaus of the snowcapped Beartooth Mountains, the campgrounds are dwarfed on the valley floor, where Limber Pine sits on the west bank of Rock Creek. The two-mile-long, hiking-only Parkside National Recreation Trail links up the four campgrounds along Rock Creek and leads 0.5 mile to Greenough Lake. Trout fishing is available at the lake and along Rock Creek. The dirt Forest Road 2004 (some use ATVs or mountain bikes on the road) departs Rock Creek Road near the campgrounds to climb onto the Hellroaring Plateau to the edge of the Absaroka-Beartooth Wilderness, where you can continue hiking on a trail for another 2.5 miles or farther cross-country with big views of alpine meadows and snowcapped peaks.

Limber Pine is a popular campground that requires reservations to get a site on weekends or holidays. Its one paved loop connects campsites that vary from full shade to partial mountain views. Black-eyed susans, sagebrush, harebells, and yellow arrowleaf balsamroot bloom between stands of limber pine. Sites 1, 2, and 10 overlook the creek and campsites in Greenough Lake Campground across the creek. Despite sitting between the highway and Rock Creek Road, the campground quiets at night.

Campsites, facilities: The campground has 10 RV or tent campsites, plus three walk-in tent-only sites (6, 7, and 11). RVs are limited to 45 feet. Facilities include picnic tables, fire rings with grills, vault toilets, drinking water, garbage service, firewood for sale, and bear boxes. The campground hosts stay at adjacent Parkside Campground. Leashed pets are permitted. A wheelchair-accessible toilet and two campsites are available.

Reservations, fees: Reservations are accepted (877/444-6777, www.recreation.gov). Campsites cost $15. An extra vehicle costs $8. Cash or check. Open mid-May-early September.

Directions: From Red Lodge, drive 11.5 miles southwest on Highway 212 to milepost 57.2. Turn right onto paved Rock Creek Road for 0.9 mile to the campground entrance on the left.

GPS Coordinates: N 45° 3.504' W 109° 24.743'

Contact: Custer National Forest, Beartooth Ranger District, 6811 Hwy. 212 S., Red Lodge, MT, 406/446-2103, www.fs.usda.gov/custer.

74 ROCK CREEK PRIMITIVE

Scenic rating: 8

in the Beartooth Mountains in Custer National Forest

Located between 7,500 feet and 8,650 feet, Rock Creek tumbles along a forest road sprinkled on both sides with short spur roads and jeep trails. These offer campers privacy and solitude, accompanied by only the sound of the creek. The U-shaped, glacier-carved valley littered with large boulders left from receding ice sweeps up several thousand feet on both sides to the high alpine plateaus of the east Beartooth Mountains. Rock Creek Road crosses into Wyoming and back before terminating at a popular trailhead. A two-mile trail climbs into a scoured rocky cirque containing Glacier Lake. Anglers go after rainbow, brook, and Yellowstone cutthroat trout in the lake as well as in Rock Creek. Rock Creek Road is a favorite of ATV riders. Mountain bikers use it, too.

Most of the dispersed primitive campsites along Rock Creek sit right on the river. You'll find sites shaded under cottonwoods and pines, in filtered sunlight in aspens, and in full sun in grassy fields with big open views of the mountains. Find most of the sites by a small sign with a tent icon; some are unmarked. Scout the dirt access roads and turnaround space before you drive in blind. Etiquette dictates one site per party.

Campsites, facilities: More than 25 primitive RV or tent campsites that can accommodate small RVs flank Rock Creek Road. Dispersed camping is permitted 300 feet on either side of the road from the centerline. The only facilities are rock fire rings. Use existing rings rather than constructing new ones. Treat river water for use. Pack out your trash. Follow Leave No

Trace principles for human waste. Leashed pets are permitted.

Reservations, fees: Reservations are not accepted. Camping is free. Open year-round, but snowbound in winter.

Directions: From Red Lodge, drive 11.5 miles southwest on Highway 212 to milepost 57.2. Turn right onto paved Rock Creek Road (Forest Road 2421). After passing Limber Pine Campground at 0.9 mile, the pavement disappears, and the road disintegrates into potholes and washboards, which require slow driving. Between Limber Pine and the road's terminus in 7.5 miles, look for spur roads and small posts with tent icons.

GPS Coordinates: N 45° 3.336' W 109° 25.018' (first primitive site)

Contact: Custer National Forest, Beartooth Ranger District, 6811 Hwy. 212 S., Red Lodge, MT, 406/446-2103, www.fs.usda.gov/custer.

A two-mile trail climbs to Glacier Lake in the Beartooth Mountains.

75 M-K

Scenic rating: 8

in the Beartooth Mountains in Custer National Forest

At 7,450 feet, M-K works as an overflow campground if Parkside, Greenough Lake, and Limber Pine are full. However, the two miles of dirt road between them is rough. Flanked by the immense above-tree-line meadow plateaus of the snowcapped Beartooth Mountains, the campground sits on the east bank of Rock Creek. At the end of Rock Creek Road (after five more miles of rough dirt road crossing into Wyoming and back), a popular two-mile trail climbs into a scoured rocky cirque containing Glacier Lake. Anglers also go after rainbow, brook, and Yellowstone cutthroat trout in the lake as well as in Rock Creek. Rock Creek Road is a favorite of ATVers; mountain bikers also use it, but they must suck the dust of

passing vehicles. M-K also sits at the south end of the two-mile, hiker-only Parkside National Recreation Trail, which leads to Greenough Lake.

M-K, favored by tenters, is a quiet, partly shaded campground with an open understory between a pine tree canopy and a pine needle and cone floor. Thanks to the lack of foliage, you can see neighbors; however, campsites are spread out for some privacy. The narrow, rough dirt road loops through the campground and connects the unnumbered sites. Those at the upper end overlook the creek, and most have huge flat spaces for multiple tents. A couple of unappealing sites flank Rock Creek Road. The sound of the creek filters through the whole campground.

Campsites, facilities: The campground has 10 RV or tent campsites. RVs are limited to 20 feet. Facilities include picnic tables, fire rings with grills, and vault toilets. Pack out your trash. Treat creek water for use. Leashed pets are permitted.

Reservations, fees: Reservations are not accepted. Camping is free. Open year-round, but snowbound in winter.

Directions: From Red Lodge, drive 11.5 miles southwest on Highway 212 to milepost 57.2. Turn right onto paved Rock Creek Road (Forest Road 2421) for 2.7 miles to the campground entrance on the right. The pavement disappears after one mile and the road disintegrates into potholes and washboards, which require slow driving.

GPS Coordinates: N 45° 2.305' W 109° 25.747'

Contact: Custer National Forest, Beartooth Ranger District, 6811 Hwy. 212 S., Red Lodge, MT, 406/446-2103, www.fs.usda. gov/custer.

76 ISLAND LAKE

Scenic rating: 10
in the Beartooth Highway in Shoshone National Forest

BEST (

At 9,600 feet on top of the Beartooth Plateau in Wyoming, Island Lake is the highest campground along the Beartooth Highway as well as the highest drive-to campground in the entire Northern Rocky Mountains. In midsummer, huge alpine meadows overflowing with fuchsia paintbrush and bluebells sprawl between windblown pines and firs. The wildflower-rimmed lake containing a tiny island provides boating for small watercraft and fishing for small trout that can't grow big in the short ice-free season. (Fishing requires a Wyoming fishing license available one mile west at Top of the World store.) Canoeists and float tubers portage 100 feet from Island Lake to Night Lake. A trail for hiking and horse-packing departs from the campground, touring the west shore and passing four more lakes within an hour of hiking. In 2.7 miles, it connects with the Beauty Lake Trail from Beartooth Lake. The trail also continues northeast into the Absaroka-Beartooth

Wilderness, linking up lakes, backpacking and mountaineering routes, and rugged, remote granite summits, but mountain bikers may ride only six miles, to the wilderness boundary. Bring DEET for the voracious mosquitoes bred in the boggy alpine meadows, prepare to be winded walking to the outhouse because of the altitude, and be ready for the regular afternoon thunderstorms that can pelt rain, hail, or snow—even in August. Set in loose-knit pine and fir clusters laced with large boulders, the campground has only a handful of campsites that can see the lake (on loop C), but trailers are not recommended on the narrow, steep loop.

Campsites, facilities: The campground has 21 RV or tent campsites. RVs are limited to 32 feet. Facilities include picnic tables, fire rings with grills, vault toilets, drinking water, garbage service, bear boxes, boat ramp, and campground hosts. Leashed pets are permitted.

Reservations, fees: Reservations are not accepted. Campsites cost $15 per unit (RV, trailer, or tent). Cash or check. Open late June-mid-September, snow permitting.

Directions: On Highway 212, drive 29 miles southwest from Red Lodge, or from Yellowstone's northeast entrance drive 33 miles east. Turn north into the campground entrance.

GPS Coordinates: N 44° 56.451' W 109° 32.311'

Contact: Shoshone National Forest, Clarks Fork Ranger District, 203A Yellowstone Ave., Cody, WY 82414, 307/527-6921, www. fs.usda.gov/shoshone.

77 BEARTOOTH LAKE

Scenic rating: 10
in the Beartooth Mountains in Shoshone National Forest

BEST (

At 9,000 feet on top of the Beartooth Plateau in Wyoming, Beartooth Lake sits below orange-streaked Beartooth Butte, a sedimentary

Hiking trails lead from Island Lake into the Absaroka Wilderness.

anomaly amid the granite Beartooth Mountains. In midsummer, huge alpine bluebell meadows flank the butte's lower slopes across Beartooth Lake, a forest- and bog-rimmed lake with a boat ramp on its south end for launching small watercraft and fishing for small trout that can't grow big in the short ice-free season. A Wyoming fishing license is required, available at the Top of the World store one mile east. From the campground, two trails angle north; one waltzes past Beauty Lake, connecting with the Island Lake trails in 2.4 miles and making a 7.9-mile loop. The loop also aims north into the Absaroka-Beartooth Wilderness, linking up lakes and backpacking and mountaineering routes, but mountain bikers may ride only five miles, to the wilderness boundary. One loop connects to Clay Butte Lookout (you can also drive to it), a 1942 fire lookout that commands a 360-degree panoramic view from 9,811 feet.

Mosquitoes breed armies here in the boggy alpine meadows: bring jumbo-sized bug juice. The air is thin; prepare to be winded walking from the lake to your campsite. Afternoon thunderstorms roll in like clockwork; be ready for August rains, hail, or snow. The quiet-at-night campground packs its three forested, partly shaded loops tight with a few sites on the A loop having peek-a-boo lake views through the trees. Step outside at night to see brilliant stars light up the sky.

Campsites, facilities: The campground has 21 RV or tent campsites. RVs are limited to 32 feet. Facilities include picnic tables, fire rings with grills, vault toilets, drinking water, garbage service, bear boxes, and campground hosts. Leashed pets are permitted.

Reservations, fees: Reservations are not accepted. Campsites cost $15 per unit (RV, trailer, or tent). Cash or check. Open late June-mid-September, snow permitting.

Directions: On Highway 212, drive 31 miles southwest from Red Lodge, or from Yellowstone's northeast entrance drive 31 miles east. Turn north into the campground entrance. GPS Coordinates: N 44° 56.614' W 109° 35.427'

Contact: Shoshone National Forest, Clarks Fork Ranger District, 203A Yellowstone

Ave., Cody, WY 82414, 307/527-6921, www. fs.usda.gov/shoshone.

78 CRAZY CREEK

Scenic rating: 7

in the Absaroka Mountains in Shoshone National Forest

At 6,900 feet, Crazy Creek Campground snuggles into the lower western slopes of the Beartooth Highway in the Absaroka Mountains in Wyoming. The campground sits at the confluence of Crazy Creek with the Clarks Fork Yellowstone River, where anglers go after trout and mountain whitefish (Wyoming license needed for fishing). Across the highway, the Crazy Lakes Trail (#612) climbs to a series of lakes in the Absaroka-Beartooth Wilderness. Crossing back into Montana in 4.5 miles, the trail splits to various lakes—destinations for day hikers, backpackers, horse-packers, and anglers. (You'll need a Montana fishing license.) A five-minute walk on the trail leads to a waterfall. Cyclists going west to east over the Beartooth Highway stay here before the climb over Beartooth Pass.

Sitting in a spruce and lodgepole pine forest, Crazy Creek offers campsites that vary between sunny and shady. Recent hazardous tree removal work thinned out some of the beetle-killed trees, opening up the forest more around the grassy sites and making it visually greener. The sunny open sites also have views of the cliffs on Jim Smith Peak. Unfortunately, the tree removal also made sites less private; however, sites 10 and 12, which work for smaller tents, have more privacy than the other campsites. Site 14 garners spectacular views of Pilot and Index Peaks. You'll hear road noise in the campground, but the highway does not permit commercial hauling through Yellowstone National Park, so noise dissipates at night.

Campsites, facilities: The campground has 16 RV or tent campsites. RVs are limited to 32 feet. Facilities include picnic tables, fire rings with grills, vault toilets, garbage service, bear boxes, and campground hosts. Bring your own drinking water, or treat creek water. Leashed pets are permitted.

Reservations, fees: Reservations are not accepted. Campsites cost $10 per unit (RV, trailer, or tent). Cash or check. Open late May-early September.

Directions: On Highway 212, drive 47 miles southwest from Red Lodge, or from the northeast entrance to Yellowstone National Park drive 15 miles east. Turn south into the campground entrance.

GPS Coordinates: N 44° 56.518' W 109° 46.429'

Contact: Shoshone National Forest, Clarks Fork Ranger District, 203A Yellowstone Ave., Cody, WY 82414, 307/527-6921, www. fs.usda.gov/shoshone.

79 FOX CREEK

Scenic rating: 8

in the Absaroka Mountains in Shoshone National Forest

At 7,100 feet, Fox Creek Campground sits on the western slopes of the Beartooth Mountains on the southern descent from the Beartooth Highway in Wyoming. While you're driving down the west side of the highway, Index and Pilot Peaks, both over 11,000 feet in elevation, jut up as prominent spires. The campground's two loops sit between the Clarks Fork Yellowstone River and the highway. You can wade-fish for trout and mountain whitefish in the nationally designated Wild and Scenic River, but you need a Wyoming fishing license.

The loose mixed forest of spruce, lodgepole pine, grand fir, and Douglas fir lends a bit of shade to the sunny campsites surrounded by grassy wildflower meadows. You'll hear some highway noise; however, the route into

Yellowstone National Park does not permit commercial trucking, so the noise quiets at night. The forest provides a thick screen, so you don't see the highway, but more open sites command views of Index and Pilot Peaks. Sites on the northeast ends of the loops sit nearest the river, but none have river views through the trees. The renovated campground now includes two extra large campsites with electrical hookups can accommodate three RVs each.

Campsites, facilities: The campground has 33 RV or tent campsites. RVs are limited to 32 feet. Facilities include picnic tables, fire rings with grills, electrical hookups, drinking water, vault toilets, garbage service, bear boxes, and campground hosts. Leashed pets are permitted.

Reservations, fees: Reservations are not accepted. Campsites cost $20 for electrical sites and $15 for other sites. Triple sites with electricity cost $60. Cash or check. Open mid-June-early September.

Directions: On Highway 212, drive 51 miles southwest from Red Lodge, or from the northeast entrance to Yellowstone National Park drive 11 miles east. Turn north into the campground entrance.

GPS Coordinates: N 44° 58.545' W 109° 50.023'

Contact: Shoshone National Forest, Clarks Fork Ranger District, 203A Yellowstone Ave., Cody, WY 82414, 307/527-6921, www.fs.usda.gov/shoshone.

80 LAKE CREEK

Scenic rating: 6
on Chief Joseph Highway in Shoshone National Forest

About 20 miles east of Yellowstone National Park, Lake Creek sits at the base of the Beartooth Mountains at 7,000 feet in Wyoming. The campground isn't a destination, but rather convenient for accessing two outstanding scenic drives with distinctly different scenery, the Beartooth Highway and Chief Joseph Highway. The Beartooth Highway climbs through rugged lake-strewn alpine plateaus while the Chief Joseph Highway winds through an arid canyon up to Dead Indian Pass. Cross-country cyclists use this campground before beginning the steep climb 3,000 feet in elevation over Beartooth Pass. Anglers can fish for brook, rainbow, and Yellowstone cutthroat trout in the Wild and Scenic-designated Clarks Fork of the Yellowstone River, which parallels Chief Joseph Highway. The Clarks Fork upstream of the campground offers experts-only Class IV-V+ white water.

Some campers prefer staying at this lower elevation campground than high on the Beartooth Plateau, as it stays warmer and drier, plus some people sleep better at lower elevations. Lake Creek fills the campground with its burbling, but not enough to drown out passing cars on the close highway. Commercial trucking noise, however, is sparse, as trucks do not climb over the Beartooth Highway or travel through Yellowstone National Park. In midsummer, the campground meadows bloom with sticky pink geraniums, wild roses, and grasses. Lodgepole pines provide partial shade. Sites 4 and 5 are tucked into more private locations under the trees, but more open sites garner mountain views.

Campsites, facilities: The campground has six RV or tent campsites. RVs are limited to 22 feet. Facilities include picnic tables, fire rings with grills, vault toilets, and bear boxes. No drinking water is available. Bring your own, or treat creek water. Pack out your trash. Leashed pets are permitted.

Reservations, fees: Reservations are not accepted. Campsites cost $10 per unit (RV, trailer, or tent). Cash or check. Open late June-early September.

Directions: From the junction of the Beartooth Highway (Hwy. 212) and Chief Joseph Highway (Hwy. 296), drive south on Highway 296 for 1.5 miles. From Cody, drive north on State Highway 120 for 16 miles and then west on Chief Joseph Highway

(Hwy. 296) for 44 miles. Turn north into the campground.

GPS Coordinates: N 44° 55.269' W 109° 42.430'

Contact: Shoshone National Forest, Clarks Fork Ranger District, 203A Yellowstone Ave., Cody, WY 82414-9313, 307/527-6921, www.fs.usda.gov/shoshone.

81 HUNTER PEAK

Scenic rating: 7

on Chief Joseph Highway in Shoshone National Forest

At 6,500 feet about 24 miles east of Yellowstone National Park, Hunter Peak Campground squeezes in between the scenic Chief Joseph Highway and the Wild and Scenic-designated Clarks Fork of the Yellowstone River in Wyoming. It sits at the base of the 9,034-foot Hunter Peak, where it attracts elk hunters in the fall. Anglers can fish the river for trout (artificial flies and lures only) from several campsites. Across the highway from the campground, the Clark's Fork Trailhead departs for a 17-mile trek along the rugged canyons of the river as it heads downstream. A 300-foot waterfall awaits about 90 minutes down the trail. The trail, a popular horse-packing route, is also open to mountain bikes and ATVs. North Crandell Trail, which departs three miles south of the campground, climbs 16 miles up North Crandell Creek into Yellowstone National Park.

Most of the campsites ring a loop on the left with the campground hosts on the right spur. The campground tucks under tall lodgepole pines and spruces on a flat grassy plateau on the river. Views from several campsites include large boulders across the river. Meadows bloom throughout the campground with penstemon, buckwheat, and pink sticky geranium. Sites 4, 5, and 6 claim river frontage, but all remaining campsites have access via trails. The sound of

the river helps you forget the road passes right above the campground, and sites vary between partly shaded and sunny.

Campsites, facilities: The campground has 10 RV or tent campsites. RVs are limited to 32 feet. Facilities include picnic tables, fire rings with grills, vault toilets, drinking water, bear boxes, garbage service, and campground hosts. Leashed pets are permitted.

Reservations, fees: Reservations are accepted (977/444-6777, www.recreation.gov). Campsites cost $15 per unit (RV, trailer, or tent). Cash or check. Open late May-mid-September; sometimes open longer, but without services.

Directions: From the junction of the Beartooth Highway (Hwy. 212) and Chief Joseph Highway (Hwy. 296), drive southeast for 4.7 miles. From Cody, drive north on State Highway 120 for 16 miles and then turn west onto Chief Joseph Highway (Hwy. 296) for 41 miles. Turn south, descending into the campground.

GPS Coordinates: N 44° 53.118' W 109° 39.306'

Contact: Shoshone National Forest, Clarks Fork Ranger District, 203A Yellowstone Ave., Cody, WY 82414-9313, 307/527-6921, www.fs.usda.gov/shoshone.

82 DEAD INDIAN CREEK

Scenic rating: 7

on Chief Joseph Highway in Shoshone National Forest

At 6,100 feet, surrounded by sagebrush hills broken by orange and white sandstones, Dead Indian Creek Campground, named for the creek and the 8,000-foot-high pass above the campground, sits on the scenic Chief Joseph Highway in between Dead Indian Pass and Sunlight Bridge in Wyoming. The Dead Indian Pass Overlook includes interpretive stories about the escape of Chief Joseph from the army and the trek of the Nez Perce across

Wyoming. The panoramic view spans the rugged country of the Beartooth Mountains to the Absaroka Range. West of the campground, the Sunlight Bridge, the highest bridge in Wyoming, crosses a deep gorge. Road cyclists pedal the switchbacking grade of the highway up to the pass. The Dead Indian Creek Trail walks a portion of the Nez Perce National Historic Trail, reaching the Clarks Fork of the Yellowstone River in less than five miles. Across the highway from the campground, a trail climbs along the creek to the summit of Dead Indian Peak.

The arid campground is divided in two parts by the creek, with five campsites on each side. Most of the campsites sit very near the creek but out of its view thanks to the thick brush. Short paths cut through the brush to the creek. Bits of shade come from cottonwoods, alder, and junipers, but most of the campsites are blazing hot in midsummer. The highway completely circles the campground; every campsite hears vehicles, but the road is not a heavy trucking route, and traffic dwindles at night. The campsites are spread out for privacy.

Campsites, facilities: The campground has 10 RV or tent campsites. RVs are limited to 32 feet. Facilities include picnic tables, fire rings with grills, vault toilets, garbage service, and campground hosts. Drinking water is not available; bring your own or treat creek water. Leashed pets are permitted.

Reservations, fees: Reservations are not accepted. Campsites cost $10 per unit (RV, trailer, or tent). Cash or check. Open late May-mid-September.

Directions: From the junction of the Beartooth Highway (Hwy. 212) and Chief Joseph Highway (Hwy. 296), drive southeast for 25 miles. From Cody, drive north on Highway 120 for 16 miles and then west on Chief Joseph Highway (Hwy. 296) for 21 miles. The campground has two entrances, both on the north side of the road and set on each side of the creek.

GPS Coordinates: N 44° 45.194' W 109° 25.132'

Contact: Shoshone National Forest, Clarks Fork Ranger District, 203A Yellowstone Ave., Cody, WY 82414-9313, 307/527-6921, www.fs.usda.gov/shoshone.

SOUTHERN YELLOWSTONE GATEWAYS

© BECKY LOMAX

Three national forests ring the southern boundaries of Yellowstone and Grand Teton National Parks. To the west, Caribou-Targhee National Forest offers spectacular "back-side" views of the Tetons. Campgrounds are smaller, more remote, and less crowded than in the national park. In the north, Island Park's plateau cradles lakes and rivers with more than 15 campgrounds. To the south and east, the Bridger-Teton National Forest surrounds Grand Teton's southern and eastern boundaries. Two high mountain ranges dominate: The Gros Ventre Mountains, with Granite Hot Springs and the Gros Ventre Landslide, while the Wind River Range contains Fremont Lake, Wyoming's second-largest natural lake. To the east, the Shoshone National Forest is the gateway from the Midwest. The Buffalo Bill Scenic Byway leads to Yellowstone's eastern entrance, where campgrounds line the arid corridor.

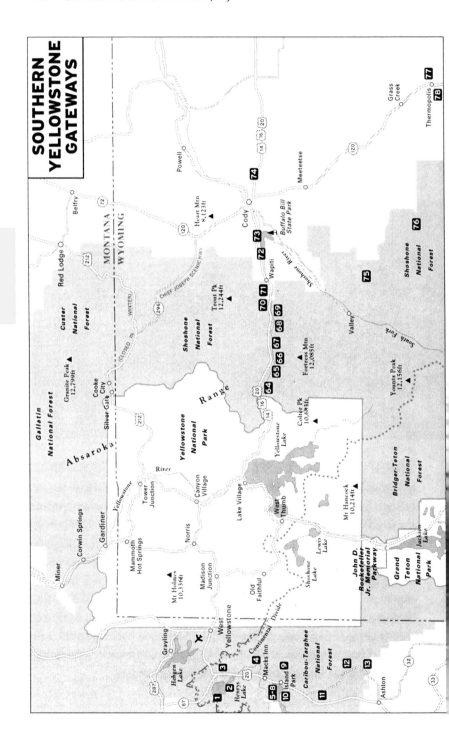

SOUTHERN YELLOWSTONE GATEWAYS

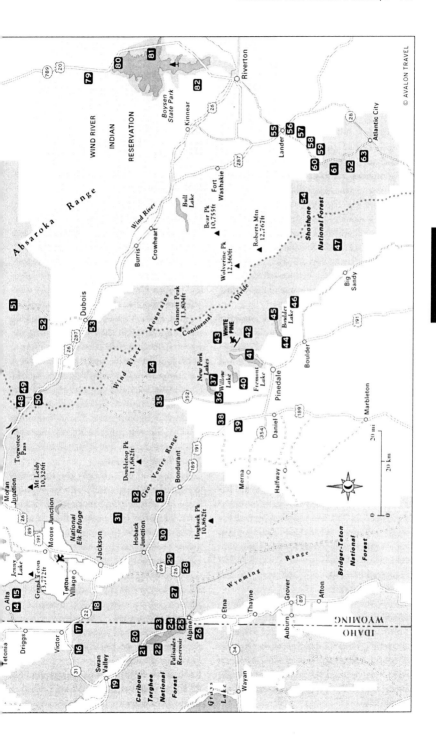

1 BILL FROME COUNTY PARK
⛴ 🛶 🚤 🎣 🏕 ♿ 🚐 ⛺

Scenic rating: 7
on Henrys Lake, Idaho

At 6,450 feet, Bill Frome County Park sits on the west side of Idaho's 6,000-acre Henrys Lake about 15 miles from the west entrance to Yellowstone National Park. A boat launch includes a cement ramp, dock, mooring, and trailer parking. Henrys Lake is popular for boating, waterskiing, and fishing for Yellowstone cutthroat, brook, and rainbow trout. You can take a scenic 25-mile dirt-road drive west to Red Rocks Pass and Red Rocks National Wildlife Refuge. You can swim, but not much beach is available because of the boating facilities.

Surrounded by sagebrush prairie, the quiet campground uses a few small perimeter aspens to help shade some of the sunny campsites and act as windbreaks for the common strong afternoon gusts. The open area, however, provides big views of the lake and the surrounding mountains, including Sawtell Peak to the south and Black Mountain to the north. A single gravel road drops through the campground to the boat launch; all campsites line up on the grass and gravel back-in parking pads in close proximity.

Campsites, facilities: The campground has 35 RV or tent campsites that can accommodate large RVs. Facilities include some rock fire rings, vault toilets (wheelchair-accessible), boat launch, pet area, firewood for sale, and campground hosts. Drinking water is not available; bring your own. Pack out your trash. Leashed pets are permitted.

Reservations, fees: Reservations are not accepted. Camping is free. Open May-October.

Directions: From the junction of Highway 20 and Highway 87, drive north on Highway 87 for 5.1 miles. Turn west and follow Henrys Lake Drive around the west side of the lake for 2.7 miles. The campground entrance sits on the left.

GPS Coordinates: N 44° 38.997' W 111° 26.275'

Contact: Fremont County, 151 West 1st North, St. Anthony, ID 83445, 208/624-7332.

2 HENRYS LAKE STATE PARK
🚶 🚴 ⛴ 🛶 🚤 🎣 🐎 🏕 ♿ 🚐 ⛺

Scenic rating: 7
on Henrys Lake, Idaho

Henrys Lake State Park, elevation 6,470 feet, sits on the southeast corner of the 6,000-acre Henrys Lake north of Island Park and 15 miles from the west entrance to Yellowstone National Park. Within a 10-minute drive, the Targhee Creek Trailhead launches a 14-mile loop past five alpine lakes at the base of Targhee Peak. A paved bicycle and walking trail loops through the park, including the wheelchair-accessible Aspen Loop Nature Trail. Guided nature walks are available. A boat ramp allows for launching onto the lake for boating, waterskiing, paddling, and fishing. The lake harbors Yellowstone cutthroat, brook, and rainbow trout. The park also has good wildlife-watching: birds, pronghorn antelope, and moose. For kids, the park has a Junior Ranger Program.

Surrounded by wetlands and sagebrush prairie, the campground's two large paved loops are on the southeast shore of Henrys Lake, where few trees provide shade or act as windbreaks for the common strong afternoon gusts. The open area, however, provides big views of the lake and the surrounding mountains, including Sawtell Peak to the south and Black Mountain to the north. Paved back-in parking pads are surrounded by mowed lawn, with campsites spread out for privacy, although you will see everyone around your site. When the winds die down, you can hear a faint truck or two on the highway.

Campsites, facilities: The campground has 43 RV or tent campsites. RVs are limited to 40 feet. Hookups are available for electricity and water. Facilities include picnic tables, fire rings with grills, flush toilets, showers, drinking water, garbage service, disposal station, firewood for sale, horseshoe pits, interpretive programs, wireless Internet, boat launch, fish-cleaning station, and campground hosts. Leashed pets are permitted. Wheelchair-accessible facilities include toilets and one campsite.

Reservations, fees: Reservations are accepted (888/922-6743 or online). Campsites cost $18-24. Park entry costs $5. Add on 6 percent Idaho sales tax. Idaho residents can buy an annual $10 passport card that covers entry and gives discounts on camping fees. Cash, check, or credit card. Open late May-mid-October.

Directions: From the junction of Highway 87 and Highway 20, drive south toward Island Park for 1.2 miles and turn right at the state park sign for 1.7 miles to the park entrance station.

GPS Coordinates: N 44° 37.127' W 111° 22.315'

Contact: Henrys Lake State Park, 3917 East 5100 North, Island Park, ID 83429, 208/558-7532, www.parksandrecreation.idaho.gov.

3 VALLEY VIEW RV PARK

🚶 🚵 🚐 ⛵ 🐴 🚗 ⛺

Scenic rating: 7

near Henrys Lake, Idaho

At 6,633 feet at the north end of Island Park, Valley View RV Park offers a convenient place to stay right on the highway for those traveling toward Yellowstone or wanting to explore the nearby Henrys Lake. Henrys Lake State Park, with a boat launch and trailer parking, sits 2.5 miles away for boating, fishing, waterskiing, canoeing, and kayaking. Nearby, the 14-mile Targhee Creek Trail loops past several forested lakes. South in Island Park, the Henry's Fork River offers fly-fishing, Harriman State Park has hiking and mountain biking trails, and scenic drives tour to Mesa Falls. The campground also sits 20 minutes

from the west entrance to Yellowstone National Park.

Baking in sun, the treeless campground offers no protection from the afternoon winds that crop up. That said, with the openness, all sites command views of the surrounding mountains, including Sawtell Peak. Some can see Henry's Lake in the distance. The campsites are level pull-throughs with small patches of grass between each site. From the campground's location by the highway, you will hear noise.

Campsites, facilities: The campground has 78 RV campsites. RVs are limited to 70 feet. Tents are allowed, too. Hookups include sewer, water, and electricity up to 50 amps. Facilities include picnic tables, flush toilets, drinking water, showers, launderette, and garbage service. Leashed pets are permitted.

Reservations, fees: Reservations are accepted. RV hookups cost $26-31. Tent sites cost $10 with no hookups or $14 with hookups. Rates are for two people. Cash or credit card. Open mid-May-September.

Directions: On Highway 20, locate Valley View RV Park 0.6-mile south of the junction with Highway 87.

GPS Coordinates: N 44° 37.614' W 111° 20.026'

Contact: Valley View RV Park, 5152 N Hwy 20, Island Park, ID 83429 208/558-7443 or 888/558-7443, http://valleyviewrv.com.

4 BIG SPRINGS

🚶 🚵 ⛵ 🐴 ♿ 🚗 ⛺

Scenic rating: 8

in Island Park in Caribou-Targhee National Forest

BEST (

At 6,400 feet, Big Springs Campground sits adjacent to Big Springs, an idyllic natural pool fed by snowmelt and rain that seeps through the Yellowstone plateau. The exceptionally clear water of the National Natural Landmark stays at 52°F year-round, providing habitat for trout, moose, bald eagles, and herons. Wheelchair-accessible trails connect the campground with the pond. A one-mile hiking-only trail (paved halfway) traverses downstream along the Henrys Fork of the Snake River. Big Springs does not permit wading, swimming, fishing, or boating along this route to protect the underwater gardens for spawning. One mile west of the campground, a river put-in allows paddlers to tour the four-mile National Recreation Water Trail, which is closed to fishing. Mountain bikers and ATV riders tour the nearby 42-mile dirt Union Pacific Railroad Right of Way Trail.

Set in a young lodgepole forest, the campground loops one paved road around its campsites, all with rough-paved pull-through parking. The campsites are spread out for privacy, and the lodgepoles are thick enough to shield sites from one another. At night, the quiet is broken only by the yipping of coyotes or the calls of herons. The spacious campsites vary between sunny (site 11) and partly shaded. Sites 1-3 view Big Springs Road.

Campsites, facilities: The campground has 15 RV or tent campsites and one large group campsite. RVs are limited to 32 feet. Facilities include picnic tables, fire rings with grills, cookstove pedestals, vault toilets (wheelchair-accessible), drinking water, garbage service, and campground hosts. Leashed pets are permitted.

Reservations, fees: Reservations are not accepted, except for the group campsite (877/444-6777, www.recreation.gov). Campsites cost $15. Extra vehicles cost $6. Cash or check. Open late May-mid-September.

Directions: From Highway 20, two entrances onto Big Springs Loop Road swing east to the campground. Coming from Henrys Lake, turn east at Island Park Village onto N. Big Springs Loop Road (Forest Road 059) for 4.3 miles mostly on dirt. Coming from Ashton, turn east at Mack's Inn onto S. Big Springs Loop Road for 4.7 paved miles. Locate the campground entrance south of the Big Springs Bridge.

GPS Coordinates: N 44° 29.849' W 111° 15.315'

Contact: Caribou-Targhee National Forest, Island Park Ranger District, 3726 Hwy. 20, Island Park, ID 83429, 208/558-7301, www.fs.usda.gov/ctnf.

5 FLAT ROCK

Scenic rating: 6

in Island Park in Caribou-Targhee National Forest, Idaho

At 6,400 feet, Flat Rock sits on the banks of the Henrys Fork of the Snake River, a blue-ribbon trout fishery. A five-minute walk leads to Mack's Inn, where you can rent canoes, kayaks, and rafts. Outfitters for fishing and horseback riding are nearby, as well as groceries, restaurants, and gas. The campground also sits at the lower end of the Henrys Fork of the Snake River National Recreation Water Trail—a four-mile paddle. Fishing is not permitted on the trail until Henrys Fork Outlet Creek; however, fishing is permitted along the riverbank at the campground, and you can launch hand-carried watercrafts from the campground. The river harbors native Yellowstone cutthroat, plus rainbow and brook trout. On Sawtell Peak, the six-mile Rock Creek Basin Trail climbs over the Continental Divide into the scenic rocky basin. For bicyclists on Highway 20, the campground is one of the most convenient with its short access.

The campground is divided into lower and upper loop (A and B loops). Loop B has electrical hookups in sites 1-9; the Loop A includes sites along the river (18-23). You can pick from sunny or shady campsites under lodgepole pines, and the grassy meadows between campsites bloom with asters in August. You'll see several other campsites from your picnic table, and both loops pick up substantial highway noise.

The Henrys Fork of the Snake River is a waterway for floating and wildlife-watching.

Campsites, facilities: The campground has nine RV campsites with electrical hookups (one is a double site) and 32 tent or RV campsites. RVs are limited to 32 feet. Facilities include picnic tables, fire rings with grills, cookstove pedestals, vault and flush toilets (wheelchair-accessible), drinking water, garbage service, and campground hosts. Leashed pets are permitted.

Reservations, fees: Reservations are accepted (877/444-6777, www.recreation.gov). Hookups cost $20. The double site costs $40. Non-hookup campsites cost $15. Extra vehicles cost $6. Cash or check. Open late May-mid-September.

Directions: From Highway 20 south of Mack's Inn at milepost 393, turn west into the campground.

GPS Coordinates: N 44° 29.993' W 111° 20.316'

Contact: Caribou-Targhee National Forest, Island Park Ranger District, 3726 Hwy. 20, Island Park, ID 83429, 208/558-7301, www. fs.usda.gov/ctnf.

6 COFFEE POT

Scenic rating: 7

in Island Park in Caribou-Targhee National Forest, Idaho

Located at 6,300 feet, Upper Coffee Pot sits on the Henrys Fork of the Snake River, a blue-ribbon trout stream. Kayakers, rafters, and canoeists can float the river one mile from Mack's Inn to the campground or five miles to the campground, starting at the upper end of the Henrys Fork of the Snake River National Recreation Water Trail. However, all boaters must take out at the campground because of the dangerous rapids downstream. Fishing is not permitted on the water trail until the confluence with the Henrys Fork Outlet Creek, but fishing is permitted at the campground. A 2.5-mile hiking trail tours the shoreline from the campground southeast to Coffee Pot Rapids. Mountain bikers and ATV riders can ride the network of old Forest Service roads around the campground.

The campground lines up in two sections along the river. The right loop contains electrical sites (8-15). Nine campsites overlook the river, but all campsites have quick access to it. Campsites at the end of each loop turnaround have the most privacy. The loose lodgepole forest and grassy meadow campground has sunny and partly shaded sites that are close enough that you'll see neighboring campers. With its location away from the highway, the only sound in the campground is the river.

Campsites, facilities: The campground has eight RV campsites with electrical hookups (one site is double) plus five RV or tent campsites. RVs are limited to 50 feet. Facilities include picnic tables, fire rings with grills, vault toilets (wheelchair-accessible), drinking water, garbage service, and campground hosts. Leashed pets are permitted.

Reservations, fees: Reservations are accepted (877/444-6777, www.recreation.gov). Hookups cost $20. Campsites cost $15. The double site costs $40. Extra vehicles cost $6. Cash or check. Open late May-mid-September.

Directions: From 0.5 mile south of Mack's Inn on Highway 20, turn west onto Forest Road 130 at milepost 392.5. Drive one mile and turn right onto Forest Road 311. Drive 0.4 mile. Turn right, and drive 0.2 mile to the campground.

GPS Coordinates: N 44° 29.442' W 111° 21.974'

Contact: Caribou-Targhee National Forest, Island Park Ranger District, 3726 Hwy. 20, Island Park, ID 83429, 208/558-7301, www.fs.usda.gov/ctnf.

◢ MCCREA BRIDGE
🚲 ⛴ 🏊 🚣 🏕 ♿ 🚌 ⛰

Scenic rating: 6
in Island Park in Caribou-Targhee National Forest, Idaho

At 6,200 feet, McCrea Bridge Campground sits where the Henrys Fork of the Snake River flows into the northeast arm of Island Park Reservoir, formed by a 1,250-foot-long dam built in 1938. The campground has a boat launch with four docks and a cement ramp, which allows access to the reservoir for boating, waterskiing, paddling, and fishing for kokanee salmon, rainbow trout, and Yellowstone cutthroat trout. Water levels drop in late summer; call the Forest Service to check on levels. Mountain bikers can tour the maze of forest roads in the area.

Sitting on the narrow arm of the reservoir, the campground flanks a western-facing hillside of lodgepole and sagebrush and looks across at summer homes. The campground has two interconnected gravel loops, with the A loop closest to the water. Three sites (3, 4, and 6) overlook the water. Several sites (2, 3, 4, 10, and 12) are wide open and sunny; the others have partial shade and some privacy created from the forest. Although the campground is removed from the trucking noise on Highway 20, the Yale-Kilgore Road is a main thoroughfare for accessing private homes on the reservoir. Most of the campsites are gravel back-ins.

Campsites, facilities: The campground has 25 RV or tent campsites. Five are double sites. RVs are limited to 32 feet. Facilities include picnic tables, fire rings with grills, vault toilets (wheelchair-accessible), drinking water, garbage service, boat launch, and campground hosts. Leashed pets are permitted.

Reservations, fees: Reservations are accepted (877/444-6777, www.recreation.gov). Campsites cost $15. Double campsites cost $30. Extra vehicles cost $6. Cash or check. Open late May-mid-September.

Directions: From Highway 20 two miles north of the Island Park Ranger Station, turn west onto Yale-Kilgore Road at milepost 389.2. Drive 2.1 miles and turn south before the bridge into the campground.

GPS Coordinates: N 44° 27.758' W 111° 24.043'

Contact: Caribou-Targhee National Forest, Island Park Ranger District, 3726 Hwy. 20,

Island Park, ID 83429, 208/558-7301, www. fs.usda.gov/ctnf.

8 BUTTERMILK
🚲 🏊 🛶 🚤 🎣 🐴 ♿ 🚐 ⛺

Scenic rating: 6
in Island Park in Caribou-Targhee National Forest, Idaho

Buttermilk Campground, elevation 6,200 feet, sits on the tip of a peninsula on Island Park Reservoir's east end. The campground is the biggest on the reservoir—empty on weekdays in early and late season, but hopping busy in peak summer. The campground's boat launch, with five docks, a double-side concrete ramp, and trailer parking, accommodates those getting onto the reservoir for boating, waterskiing, paddling, and fishing. Anglers go after kokanee salmon, rainbow trout, and Yellowstone cutthroat trout. Mountain bikers and ATVers ride the local network of forest roads.

Buttermilk spreads the partly shaded campsites out, but you can see through the trees to the neighbors. Although the access to the campground is via paved road, the campground loops and parking pads, mostly backins, are gravel. Only three sites in loop A and five sites in loop B have peek-a-boo views of the water through the trees. After the boating stops, the campground is quiet at night. Paths cut from the campground loops to the water.

Campsites, facilities: The campground has 47 RV or tent campsites, five double campsites, and one group site. (As of 2013, only 25 are available to the public.) One additional RV campsite (site 38) has a hookup for electricity. RVs are limited to 45 feet. Facilities include picnic tables, fire rings with grills, vault toilets (wheelchair-accessible), drinking water, tent platforms, garbage service, a boat launch, and campground hosts. Leashed pets are permitted.

Reservations, fees: Reservations are accepted (877/444-6777, www.recreation.gov). Campsites cost $15. The electrical hookup site costs $20, and double sites cost $30. Extra vehicles cost $6. Cash or check. Open late May-mid-September.

Directions: From Highway 20 two miles north of the Island Park Ranger Station, turn west onto Yale-Kilgore Road at milepost 389.2. Drive 1.9 miles and turn south onto Buttermilk Road for 2.5 miles. Turn right into the campground.

GPS Coordinates: N 44° 25.934' W 111° 25.568'

Contact: Caribou-Targhee National Forest, Island Park Ranger District, 3726 Hwy. 20, Island Park, ID 83429, 208/558-7301, www. fs.usda.gov/ctnf.

9 BUFFALO
🚲 🛶 🚤 🎣 🐴 ♿ 🚐 ⛺

Scenic rating: 7
in Island Park in Caribou-Targhee National Forest, Idaho

At 6,200 feet, Buffalo is the largest national forest campground in the Island Park area and the one that sees the most visits. The campground sits right on the Buffalo River, where anglers go after a variety of trout. A wheelchair-accessible boardwalk and fishing platforms sit adjacent to the G loop. Kayakers, canoeists, tubers, and rafts float the river. Boaters, water-skiers, and anglers can access Island Park Reservoir via the Island Park boat ramp, two miles from the campground. Cyclists on Highway 20 use this campground for its convenience to the highway. Evening interpretive programs include appearances by Smokey Bear.

A paved road winds through the seven loops of Buffalo Campground with paved pull-through or back-in parking pads. Surrounded by grass, fireweed, and purple asters, the campsites are partly shaded by doghair lodgepole and aspens, which also make the sites semiprivate. A and B loops sit closest to the highway, which rumbles with commercial trucking. Loops A, D, F, and G each have a handful of campsites that border the river, although trees, serviceberries, and willows block some views. G5 has the best river view.

Campsites, facilities: The campground has 127 RV or tent campsites, including 12 sites with electricity, four double campsites, and one group site. RVs are limited to 45 feet. Facilities include picnic tables, fire rings with grills, flush and vault toilets (wheelchair-accessible), drinking water, tent platforms, garbage service, an amphitheater for interpretive programs, and campground hosts. Leashed pets are permitted.

Reservations, fees: Reservations are accepted (877/444-6777, www.recreation.gov). Campsites cost $15. Electrical hookups cost $20; double sites cost $40. Extra vehicles cost $6. Cash or check. Open late May-mid-September.

Directions: On Highway 20, drive 0.25 mile north of the Island Park Ranger Station to milepost 387.5. Turn east off the highway into the campground.

GPS Coordinates: N 44° 25.571' W 111° 22.119'

Contact: Caribou-Targhee National Forest, Island Park Ranger District, 3726 Hwy. 20, Island Park, ID 83429, 208/558-7301, www.fs.usda.gov/ctnf.

10 BOX CANYON

🏃 🚴 🛶 🚤 ⛵ 🎣 ♿ 🚐 ⛺

Scenic rating: 7

in Island Park in Caribou-Targhee National Forest, Idaho

Located at 6,320 feet, Box Canyon sits on the Henrys Fork of the Snake River. Trout anglers favor the blue-ribbon fishery for its wild Yellowstone cutthroat and rainbow trout. In this section, the river is catch-and-release only with barbless hooks. Box Canyon is also a favorite section of the river for rafts, kayaks, and experienced canoeists with its Class II rapids. The two-hour float goes from the Island Park Dam Road launch to Last Chance. Mountain bikers tour the maze of dirt Forest Service roads in the area, and hikers can walk Box Canyon via a three-mile trail along its rim.

Box Canyon is one of the best campgrounds in Island Park for those who like privacy and seclusion. One gravel loop accesses all the campsites with gravel back-in parking pads. Set back from the highway, the quiet campground has spacious campsites tucked into shade of lodgepoles and Douglas firs. The large, grassy sites spread out for privacy surrounded by purple asters, huckleberries, and serviceberries. Several campsites sit near the river, without views of the water, but with paths cutting through the trees to the riverbank.

Campsites, facilities: The campground has 19 RV or tent campsites, including two double sites. RVs are limited to 32 feet. Facilities include picnic tables, fire rings with grills, vault toilets (wheelchair-accessible), drinking water, garbage service, tent platforms, and campground hosts. Leashed pets are permitted.

Reservations, fees: Reservations are not accepted. Campsites cost $15; double campsites cost $30. Extra vehicles cost $6. Cash or check. Open late May-mid-September.

Directions: From Highway 20 one mile south of the Island Park Ranger Station, turn west at milepost 386 onto the gravel Forest Road 134 for 0.4 mile. Turn right onto Forest Road 284 for one mile to reach the campground entrance.

GPS Coordinates: N 44° 24.584' W 111° 23.799'

Contact: Caribou-Targhee National Forest, Island Park Ranger District, 3726 Hwy. 20, Island Park, ID 83429, 208/558-7301, www.fs.usda.gov/ctnf.

11 RIVERSIDE

🏃 🚴 🛶 🚤 ⛵ 🎣 ♿ 🚐 ⛺

Scenic rating: 8

in Island Park in Caribou-Targhee National Forest, Idaho

BEST (

At 6,200 feet, Riverside is Island Park's

southernmost campground. It sits five miles south of Harriman State Park ($4 for entrance), a wildlife refuge where you can see elk, moose, sandhill cranes, and trumpeter swans. The park is also renowned for its blue-ribbon fishery, and it holds 20 miles of trails for hikers and mountain bikers. Guided horseback trail rides and tours of historical ranch buildings are also available. From the campground, you can fish the Henrys Fork of the Snake River. Upstream of the campground is catch-and-release only with barbless hooks. Downstream of the campground there's a two-fish limit. Expert boaters can launch from the campground to float Cardiac Canyon to Hatchery Ford; less skilled boaters should float the upstream section seven miles from Last Chance to take out at the campground.

The campground sprawls in several interconnected loops. The A sites line up along the river, with many of them overlooking the water and the volcanic rockfalls flanking the opposite shore. While many of these grab the views, they do so at a cost to privacy as they are more sunny and open amid small stands of aspens and lodgepoles. Those seeking privacy and shade will find both in the hillside camps of loops B and C under tall lodgepoles. The river froths here, filling the campground with its sound.

Campsites, facilities: The campground has 56 RV or tent campsites, plus one double site and one group campsite. (As of 2013, only 34 sites are available to the public.) Fifteen sites have paved parking pads and patios that are wheelchair-accessible. RVs are limited to 35 feet. Facilities include picnic tables, fire rings with grills, cookstove pedestals, vault toilets, drinking water, garbage service, and campground hosts. Leashed pets are permitted. Wheelchair-accessible toilets are available.

Reservations, fees: Reservations are accepted (877/444-6777, www.recreation.gov). Campsites cost $15. Double sites cost $30. Extra vehicles cost $6. Cash or check. Open late May-mid-September.

Directions: From Highway 20 about 16 miles

north of Ashton, turn east off the highway at milepost 375.6. Head southeast on the narrow, rough-paved Forest Road 304 for 0.8 mile to the campground entrance.

GPS Coordinates: N 44° 15.999' W 111° 27.482'

Contact: Caribou-Targhee National Forest, Island Park Ranger District, 3726 Hwy. 20, Island Park, ID 83429, 208/558-7301, www.fs.usda.gov/ctnf.

12 GRANDVIEW

Scenic rating: 9

in Island Park in Caribou-Targhee National Forest, Idaho

BEST (

Located on the Mesa Falls Scenic Byway at 5,900 feet, Grandview perches on the lip of a deep canyon that houses the Henrys Fork of the Snake River where it roars through Mesa Falls. A four-wheel-drive road drops from the

Lower Mesa Falls on the Henrys Fork of the Snake River

back of the campground 0.5 mile to the river for fishing, rafting, or kayaking. The route also makes a good hike, since the climb back up gains 500 feet in elevation. From the campground, a two-minute walk leads to the overlook for the 65-foot-high Lower Mesa Falls, but the larger 114-foot-high and 300-foot-wide Upper Mesa Falls thunders about a mile upstream, looking like a smaller clone of Niagara Falls. At the site ($5 or federal access passes), paths lead to decks overlooking various points of the falls, including the lip.

The campground sits in a loose forest of fir, aspen, and lodgepole trees with brushy mountain ash and willows lending a thick understory. The short gravel road puts the partly shaded campsites close to each other, but the underbrush lends privacy. Once the day traffic on the scenic byway disappears, the campground is so quiet that you can hear the faint roar of Lower Mesa Falls below in the canyon.

Campsites, facilities: The campground has nine RV or tent campsites (two are double sites). RVs are limited to 28 feet. Facilities include picnic tables, fire rings with grills, cookstove pedestals, electrical hookups, vault toilets (wheelchair-accessible), drinking water, garbage service, and campground hosts. Leashed pets are permitted.

Reservations, fees: Reservations are not accepted. Campsites cost $20. Double sites cost $40. Extra vehicles cost $6. Cash or check. Open from late May–October.

Directions: From Highway 20 one mile north of Harriman State Park, turn east onto the Mesa Falls Scenic Byway (also Route 47 and Forest Road 294) and drive south for 14 miles. Or from Ashton, drive the byway 16 miles northeast. The campground entrance is on the southwest side of the byway adjacent to Lower Mesa Falls Overlook and 0.5 mile southeast from the entrance to Upper Mesa Falls. GPS Coordinates: N 44° 10.506' W 111° 18.837'

Contact: Caribou-Targhee National Forest, Island Park Ranger District, 3726 Hwy. 20, Island Park, ID 83429, 208/558-7301, www.fs.usda.gov/ctnf.

13 WARM RIVER

🏕️ 🚴 ⛵ 🛶 🏊 🎣 🥾 ♿ 🚐 ⛰️

Scenic rating: 6

in Island Park in Caribou-Targhee National Forest, Idaho

BEST (

At 5,200 feet along the Mesa Falls Scenic Byway, Warm River Campground sits adjacent to a tiny burg of three houses. The river's slow-moving water is popular for swimming, floating with tubes, paddling, and rafting. Fed by water from the Yellowstone plateau via underground springs, the clear water maintains a year-round temperature of 50°F. Wading anglers go after native trout, and a wheelchair-accessible fishing platform is available. The campground is also the south entrance to the 42-mile Railroad Right of Way Trail, which includes one tunnel, with its first two miles open only to hikers and mountain bikers.

Surrounded by sagebrush and aspen slopes, the popular campground tucks into a lush river corridor. Many of the grassy campsites sit right on the Warm River. Mature willows provide shade for some of the sites, but the lack of understory allows you to see other campers. The campground is in several sections: a collection of shady RV sites, walk-in tent sites, a large group pavilion, and a sunny loop of campsites accessed via a narrow bridge across the river. Once the byway traffic dies at night, the campground quiets to the sound of the river and birds.

Campsites, facilities: The campground has 13 RV campsites, 12 tent campsites, one double site, and one group site. RVs are limited to 40 feet. Facilities include picnic tables, fire rings with grills, pedestal grills, cookstove pedestals, vault toilets, drinking water, garbage service, horseshoe pits, tent pads, and campground hosts. Leashed pets are permitted.

Wheelchair-accessible facilities include toilets and one campsite with electricity (site 13).
Reservations, fees: Reservations are accepted (877/444-6777, www.recreation.gov). Campsites cost $15. The double site costs $30. Extra vehicles cost $6. The accessible electrical hookup site costs $19-21. Cash or check. Open late May-mid-September.
Directions: From Highway 20 one mile north of Harriman State Park, turn east onto the Mesa Falls Scenic Byway (also Route 47 and Forest Road 294) and drive south for 20 miles. At milepost 8.9, turn east along the river and drive 0.5 mile into the campground. From Ashton, you can also head north on the byway for about nine miles to reach the campground. GPS Coordinates: N 44° 7.208' W 111° 18.814'
Contact: Caribou-Targhee National Forest, Island Park Ranger District, 3726 Hwy. 20, Island Park, ID 83429, 208/558-7301, www.fs.usda.gov/ctnf.

14 REUNION FLATS

Scenic rating: 9

in the Teton Mountains in Caribou-Targhee National Forest, Wyoming

Located at 6,900 feet, Reunion Flats sits on the west flank of the Teton Mountains. It is the closest campground to Grand Targhee Resort, which offers summer scenic lift rides, horseback riding, and lift-accessed mountain biking and hiking. You'll stare at Grand Teton from Targhee's slopes. The resort's annual bluegrass festival takes place in late August. Trailheads into the Jedediah Smith Wilderness and Grand Teton National Park depart 1.8 miles to the east near Teton Canyon Campground. Because of the Yellowstone cutthroat trout's spawning, fishing is not permitted in Teton Creek until July 1.

While a pine, fir, and aspen forest surrounds the campground, many of the grassy sites are open, allowing big views of Teton Canyon and the tips of the Teton Mountains in the distance. Paths connect to Teton Creek, which runs past the campground. The spacious sites have flat, roomy spots for tents. Unfortunately, the individual sites sit in between the large group camping sites, but if large groups are not present, the campground is very quiet.
Campsites, facilities: The campground has four RV or tent campsites, one tent campsite, and three large group sites. RVs are limited to 60 feet. Facilities include picnic tables, fire rings with grills, vault toilets (wheelchair-accessible), drinking water, and garbage service. Leashed pets are permitted.
Reservations, fees: Reservations are accepted (877/444-6777, www.recreation.gov). Campsites cost $12. Group sites cost $50. Extra vehicles cost $6. Cash or check. Open late May-September.
Directions: From Highway 33 in Driggs, Idaho, turn east at Little Street/Ski Hill Road for one mile to a Y intersection. Bear left onto Ski Hill Road and go 5.6 miles, passing Alta and the state line into Wyoming, to the campground sign. Turn right onto the gravel Forest Road 009 and drive 2.7 miles, turning right into the campground. GPS Coordinates: N 43° 45.449' W 110° 57.032'
Contact: Caribou-Targhee National Forest, Teton Basin Ranger District, 515 S. Main, Driggs, ID 83422, 208/354-2312, www.fs.usda.gov/ctnf.

15 TETON CANYON

Scenic rating: 9

in the Teton Mountain in Caribou-Targhee National Forest, Wyoming

At 6,960 feet, Teton Canyon Campground sits on the edge of the Jedediah Smith Wilderness on the west flank of the Teton Mountains. En route to the campground, the scenic drive, which enters Wyoming, lends views of Grand

Teton National Park's rugged panorama of peaks. From the campground, a popular trailhead departs into the wilderness via the South and North Forks of Teton Creek. Reach Alaska Basin Lakes in seven miles, Grand Teton National Park in nine miles, or 11,106-foot Table Mountain in six miles for views of the Grand Teton. Stock facilities sit 0.1 mile west of the campground. Surrounding granitic rock outcroppings and cliffs have rock-climbing routes. Teton Creek is closed to fishing until July 1.

The campground's two interconnected loops provide different environments. The southern loop weaves through a thick conifer forest that shades the campsites dark, keeping them cool and protected from the elements. Teton Creek flows nearest sites 6-8, and most of the sites are gravel back-ins. The open understory permits some views of nearby campers. Campsites in the north loop ring an open wildflower field dotted with only a handful of aspens. While the open sites, most of which are pull-throughs, do not afford privacy, they command views of the canyon's cliffs and sweeping mountain slopes. The trailhead draws in day hikers, but at night, the campground is ultra quiet.

Campsites, facilities: The campground has 20 RV or tent campsites. RVs are limited to 24 feet. Facilities include picnic tables, fire rings with grills, vault toilets, drinking water, garbage service, and campground hosts. Bring your own firewood. Leashed pets are permitted.

Reservations, fees: Reservations are accepted (877/444-6777, www.recreation.gov). Campsites cost $12. The double site costs $24. Extra vehicles cost $6. Cash or check. Open late May-September.

Directions: From Highway 33 in Driggs, Idaho, turn east at Little Street/Ski Hill Road for one mile to a Y intersection. Bear left onto Ski Hill Road and go 5.6 miles, passing Alta and the state line into Wyoming, to the campground sign. Turn right onto the gravel Forest Road 009 and drive 4.3 miles, turning right into the campground.

GPS Coordinates: N 43° 45.411' W 110° 55.258'
Contact: Caribou-Targhee National Forest, Teton Basin Ranger District, 515 S. Main, Driggs, ID 83422, 208/354-2312, www.fs.usda.gov/ctnf.

16 PINE CREEK

Scenic rating: 8

in the Big Hole Mountains in Caribou-Targhee National Forest, Idaho

At 6,600 feet, Pine Creek sits nearly at the summit of Pine Creek Pass over the Big Hole Mountains. A trail along the crest of the Big Hole Mountains departs northward just west of the pass. Hikers use the trail for its expansive views across the Teton Valley to the Grand Teton and Teton Mountains. Mountain bikers ride the 17 miles across the crest trail to the Horseshoe Canyon Trailhead west of Driggs.

The curvy gravel campground road and back-in gravel parking pads may pose difficulties for those with large trailers, but spacious, spread-out campsites make it appealing. A mixed forest of firs, lodgepoles, and aspens provides a thick overhead canopy for shade. Pink wild roses and a brushy understory shield the campground from the highway, but Pine Creek Summit is not a major thoroughfare for trucking, so night traffic is minimal. Sites 1 and 2 sit closest to the road. Two of the campsites have small bridges crossing the creek to their tables and tent spaces.

Campsites, facilities: The campground has 10 RV or tent campsites. RVs are limited to 30 feet. Facilities include picnic tables, fire rings, and vault toilets. No water is available; bring your own. When the creek through the campground is running, treat its water. Pack out your trash. Leashed pets are permitted.

Reservations, fees: Reservations are not accepted. Campsites cost $8. Extra vehicles cost $5. Cash or check. Open late May-mid-September.

Directions: From Victor, drive Highway 31 southwest for six miles. Turn left into the campground. Coming from Swan Valley, locate the campground entrance about 0.7 mile on the east side of Pine Creek Pass.

GPS Coordinates: N 43° 34.388' W 111° 12.322'

Contact: Caribou-Targhee National Forest, Teton Basin Ranger District, 515 S. Main, Driggs, ID 83422, 208/354-2312, www. fs.usda.gov/ctnf.

17 MIKE HARRIS

Scenic rating: 8

in the Big Hole Mountains in Caribou-Targhee National Forest, Idaho

At 6,560 feet, Mike Harris Campground sits in the Big Hole Range south of Victor. At the bottom of the long, 10 percent grade climb over Teton Pass, the campground is popular with hikers and mountain bikers. With the trailhead departing from the 90-degree bend in the campground entrance road, the Mikesell Canyon Trail (#049) climbs four miles to the top of 8,987-foot Oliver Peak for views of the southern Teton Mountains. Another four-mile stretch crosses the state line into Wyoming to connect with Mosquito Pass on the Teton Crest. Stream fishing is available in Trail Creek adjacent to the highway.

The one gravel campground loop tucks under a green canopy of firs, lodgepole pines, and aspens, with two gravel pull-throughs and the remainder back-in parking pads. Meadows of grass, paintbrush, and fireweed weave through the trees, which partly shade the campsites. The roomy campsites are spread out for privacy, but spaces for tents are small. With its proximity to the highway, morning and evening noise is abundant with the commuter traffic from the Teton Valley to Jackson Hole.

Campsites, facilities: The campground has 10 RV or tent campsites. RVs are limited to 30 feet. Facilities include picnic tables, fire rings with grills, pedestal grills, vault toilets (wheelchair-accessible), bear boxes, garbage service, and a campground host. No drinking water is available; treat stream water. Leashed pets are permitted.

Reservations, fees: Reservations are accepted (877/444-6777, www.recreation.gov). Campsites cost $8. Extra vehicles cost $5. Cash or check. Open mid-May-mid-September.

Directions: From Victor, drive southeast on Highway 33 for 3.8 miles. At milepost 153.5, turn west for 300 feet, and turn south for 0.3 mile, arcing right into the campground. Coming from Teton Pass, locate the turnoff 1.5 miles northwest of the Idaho-Wyoming state line.

GPS Coordinates: N 43° 33.371' W 111° 4.136'

Contact: Caribou-Targhee National Forest, Teton Basin Ranger District, 515 S. Main, Driggs, ID 83422, 208/354-2312, www. fs.usda.gov/ctnf.

18 TRAIL CREEK

Scenic rating: 8

in Big Hole Mountains in Caribou-Targhee National Forest, Wyoming

Located at 6,600 feet, Trail Creek Campground sits in the Big Hole Mountains on the highway over Teton Pass. It is convenient for those traveling over the pass to reach Grand Teton and Yellowstone National Parks, but those who drive the steep road with trailers will feel its 10 percent grade. The trailhead at Coal Creek Meadows leads through the Jedediah Smith Wilderness to the Teton Crest Trail, with views north to the Grand Teton. A three-mile steady climb reaches the meadows. Cyclists traveling over Teton Pass use this campground for its convenience to the highway, and mountain bikers use the nearby national forest trails.

The campground road parallels the highway, squeezed by traffic on the north and Trail Creek on the south. Most of the campsites are open to the highway, which buzzes with commuters traveling between Teton Valley and Jackson Hole in the morning and evening. At night, after the traffic dies down, you can hear the creek. The sunny campsites have little privacy; however, a few snuggled against the aspen and fir forest carve out little private nooks. Surrounded by pink fireweed in midsummer, the grassy campsites are spread out, with big, flat tent spaces available. Six of the campsites have gravel pull-through parking pads.

Campsites, facilities: The campground has 10 RV or tent campsites. RVs are limited to 40 feet. Facilities include picnic tables, fire rings with grills, vault toilets (wheelchair-accessible), bear boxes, garbage service, drinking water, and campground hosts. Leashed pets are permitted.

Reservations, fees: Reservations are accepted (877/444-6777, www.recreation.gov). Campsites cost $8. Extra vehicles cost $5. Cash or check. Open mid-May-September.

Directions: From Victor, drive southeast on Highway 33 for 5.6 miles. At milepost 155, turn south into the campground. Coming from Teton Pass, locate the turnoff 3.5 miles past the Coal Creek Meadows pullout.

GPS Coordinates: N 43° 32.462' W 111° 2.477'

Contact: Caribou-Targhee National Forest, Teton Basin Ranger District, 515 S. Main, Driggs, ID 83422, 208/354-2312, www.fs.usda.gov/ctnf.

19 FALLS

Scenic rating: 7

on the Snake River in Caribou-Targhee National Forest, Idaho

At 5,282 feet, Falls Campground sits on old river bars that once were under the Snake River, but now form a series of wooded islands—home to eagles, deer, and moose. The river is a favorite for anglers, canoers, kayakers, and rafters. Nearby Conant Boat Ramp offers a place to launch for floating, and anglers can fish from the campground. Nearby, the falls that gives the campground its name tumbles from Falls Creek 60 feet over a travertine outcrop into the river. The river's edge is a favorite spot for photographing the falls.

The quiet campground sits on a cottonwood-covered river bar where a small braid of the Snake River flows past several grassy campsites. One double campsite has views of the river spur while others have short trails through the brush to access it. You'll have your choice of partly shaded and sunny campsites. A few pull-through sites are available.

Campsites, facilities: The campground has 16 RV or tent campsites, five double campsites, one tent site, and one large group campsite. RVs are limited to 45 feet. Facilities include picnic tables, fire rings with grills, vault toilets, drinking water, garbage service, firewood for sale, and campground hosts. Leashed pets are permitted.

Reservations, fees: Reservations are accepted (877/444-6777, www.recreation.gov). Campsites cost $12. Extra vehicles cost $6. Double campsites cost $24. Cash or check. Open May-September.

Directions: Coming from Idaho Falls on Highway 26, drive 45 miles and turn right just before the bridge crossing the Snake River. Coming from Swan Valley, drive west on Highway 26 for 3.4 miles to the bridge crossing the Snake River and turn left. Drive Forest Road 058 for 2.4 miles and turn north into the campground.

GPS Coordinates: N 43° 25.957' W 111° 21.749'

Contact: Caribou-Targhee National Forest, Palisades Ranger District, 3659 E. Ririe Hwy., Idaho Falls, ID 83401, 208/523-1412, www.fs.usda.gov/ctnf.

20 PALISADES CREEK
🏃 🛶 🏕 🚐 ⛰

Scenic rating: 7

in the Snake River Mountains in
Caribou-Targhee National Forest, Idaho

At 5,550 feet, Palisades Creek Campground
snuggles into the Palisades Creek Canyon
at the base of 10,000-foot-high peaks of the
Snake River Range. It houses the most popular
trail in the range, busy on hot summer days
when hikers head to the cool subalpine lakes
for fishing and swimming. A gentle trail leads
four miles to Lower Palisades Lake, surrounded by willow brush, and continues through
Waterfall Canyon to the larger Upper Palisades
Lake with its scenic shoreline (7.5 miles total).
The trailhead departs from the east side of
the campground. A stock ramp is available
at the separate trailhead for horses. You can
often see mountain goats on the canyon cliffs
high above the trail and moose at the lakes.
Anglers enjoy the lakes and Palisades Creek
for its native cutthroat trout.

The tiny campground tucks its loop into
a shady forest of mixed conifers at the bottom of the Palisades Creek Canyon. The creek
runs adjacent to the campground. Underbrush
and small trees contribute to the privacy of
the campsites. Once day hikers depart, the
campground is very quiet, prized by those who
seek solitude.

Campsites, facilities: The campground has
five RV or tent campsites and two double
campsites. RVs are limited to 22 feet. Facilities include picnic tables, fire rings with grills,
vault toilets, drinking water, garbage service,
firewood for sale, and campground hosts.
Leashed pets are permitted.

Reservations, fees: Reservations are not accepted. Campsites cost $12. Extra vehicles cost
$6. Double campsites cost $24. Cash or check.
Open May-September.

Directions: On Highway 26, drive 7.1 miles
south of Swan Valley. Turn north onto Palisades Creek Road (Forest Road 255) for two
dirt miles to the campground entrance, passing
the hiker parking for the trailhead just before
the entrance. Coming from the south on the
highway, locate the turnoff 3.7 miles north of
Palisades Dam.

GPS Coordinates: N 43° 23.803' W 111°
12.892'

Contact: Caribou-Targhee National Forest,
Palisades Ranger District, 3659 E. Ririe Hwy.,
Idaho Falls, ID 83401, 208/523-1412, www.
fs.usda.gov/ctnf.

21 RIVERSIDE PARK
🏃 🏊 🛶 ⛴ 🎣 🏕 ♿ 🚐 ⛰

Scenic rating: 7

on the Snake River in Caribou-Targhee
National Forest

Riverside Park, elevation 5,400 feet, sits on
the South Fork of the Snake River below Palisades Dam. Fishing is available right from
the campground. The river in this stretch,
referred to as the South Fork, is renowned for
its fly-fishing, which runs from early July in
to autumn. Drift boats full of anglers fishing
for trout float from the dam downstream to
Swan Valley. The Class II river also works
for scenic floats in rafts, kayaks, tubes, and
canoes. American pelicans, sandhill cranes,
golden eagles, and moose frequent the area.
Designated as a National Important Bird
Area, the river corridor is home to the largest riparian cottonwood forest in the West,
which provides habitat for 126 bird species, including 21 raptors. A boat ramp is
also available for launching onto the nearby
Palisades Reservoir.

The campground squeezes in between the
river and the highway, with road noise pervasive. Built on a flat river bar, the location
offers roomy campsites with big, flat, raised
gravel tent platforms. The electrical hookup
sites are very open, sunny, back from the river,
and lined up in parking-lot fashion. The other
campsites sit partly shaded on a loop in the

cottonwoods down by the river. Several sites overlook the river.

Campsites, facilities: The campground has 22 RV or tent campsites, plus 10 double campsites. Pull-through sites can accommodate large RVs. Nine RV campsites have electrical hookups. Facilities include picnic tables, fire rings with grills, flush and vault toilets (wheelchair-accessible), drinking water, garbage service, firewood for sale, tent platforms, disposal station ($5), and campground hosts. Leashed pets are permitted.

Reservations, fees: Reservations are not accepted. Campsites cost $12 for single sites and $24 for double sites. Electrical hookups cost $17. Extra vehicles cost $6. Cash or check. Open May-September.

Directions: On Highway 26, drive eight miles south of Swan Valley. At milepost 387, turn west into the campground. Coming from the south on the highway, locate the turnoff one mile north of Palisades Dam.

GPS Coordinates: N 43° 20.424' W 111° 12.319'

Contact: Caribou-Targhee National Forest, Palisades Ranger District, 3659 E. Ririe Hwy., Idaho Falls, ID 83401, 208/523-1412, www.fs.usda.gov/ctnf.

22 CALAMITY

Scenic rating: 7

on Palisades Reservoir in Caribou-Targhee National Forest, Idaho

Located at 5,660 feet, Calamity Campground is the largest of the campgrounds on Palisades Reservoir, dividing the Snake River and Caribou Mountains. The campground sits on the northwest corner of the reservoir, south of Palisades Dam. Warnings on the dam will note concerns for motorists and campers on the gravel access road where it passes through a landslide. The reservoir is popular for fishing, swimming, boating, waterskiing, paddling,

and sailing. The boat launch includes concrete ramps, a dock, and trailer parking. The campground's location across the reservoir from the highway makes it quieter than other reservoir campgrounds and it has huckleberries in season.

Built on a steep hillside with constructed steps and gravel terraces for campsites, the campground has three loops. The spacious campsites have big, flat spaces for tents with a forest of aspen, fir, and lodgepoles adds partial shade and privacy to some sites; others are sunny with views of the reservoir. You can hear faint trucking noise from the highway across the reservoir. Loop C, on a steeper hillside with more privacy, has the best views.

Campsites, facilities: The campground has 40 RV or tent campsites and one double campsite. RVs are limited to 40 feet. Facilities include picnic tables, fire rings with grills, vault toilets (wheelchair-accessible), drinking water, garbage service, firewood for sale, boat launch, and campground hosts. Leashed pets are permitted.

Reservations, fees: Reservations are accepted (877/444-6777, www.recreation.gov). Campsites cost $12. Double sites cost $24. Extra vehicles cost $6. Cash or check. Open May-September.

Directions: From Alpine Junction, where Highway 26 and Highway 89 join on the Snake River, drive 18.5 miles northwest on Highway 26. At milepost 388, turn west over the dam on Bear Creek Road (Forest Road 058) and drive one mile of rough dirt road, veering left into the campground. Coming from the north on the highway, locate the turnoff at Palisades Dam.

GPS Coordinates: N 43° 19.641' W 111° 12.922'

Contact: Caribou-Targhee National Forest, Palisades Ranger District, 3659 E. Ririe Hwy., Idaho Falls, ID 83401, 208/523-1412, www.fs.usda.gov/ctnf.

23 BIG ELK CREEK

Scenic rating: 7

on Palisades Reservoir in Caribou-Targhee
National Forest, Idaho

At 5,680 feet, Big Elk Creek Campground sits on Palisades Reservoir in a forested side canyon below the 10,000-foot-high peaks of the Snake River Mountains. The campground sits on an arm of the reservoir that fills with water in early summer, but dwindles to a dry basin in late summer. It is close enough to launch boats from two nearby primitive ramps or the concrete ramps at Blowout or Calamity Campgrounds. The reservoir is popular for fishing, swimming, boating, waterskiing, paddling, and sailing. The campground's location in a side canyon makes it quieter than the Palisades campgrounds right on the highway. Big Elk Creek Road terminates 0.4 mile farther at a trailhead with a stock ramp. A gentle trail for hikers, bikers, and horseback riders heads up the creek canyon, reaching Dry Canyon in 2.5 miles, Hells Hole Canyon in 3.4 miles, and Idaho-Wyoming border in 4.5 miles.

The grassy campground loops on an open, sunny, south-facing gentle slope. A few conifers sprinkle through the campground but provide minimal shade. Surrounded by a large sagebrush field, the wide-open sites garner big views of the Big Elk Creek drainage, but at the cost of privacy, and some sites are quite close together. A gravel road loops through the campground to access gravel and grass parking pads. Overflow primitive camping is available at Little Elk Creek boat ramp.

Campsites, facilities: The campground has 10 RV or tent campsites, plus five double sites and three large group campsites. RVs are limited to 22 feet. Facilities include picnic tables, fire rings with grills, vault toilets (wheelchair-accessible), drinking water, garbage service, firewood for sale, and campground hosts. Leashed pets are permitted.

Reservations, fees: Reservations are only accepted for group campsites (877/444-6777, www.recreation.gov). Campsites cost $12. Double sites cost $24. Large group sites cost $50. Extra vehicles cost $6. Cash or check. Open May-September.

Directions: From Alpine Junction, where Highway 26 and Highway 89 join on the Snake River, drive 15.1 miles northwest on Highway 26. At milepost 390.8, turn north onto Big Elk Creek Road (Forest Road 262) and drive 1.6 miles. The campground entrance is on the left. Coming from the north on the highway, locate the turnoff about 3.4 miles southeast of Palisades Dam.
GPS Coordinates: N 43° 19.331' W 111° 7.051'
Contact: Caribou-Targhee National Forest, Palisades Ranger District, 3659 E. Ririe Hwy., Idaho Falls, ID 83401, 208/523-1412, www.fs.usda.gov/ctnf.

24 BLOWOUT

Scenic rating: 7

on Palisades Reservoir in Caribou-Targhee
National Forest, Idaho

At 5,800 feet, Blowout Campground is situated on the northeast side of the 16,000-acre Palisades Reservoir, surrounded by steep forested mountains. With its location, it is one of the most popular campgrounds on the lake. Fed by the Snake River, the reservoir, which is known for wind and summer thunderstorms, is popular for fishing, swimming, boating, waterskiing, paddling, and sailing. The campground's large boat launch includes a double-wide concrete ramp, dock, and trailer parking. The reservoir harbors cutthroat, brown, and lake trout, along with kokanee salmon. Thanks to its location on the highway, cross-country cyclists find this campground convenient. In fall, the hillsides around the lake light up with color—especially when the aspens turn gold.

The aspen and lodgepole forest provides partial shade for the tight campsites with gravel back-in parking pads; you'll have your pick between sites overlooking the reservoir and varying amounts of privacy. Only small spaces for tents are available. Unfortunately, sites 2 and 15 plop next to the highway and chain-link fence. This campground picks up road noise during the night from commercial trucking on the highway. Overflow parking for large RVs is available at the boat launch.

Campsites, facilities: The campground has 11 RV or tent campsites, plus four double campsites. RVs are limited to 32 feet. Facilities include picnic tables, fire rings with grills, vault toilets (wheelchair-accessible), drinking water, garbage service, boat launch, firewood for sale, and campground hosts. Leashed pets are permitted.

Reservations, fees: Reservations are not accepted. Campsites cost $12. Double sites cost $24. Extra vehicles cost $6. Cash or check. Open mid-May-mid-September.

Directions: From Alpine Junction, where Highway 26 and Highway 89 join on the Snake River, drive 12 miles northwest on Highway 26. At milepost 394, turn south into the campground. Coming from the north on the highway, locate the campground entrance about 6.5 miles southeast of Palisades Dam. GPS Coordinates: N 43° 17.131' W 111° 7.350'

Contact: Caribou-Targhee National Forest, Palisades Ranger District, 3659 E. Ririe Hwy., Idaho Falls, ID 83401, 208/523-1412, www.fs.usda.gov/ctnf.

25 ALPINE

Scenic rating: 7

on Palisades Reservoir in Caribou-Targhee National Forest, Wyoming

Located at 5,692 feet, Alpine Campground sits at the head of the 16,000-acre Palisades Reservoir, surrounded by steep forested mountains. Anglers will need to ensure they have the appropriate state licenses depending on where they drop in lines. The reservoir, fed by the Snake River, is shallow along the shoreline near the campground. When the lake water level drops low in late August, the area in front of the campground can become a muddy maze of braided streams. The reservoir is popular for fishing, swimming, paddling, and boating. The closest boat ramp is in the town of Alpine. Another is located midlake on the east side at Indian Creek. The reservoir harbors cutthroat, brown, and lake trout along with kokanee salmon. Because of its location on the highway, cross-country cyclists find this campground convenient.

The campground tucks into a loose lodgepole pine, aspen, and spruce forest, which admits partial and full sun to campsites. Contrary to the surrounding steep hillsides, the campground is in flatter terrain. High undergrowth blooming with pink fireweed under the forest canopy gives the roomy, grassy campsites privacy. With the highway so close—a commercial trucking route—road noise enters the campground.

Campsites, facilities: The campground has 16 RV or tent campsites, plus six double campsites and three large group campsites. RVs are limited to 45 feet. Facilities include picnic tables, fire rings with grills, vault toilets (wheelchair-accessible), drinking water, firewood for sale, garbage service, and campground hosts. Leashed pets are permitted.

Reservations, fees: Reservations are accepted (877/444-6777, www.recreation.gov). Campsites cost $12. Double sites cost $24. Group campsites cost $50. Extra vehicles cost $6. Cash or check. Open late May-mid-September.

Directions: From Alpine Junction, where Highway 26 and Highway 89 join on the Snake River, drive two miles northwest on Highway 26. At milepost 402, turn south into the campground. Coming from the north on the highway, look for the campground entrance 0.5 mile southeast of Forest Road 402. GPS Coordinates: N 43° 11.817' W 111° 2.483'

Contact: Caribou-Targhee National Forest, Palisades Ranger District, 3659 E. Ririe Hwy.,

Idaho Falls, ID 83401, 208/523-1412, www. fs.usda.gov/ctnf.

26 MCCOY CREEK

Scenic rating: 7

on Palisades Reservoir in Caribou-Targhee National Forest, Idaho

Located at 5,682 feet in the Caribou Mountains, McCoy Creek Campground sits where McCoy Creek flows into the 16,000-acre Palisades Reservoir. Owing to the campground's location at the head of the lake, the lake water drops low in August, leaving bare slopes rimming the reservoir. A primitive boat ramp off the second campground spur works for launching hand-carried watercraft like canoes, kayaks, and rafts. The reservoir harbors cutthroat, brown, and lake trout along with kokanee salmon, and anglers can fish McCoy Creek, too. Swimmers can cool off at the reservoir.

Two separate gravel spurs with turnarounds form the campground. Partly shaded to sunny campsites tuck into a mixed conifer forest. The location at the southeast corner of the reservoir defines quiet because of its distance from the highway.

Campsites, facilities: The campground has 17 RV or tent campsites. RVs are limited to 25 feet. Facilities include picnic tables, fire rings with grills, vault toilets (wheelchair-accessible), drinking water, firewood for sale, garbage service, and campground hosts. Leashed pets are permitted.

Reservations, fees: Reservations are not accepted. Campsites cost $12. Extra vehicles cost $6. Cash or check. Open May-September.

Directions: From Alpine Junction, where Highway 26 and Highway 89 join on the Snake River, drive southeast on Highway 89 for 3.7 miles. Turn right onto Salt River-McCoy Road (Forest Road 087) and drive 6.7 miles to the first campground entrance

on the right. The second entrance sits 0.25 mile further.

GPS Coordinates: N 43° 11.075' W 111° 6.080'

Contact: Caribou-Targhee National Forest, Palisades Ranger District, 3659 E. Ririe Hwy., Idaho Falls, ID 83401, 208/523-1412, www. fs.usda.gov/ctnf.

27 WOLF CREEK

Scenic rating: 8

in Snake River Canyon in Bridger-Teton National Forest

In the Wyoming Range, Wolf Creek Campground sits at 5,800 feet at the southwest end of the Snake River Canyon. The canyon walls narrow, forcing the campground to climb a hillside, but this Class III stretch of river through the canyon, designated as Wild and Scenic, is favored by kayakers and rafters for eight miles of white water. Taco Hole kayak playboat area is 3.5 miles northwest of the campground. Anglers on the shore or in drift boats go after brown and Yellowstone cutthroat trout. Outfitters for fishing and rafting are available in Hoback Junction. The Wolf Creek Trailhead, 1.5 miles east of the campground, leads eight miles to Red Pass on the west side of 9,483-foot Wolf Mountain. The campsite's highway location is convenient for cross-country cyclists.

The campground does not afford enjoyment of the river from campsites, but a few paths across the highway lead to the shore. On a hillside, the campsites have views of the highway, power lines crossing above the campground, and the river. The gravel road accesses three loops with gravel parking pads. Loop C climbs the farthest above the highway, with its upper campsites having views of the cliffs across the canyon. A few firs for shade sprinkle across the sagebrush hillside, blooming with fireweed and mountain hollyhock.

Campsites, facilities: The campground has 20 RV or tent campsites. RVs are limited to midsized rigs. Facilities include picnic tables, fire rings with grills, vault toilets (wheelchair-accessible), drinking water, bear boxes, garbage service, tent platforms, and campground hosts. Leashed pets are permitted.

Reservations, fees: Reservations are not accepted. Campsites cost $15. Cash or check. Open late June-August.

Directions: On Highway 26/89/6, from Hoback Junction drive southwest for 16 miles, or from Alpine drive seven miles northeast. At milepost 124.9, turn north into the campground.

GPS Coordinates: N 43° 11.931' W 110° 54.017'

Contact: Bridger-Teton National Forest, Jackson Ranger District, 25 Rosencrans Ln., Jackson, WY 83001, 307/739-5400, www.fs.usda.gov/btnf.

28 STATION CREEK

Scenic rating: 8

in Snake River Canyon in Bridger-Teton National Forest

Located at 5,800 feet in the Wyoming Range, the popular Station Creek Campground sits midway in the Snake River Canyon. The canyon walls narrow, forcing the campground onto a bluff above the river without access to the shore. The Class III stretch of river through the canyon, designated as Wild and Scenic, is favored by kayakers and rafters for its eight miles of white water, which peaks in early June. Water rips through Big Kahuna, Lunch Counter, and Ropes rapids. The campground is convenient for floaters as it sits midway between the put-in at West Table launch site and take-out at Sheep Gulch. Taco Hole, a kayak playboat area with a 30-foot-wide wave hole and the accompanying Burrito Hole, sits 0.5 mile west. Anglers, floating the upper section

of the river in drift boats, go after brown and Yellowstone cutthroat trout. Station Creek Trail departs across the highway. Outfitters for fishing and rafting are available in Hoback Junction. The highway location is convenient for cross-country cyclists.

Station Creek Campground sits high above the Snake River on a bluff, with half of its campsites (3-10) overlooking the river. The drop to the river is so steep that fences rim the ledges. Lodgepole pines and firs shade the campsites, which are ringed with meadows of fireweed. The sites sit within view of neighboring campers, and road noise competes with the roar of the river.

Campsites, facilities: The campground has 16 RV or tent campsites and a large group campsite across the highway. RVs are limited to midsized rigs. Facilities include picnic tables, fire rings with grills, pedestal grills, vault toilets (wheelchair-accessible), drinking water, bear boxes, garbage service, tent platforms, and campground hosts. Leashed pets are permitted.

Reservations, fees: Reservations are only accepted for the large group site (877/444-6777, www.recreation.gov). Campsites cost $15. Cash or check. Open late May-August.

Directions: On Highway 26/89/6, from Hoback Junction drive southwest for 12 miles, or from Alpine drive 11 miles northeast. At milepost 128.7, turn south into the campground.

GPS Coordinates: N 43° 12.296' W 110° 50.074'

Contact: Bridger-Teton National Forest, Jackson Ranger District, 25 Rosencrans Ln., Jackson, WY 83001, 307/739-5400, www.fs.usda.gov/btnf.

29 EAST TABLE CREEK

Scenic rating: 8

in Snake River Canyon in Bridger-Teton National Forest

At 5,800 feet in the Wyoming Range, East

Table Campground sits toward the upper end of the Snake River Canyon. Even though this is the only Snake River Canyon campground that accesses the water, boat launching is not permitted from the campground. Instead, launch from the huge West Table boat ramp west of the campground or for hand-carried watercraft, use the adjacent East Table primitive boat ramp. The river, designated as Wild and Scenic, is calmer above the campground, where anglers float drift boats from Hoback Junction to fish for brown and Yellowstone cutthroat trout. You can also fish from the shore along the campground and wade-fish in late summer. Below the campground, an eight-mile stretch of Class III white water amuses kayakers and rafters. Outfitters for fishing and rafting are available in Hoback Junction. The campground's highway location is convenient for cross-country cyclists, and hikers can access the East Table Creek Trail across the highway.

The campground sits on a large, aspen- and lodgepole-covered river bar crisscrossed with paths leading to the water. Eight campsites overlook the river. Tall, mature pines shade many of the campsites, but with little understory, you'll see neighbors. Road noise competes with the sound of the river. If the campground is full, you can use the primitive overflow sites and walk-in tent campsites across the highway, but no services are available. Hunters can reserve the overflow site in fall (307-739-5427).

Campsites, facilities: The campground has 18 RV or tent campsites. RVs are limited to midsized rigs. Facilities include picnic tables, fire rings with grills, pedestal grills, vault toilets (wheelchair-accessible), drinking water, bear boxes, garbage service, tent platforms, and campground hosts. Leashed pets are permitted.
Reservations, fees: Reservations are not accepted. Campsites cost $15. Cash or check. Open late May-August.
Directions: On Highway 26/89/6, from Hoback Junction drive southwest for 11 miles, or from Alpine drive 12 miles northeast. At milepost 130, turn south into the campground.

GPS Coordinates: N 43° 12.762' W 110° 48.459'
Contact: Bridger-Teton National Forest, Jackson Ranger District, 25 Rosencrans Ln., Jackson, WY 83001, 307/739-5400, www.fs.usda.gov/btnf.

30 HOBACK

🚶 🚵 🛶 🛏 ⛴ 🏕 🚐 ⛺

Scenic rating: 8

in Hoback Canyon in Bridger-Teton National Forest

In the Gros Ventre Range, Hoback Campground tucks at 6,200 feet into deep gray- and red-cliffed Hoback Canyon, where ospreys fish the Hoback River. Trout fishing runs sluggish during June runoff, but during the salmon fly hatch in early July, fishing picks up. Designated Wild and Scenic, the Hoback froths with Class I-III white water through the canyon. You can put in at the campground and take out at Hoback Junction, or put in at Granite Creek and take out at the campground. Because of its white-water sections, this river requires some skill to navigate by kayak or raft. This highway campground attracts cross-country cyclists, and across the highway, a trail climbs partway up Cream Puff Peak.

Tucked under big spruce, firs, and aspens, the campground squeezes in between the highway and the river; a couple campsites, such as site 7, suffer right near the highway noise. Open, sunny campsites are interspersed with partly shaded campsites, offering campers a choice. Those in the open garner views of the canyon walls. Five sites enjoy river frontage. A paved road loops through the campground with paved back-in parking pads.
Campsites, facilities: The campground has 13 RV or tent campsites. RVs are limited to midsized rigs. Facilities include picnic tables, fire rings with grills, pedestal grills, vault toilets (wheelchair-accessible), drinking water, bear boxes, garbage service, and campground hosts. Leashed pets are permitted.

Reservations, fees: Reservations are not accepted. Campsites cost $15. Cash or check. Open late May-September.
Directions: From Hoback Junction, drive eight miles southeast on Highway 189/191. At milepost 155.5, turn south into the campground.
GPS Coordinates: N 43° 16.876' W 110° 35.628'
Contact: Bridger-Teton National Forest, Jackson Ranger District, 25 Rosencrans Ln., Jackson, WY 83001, 307/739-5400, www.fs.usda.gov/btnf.

31 GRANITE CREEK

Scenic rating: 9
in the Gros Ventre Mountains in Bridger-Teton National Forest

BEST (
Located at 6,870 feet, Granite Creek

Campground lies below the massive Open Door rock slab, a slice of orange rock with a horizontal hole like a doorway. Granite Hot Springs (307/734-7400, open late May-October) and Granite Falls sit within one mile. The hot springs (with a changing room, restrooms, and outdoor cement pool built by the CCC in 1933) heats to 93°F in the summer, when rains and snowmelt dilute the hot water, and to 112°F in the winter. Primitive hot pools also sit below Granite Falls. Granite Creek flows past the campground, although its thick willows make wade-fishing for Yellowstone cutthroat trout and mountain whitefish more difficult. Granite Creek Trail runs along the opposite side of the river from the bridge south of the campground two miles to the falls and hot springs before continuing farther north into the Gros Ventre Wilderness. Rafting and kayaking—best late May-mid-June—start at the wooden bridge seven miles up the road from the highway.

Granite Creek Hot Springs is a pool constructed in 1933 by the Civilian Conservation Corps in Bridger-Teton National Forest.

Several campsites on the campground's three loops have views of the Open Door. Large lodgepoles and subalpine firs shade most of the campsites, except for a handful of sunny, open sites in loop A. The sites are spaced out for privacy—many with spacious tent areas—but with forest pine needle and duff floors, the minimal vegetation between sites lets you see neighboring campers. Despite the narrow high elevation canyon, sandhill cranes fly in over the willows around the creek, squawking as they land.

Campsites, facilities: The campground has 53 RV or tent campsites. RVs are limited to midsized rigs. Facilities include picnic tables, fire rings with grills, pedestal grills, vault toilets (wheelchair-accessible), drinking water, bear boxes, garbage service, tent platforms, and campground hosts. Leashed pets are permitted.

Reservations, fees: Reservations are not accepted. Campsites cost $15. Cash or check. Open late May-September.

Directions: From Hoback Junction, drive 11 miles southeast on Highway 189/191. Turn north onto bumpy dirt Granite Creek Road (Forest Road 30500) for 8.6 miles to the campground entrance on the right.

GPS Coordinates: N 43° 21.567' W 110° 26.802'

Contact: Bridger-Teton National Forest, Jackson Ranger District, 25 Rosencrans Ln., Jackson, WY 83001, 307/739-5400, www.fs.usda.gov/btnf.

32 GRANITE CREEK PRIMITIVE

Scenic rating: 9

in the Gros Ventre Mountains in Bridger-Teton National Forest

Located 6,400 to 6,850 feet, Granite Creek primitive campsites are popular for their beauty, solitude, and quiet as well as options for camping in shoulder seasons when Granite Creek Campground is closed. Granite Hot Springs (307/734-7400, open late May-October) and Granite Falls (with primitive hot pools at the base) sit at the end of the 10-mile dirt road. From the hot springs, Granite Creek Trail runs two miles along the river south past the falls and also north into the Gros Ventre Wilderness. At primitive campsites, anglers wade-fish for Yellowstone cutthroat trout and mountain whitefish in Granite Creek. Rafters and kayakers float the river's bottom seven miles, best from late May to mid-June.

All campsites command river frontage along Granite Creek. The first few sit within sight of the road, but the upper ones tuck into private locations behind aspens, firs, and pines. Some have sweeping views of the Gros Ventre Mountains at the end of the drainage. Many of the spur accesses are narrow and rough; scout them first.

Campsites, facilities: The area has 12 RV or tent campsites; some can accommodate midsized RVs. Facilities include rock fire rings. Bring your own drinking water, or treat creek water. Pack out your trash. Use Leave No Trace principles for managing human waste. Pets are permitted.

Reservations, fees: Reservations are not accepted. Camping is free. Open May-early November.

Directions: From Hoback Junction, drive 11 miles southeast on Highway 189/191. Turn north onto the bumpy dirt Granite Creek Road (Forest Road 30500). Locate the entrances to the primitive campsites on the right side of the road along the seven miles after milepost 1.3 and 1.3 miles before the end of the road, where a sign denotes the end of primitive camping.

GPS Coordinates: N 43° 17.833' W 110° 30.115' (first primitive site)

Contact: Bridger-Teton National Forest, Jackson Ranger District, 25 Rosencrans Ln., Jackson, WY 83001, 307/739-5400, www.fs.usda.gov/btnf.

33 KOZY

Scenic rating: 8

in Hoback Canyon in Bridger-Teton National Forest

At 6,500 feet in the Gros Ventre Mountains, tiny Kozy Campground tucks into deep gray- and red-cliffed Hoback Canyon, where ospreys fish the Hoback River. Trout fishing runs sluggish during June runoff, but during the salmon fly hatch in early July, fishing picks up. Designated Wild and Scenic, the Hoback froths with Class I-III white water through the canyon. You can put in at the campground and take out at Hoback Junction, or put in at Bondurant and take out at the campground. Considering its white-water sections, this river requires some skill to navigate by kayak or raft. West of the campground, the Shoal Creek trail climbs to a falls, a lake, and the Gros Ventre Wilderness. The campground attracts cross-country cyclists because of the highway location.

The tiny campground, with a paved road and parking pads, nestles in Hoback Canyon, squeezed between the highway and the river. It's close to the highway, and even the river can't drown out the trucking noise at night. Surrounded by sagebrush and pine slopes, the campground tucks several of the campsites into the loose forest, but you can still see the highway as well as other campers. Five sites claim river frontage. At the end of the turnaround loop, one site offers the most privacy.

Campsites, facilities: The campground has eight RV or tent campsites. RVs are limited to midsized rigs. Facilities include picnic tables, fire rings with grills, pedestal grills, vault toilets (wheelchair-accessible), drinking water, bear boxes, and garbage service. Leashed pets are permitted.

Reservations, fees: Reservations are not accepted. Campsites cost $12. Cash or check. Open late May-mid-September.

Directions: From Hoback Junction, drive 13 miles southeast on Highway 189/191. At milepost 151.9, turn north into the campground. GPS Coordinates: N 43° 16.217' W 110° 31.021'

Contact: Bridger-Teton National Forest, Jackson Ranger District, 25 Rosencrans Ln., Jackson, WY 83001, 307/739-5400, www.fs.usda.gov/btnf.

34 GREEN RIVER LAKE

Scenic rating: 10

in the Wind River Mountains in Bridger-Teton National Forest

Green River Lake Campground, elevation 8,080 feet, is a prized spot for campers on Lower Green River Lake. Stunning views at the lake often yield reflections of the blocky Squaretop Mountain, and rugged peaks over 11,000-feet that surround the campground. With stock facilities available, trails depart for several destinations, including one only for hikers and horseback riders that saunters in three gentle miles to Upper Green River Lake in the Bridger Wilderness. It is also part of the Continental Divide Trail. Mountain bikers can access trail outside the wilderness and old forest roads. Anglers can fish for trout in the Green River and the lakes. Using a primitive ramp, boaters and paddlers can launch onto the two-mile-long Green River Lake. When conditions are right, paddlers can travel upstream into Upper Green River Lake, paddling or pulling canoes or kayaks while walking streamside. Swimmers should prepare for chilly water in the lake.

Prepare for thick mosquitoes and biting flies at this remote quiet campground, tucked in a lush green valley around two loops. While lodgepoles occlude views of the lake from most campsites, several campsites command views of Squaretop Mountain and surrounding peaks—scenery worth giving up sheltered privacy to enjoy. A trail descends from the lower loop to the beach of Green River Lake. Primitive and overflow camping is also available at many sites along the Green River on the way up to Green River Lakes; campers at these dispersed sites should use previous fire rings, treat water taken from the river, pack out trash, and use Leave No Trace responsibility with human waste.

Campsites, facilities: The campground has 39 RV or tent campsites plus three large group campsites. RVs are limited to 35 feet. Facilities include picnic tables, fire rings with grills, vault toilets, drinking water, bear boxes, and campground hosts. Pack out your trash. Leashed pets are permitted. Wheelchair-accessible toilets are available.

Reservations, fees: Reservations are accepted only for the group campsites (877/444-6777, www.recreation.gov). Campsites cost $12. Cash or check. Open mid-June-mid-September.

Directions: From seven miles west of in Pinedale on Highway 191, turn north onto State Highway 352 for 28 miles where the pavement ends, and the gravel road becomes Forest Road 650. Drive for 23 miles, staying to the right of the river at junctions, to the campground entrance on the right.

GPS Coordinates: N 43° 18.905' W 109° 51.808'

Contact: Bridger-Teton National Forest, Pinedale Ranger District, 29 E. Fremont Lake Rd., Pinedale, WY 82941, 307/367-4326, www.fs.usda.gov/btnf.

35 WHISKEY GROVE

Scenic rating: 8
in the Wind River Mountains in Bridger-Teton National Forest

Whiskey Grove Campground sits at 7,720 feet along the Upper Green River. Anglers can fish the Green River for brook and rainbow trout. The nearby Kendall Warm Springs (no swimming or fishing) harbors dace, a tiny fish

listed on the Endangered Species List for its rarity. The fish lives in the 85°F spring water that streams down into the Green River. The campground sits just south of a fork with two scenic back-road drives in the Wind River Mountains. One route follows the Green River to Green River Lakes. The other crosses the mountains over the 9,664-foot Union Pass.

The campground sits on the south rim of an oxbow in the Green River. A pine forest casts partial shade on the campground, but with little undergrowth, you'll see some neighbors. Several sites have river frontage, with views of the water.

Campsites, facilities: The campground has nine RV or tent campsites. RVs are limited to 35 feet. Facilities include picnic tables, fire rings, vault toilets, and drinking water from a hand pump. Pack out your trash. Leashed pets are permitted.

Reservations, fees: Reservations are not accepted. Campsites cost $7. Cash or check. Open mid-June-mid-September.

Directions: From seven miles west of in Pinedale on Highway 191, turn north onto State Highway 352 for 28 miles where the pavement ends, and the gravel road becomes Forest Road 650. Drive three miles and turn left into the campground.

GPS Coordinates: N 43° 15.337' W 110° 1.550'

Contact: Bridger-Teton National Forest, Pinedale Ranger District, 29 E. Fremont Lake Rd., Pinedale, WY 82941, 307/367-4326, www.fs.usda.gov/btnf.

36 NEW FORK LAKE

Scenic rating: 8
in the Wind River Mountains in Bridger-Teton National Forest

New Fork Lake Campground sits at the foot of a scenic lake at 7,850 feet. New Fork Lake tucks into a steep-walled canyon that descends from Dome Peak following the route of a glacier. While you can launch hand-carried canoes or kayaks from the campground, a cement boat ramp with trailer parking sits partway up the lake, requiring a 1.5-mile drive, and serving to launch motorized boats (no Jet Skis permitted). In the lake, anglers go after a variety of trout as well as kokanee salmon. Several beaches at the lake's foot offer places for family water play and swimming.

The campground tucks its one loop in a grove of aspens that chatter in the breeze. The sites are all back-ins, and the narrow loop can pose problems for some RVs; scouting is advised. A few campsites have views of the lake and dramatic canyon, but all gain privacy from the thick understory.

Campsites, facilities: The campground has 15 RV or tent campsites plus one large group campsites. RVs are limited to 30 feet. Facilities include picnic tables, fire rings with grills, vault toilets, and campground hosts. Bring your own drinking water, or treat lake water. Pack out your trash. Leashed pets are permitted. Wheelchair-accessible toilets are available.

Reservations, fees: Reservations are accepted (877/444-6777, www.recreation.gov). Campsites cost $7. Cash or check. Open June-mid-September.

Directions: From seven miles west of in Pinedale on Highway 191, turn north onto State Highway 352 for about 14 miles. Turn right onto the gravel New Fork Lake Road for 3.3 miles. Turn right onto Forest Road 753 for 0.1-mile and left into the campground.
GPS Coordinates: N 43° 4.950' W 109° 57.966'

Contact: Bridger-Teton National Forest, Pinedale Ranger District, 29 E. Fremont Lake Rd., Pinedale, WY 82941, 307/367-4326, www.fs.usda.gov/btnf.

37 NARROWS

Scenic rating: 9

in the Wind River Mountains in Bridger-Teton National Forest

At 7,900 feet, the Narrows Campground overlooks New Fork Lake, a lake nearly split in two by a pair of peninsulas. You can swim the narrow waterway—only a couple hundred feet—that separates the two peninsulas, but be prepared for cold water. The lake tucks into a steep-walled canyon that descends from Dome Peak following the route of a glacier. A cement boat ramp with trailer parking sits one mile before the campground, offering a place to launch motorboats, canoes, and kayaks (no Jet Skis permitted). In the lake, anglers go after a variety of trout as well as kokanee salmon. A trailhead with stock facilities departs from the campground to head up the lake and into the Bridger Wilderness.

The quiet hillside campground flanks the north slope at the Narrows. Most of the campsites overlook the lake and garner views of the canyon and mountains at the head of the lake. Amid aspens, the campground's two spurs pack the grassy campsites close to each other.

Campsites, facilities: The campground has 18 RV or tent campsites. RVs are limited to 30 feet. Facilities include picnic tables, fire rings with grills, vault toilets, drinking water, and campground hosts. Leashed pets are permitted. Wheelchair-accessible toilets are available.

Reservations, fees: Reservations are accepted (877/444-6777, www.recreation.gov). Campsites cost $12. Cash or check. Open June-mid-September.

Directions: From seven miles west of in Pinedale on Highway 191, turn north onto State Highway 352 for about 14 miles. Turn right onto the gravel New Fork Lake Road for four miles. Veer right for two miles along the lake until the road terminates in the campground.

GPS Coordinates: N 43° 6.288' W 109° 56.557'

Contact: Bridger-Teton National Forest, Pinedale Ranger District, 29 E. Fremont Lake Rd., Pinedale, WY 82941, 307/367-4326, www.fs.usda.gov/btnf.

38 GREEN RIVER WARREN BRIDGE ACCESS AREA

🛶🚣🎣🏕🚐⛺

Scenic rating: 8

on the Green River

BEST(

Located between 7,600 and 8,000 feet, the Green River floats through a series of convoluted oxbows in its gentle descent through the valley from the Wind River Mountains. Nine miles of mini campgrounds line the river's western shore at 12 developed river access points. During early-summer high water, the river runs at Class I-II, good for canoes, rafts, drift boats, and kayaks. Late-summer low water may require negotiating gravel bars. In this reputable fishery, anglers go after rainbow, brown, and Yellowstone cutthroat trout via wade-fishing or by boat in the river. Boat ramps—which work for standard trucks and cars with trailers—are provided at four of the river access sites. Most vehicles can reach the river access sites, but wet, muddy conditions may require four-wheel drive, and many require steep descents.

The sunny campgrounds offer quiet places away from hordes of people. But in the height of the boating season, you will see plenty of river traffic and day-use visitors. At night, the campgrounds are very quiet. Sagebrush prairies cover the slopes around the campgrounds, with brushy willows along the riverbanks. Be ready to cope with biting blackflies.

Campsites, facilities: The river access area has 12 locations on the west side of the Green River with 23 RV or tent campsites. Five of the river accesses (3, 4, 7, 10, and 12) can accommodate large RVs; the others can only fit RVs less than 31 feet. Vehicles must be parked at least 50 feet from the water. Facilities include picnic tables, fire rings with grills, vault toilets, and boat ramps at sites 1, 2, 4, and 12. Drinking water is not available. Bring your own, or treat river water. Pack out your trash. Leashed pets are permitted.

Reservations, fees: Reservations are not accepted. Camping is free. Open mid-May-September.

Directions: From 20 miles north of Pinedale on Highway 191, turn east onto the gravel road north of Warren Bridge over the Green River. Road conditions vary, depending on the season. The 12 river access locations are on the right side of the road in the nine miles upstream from Warren Bridge. GPS Coordinates for first site: N 43° 1.713' W 110° 6.365'

Contact: Bureau of Land Management, Pinedale Field Office, 1625 W. Pine St., Pinedale, WY 82941, 307/367-5300, www.blm.gov/wy/st/en/field_offices/Pinedale/recreation/developed_sites.html.

39 WARREN BRIDGE

🛶🚣🎣🏕♿🚐⛺

Scenic rating: 8

on the Green River

At 7,250 feet, Warren Bridge Campground sits on a broad sagebrush prairie between the Wind River Mountains and the Wyoming Range. It flanks the upper Green River en route to its confluence in Utah with the Colorado River. Across Warren Bridge, a gravel road parallels the Class I and II river upstream with 12 different places to launch drift boats, kayaks, rafts, or canoes. High water runs in early summer, but even as the water level drops, the river remains floatable through August. September flows may require pulling boats over shallow gravel bars. Wildlife—particularly sage grouse and pronghorn antelope—use the prairies around the river. Anglers go after rainbow, Yellowstone cutthroat, and brown trout in the Green.

Warren Bridge Campground is adjacent to the highway, where commercial trucking delivers noise to the campground at night. Only the howling wind can drown out the highway. The sagebrush and purple lupine plateau can be hot or windy, but the treeless campground offers big views of the Wyoming Range and the Wind River Mountains. The wide-open prairie offers no natural fences between sites, but they are spaced out for privacy.

Campsites, facilities: The campground has 16 RV or tent campsites. Large RVs can fit in the pull-through sites. Facilities include picnic tables, fire rings with grills, pedestal grills, vault toilets (wheelchair-accessible), drinking water, disposal station, and campground hosts. Leashed pets are permitted.

Reservations, fees: Reservations are not accepted. Campsites cost $10. Use of the waste disposal costs $5. Cash or check. Open mid-May-September.

Directions: From 20 miles north of Pinedale on Highway 191, turn southwest into the campground at milepost 120—just south of the bridge over the Green River.

GPS Coordinates: N 43° 1.076' W 110° 7.109'

Contact: Bureau of Land Management, Pinedale Field Office, 1625 W. Pine St., Pinedale, WY 82941, 307/367-5300, www.blm.gov/wy/st/en/field_offices/Pinedale/recreation/developed_sites.html.

40 WILLOW LAKE

Scenic rating: 7

in the Wind River Mountains in Bridger-Teton National Forest

Willow Lake Campground offers a way to explore a less visited lake. The 4.5-mile-long glacially carved lake sits in a more arid basin from neighboring lakes. A primitive ramp allows for launching onto the lake for boating, paddling, or fishing. Swimming is okay here. Anglers also enjoy fly-fishing in Willow Creek. The head of the lake touches the Bridger Wilderness, and trails access peaks, lakes, and the interior mountains. The campground is popular with hunters.

This unmaintained campground is not for everyone as the Forest Service does little upkeep. Nevertheless, its location offers quiet and solitude at the foot of the lake where sagebrush surrounds campsites tucked into aspen groves.

Campsites, facilities: The campground has six RV or tent campsites. RVs are limited to 25 feet. Facilities include picnic tables, fire pits, pit toilets, and boat launch. Bring your own drinking water, or treat lake water. Leashed pets are permitted.

Reservations, fees: Reservations are not accepted. Camping is free. Open June-early September.

Directions: In Pinedale, take Jackson Street north until it turns into Willow Lake Road. Drive about 10 miles to the national forest boundary. After the boundary, veer left and drive about four miles to the lake on a rough gravel road. Find the campground entrance on the southwest shore.

GPS Coordinates: N 42° 59.334' W 109° 43.936'

Contact: Bridger-Teton National Forest, Pinedale Ranger District, 29 E. Fremont Lake Rd., Pinedale, WY 82941, 307/367-4326, www.fs.usda.gov/btnf.

41 FREMONT LAKE

Scenic rating: 8

in the Wind River Mountains in Bridger-Teton National Forest

Fremont Lake Campground, elevation 7,500 feet, sits on the east shore of Fremont Lake, where the landscape changes from sagebrush prairie to forest. The nine-mile-long and 600-foot-deep, glacier-carved lake, which supplies Pinedale's water, is the second-largest natural lake in Wyoming. The lake is popular for boating, sailing, waterskiing, Jet Skiing, swimming, kayaking, canoeing, and fishing for lake, rainbow, and brown trout. The newly reconstructed boat launch has a concrete ramp, dock, and trailer parking. Sandy swimming beaches rim part of the campground shore. Mornings bring calm water; winds usually pick up in the afternoon with whitecaps, and late afternoon thunderstorms are common. Accessible by boat, short hiking trails into the Bridger Wilderness depart from the head of the lake. The location of the campground near the lake's upper canyon blocks views of the snow-covered peaks of the Wind River Range; drive or boat to the lake's south end for the stunning views.

Fremont Lake, the second largest natural lake in Wyoming, tucks into the Wind River Mountains.

Reconstructed in 2013 with upgraded toilets, a group campsite, and pull-throughs for larger RVs, the campground—the largest in the Pinedale area—offers a mix of shaded, partly shaded, and sunny campsites with paved parking aprons sprawled in several loops along the lakeshore hillside. A mixed forest of Douglas fir, junipers, spruce, and aspens provides the shade for some sites; others are surrounded by brushy growth of wild roses, sagebrush, balsamroot, and willows. From some campsites, you can see the neighbors; very few campsites have lake views.

Campsites, facilities: The campground has 54 RV or tent campsites. RVs are limited to 45 feet. Facilities include picnic tables, fire rings with grills, vault and pit toilets, drinking water, boat launch, and campground hosts. Leashed pets are permitted. Wheelchair-accessible facilities include toilets and six campsites.

Reservations, fees: Reservations are highly recommended (877/444-6777, www.recreation.gov). Campsites cost $12. Cash or check. Open late May-early September.

Directions: From Highway 191 in Pinedale, turn northeast onto Fremont Lake Road for four miles. At the T junction, turn left for 0.2 mile. At the Y junction, turn right for 3.1 miles to the campground entrance on the left. GPS Coordinates: N 42° 56.415' W 109° 47.814'

Contact: Bridger-Teton National Forest, Pinedale Ranger District, 29 E. Fremont Lake Rd., Pinedale, WY 82941, 307/367-4326, www.fs.usda.gov/btnf.

42 HALF MOON LAKE

Scenic rating: 7

in the Wind River Mountains in Bridger-Teton National Forest

Half Moon Lake Campground sits at 7,600 feet on the three-mile-long lake. A boat ramp on the north shore, located 0.2 miles from the campground, includes room for trailer parking and launching motorboats, canoes, or kayaks. Hiking trails depart from the road's end at the lake's northeast corner; the trail tours around the head of the lake, climbing over the ridge, connecting with Fayette Lake (3 miles), and linking with trails into the Bridger Wilderness. Families can enjoy the sandy beach at the campground for swimming and playing in the water. The narrow winding Skyline Drive is worth the nine-mile drive up to Elkhart Park for the views of the Wind River Mountains and Bridger Wilderness; from there, a 10-mile-round trip trail leads to Photographer's Point.

The campground curls one main loop in the willows on the west end of the lake. The trees and brush leave the campsites with no views of the lake. However, several campsites sit very close to lake, where the sandy beach offers a place to swim, fish, and moor boats. The tight campground loop cramps large RVs, and overgrowth scrunches places for setting up tents.

Campsites, facilities: The campground has 15 RV or tent campsites and one tent-only site. RVs are limited to 40 feet. Facilities include picnic tables, fire rings, vault toilets, and boat launch. Bring your own drinking water, or treat lake water. Leashed pets are permitted.

Reservations, fees: Reservations are not accepted. Camping costs $7. Open June-early September.

Directions: From Highway 191 in Pinedale, turn northeast onto Fremont Lake Road for four miles. Continue straight onto Skyline Drive for 3.8 miles. Turn right and drive on the dirt Forest Road 114 for 1.1 miles and turn right to reach the campground entrance. GPS Coordinates: N 42° 56.206' W 109° 45.666'

Contact: Bridger-Teton National Forest, Pinedale Ranger District, 29 E. Fremont Lake Rd., Pinedale, WY 82941, 307/367-4326, www.fs.usda.gov/btnf.

43 TRAIL'S END

Scenic rating: 8

in the Wind River Mountains in Bridger-Teton National Forest

At 9,300 feet, Trail's End Campground has the distinction of being the highest vehicle-accessed campground in the Wind River Mountains. Also known as Elkhart, the area is a leap off point into the Bridger Wilderness, with alpine wildflower meadows interspersed with forests splayed out on gray rocky monoliths. Trails depart for lakes and connect eventually with the Continental Divide. Anglers may want to hike two miles to Long Lake to fish for trout. But the best day hike destination heads five miles to Photographer's Point, where expansive views include rugged peaks over 13,000 feet. Horse facilities including corrals are available at the trailhead. During the summer, the Forest Service maintains an information A-frame at Elkhart. The campground attracts hunters in fall.

Be ready for the high elevation of this campground. Just walking to the toilet will tucker you out if you aren't acclimatized to the altitude. In midsummer, the campground can fill up; plan to arrive early to get a spot. Otherwise, you can camp in several primitive sites on Skyline Drive. While plenty of spectacular views await hikers, those sticking to the campground will see mostly meadows and forest rather than peaks. Be ready for voracious mosquitoes.

Campsites, facilities: The campground has eight RV or tent campsites. RVs are limited to 20 feet. Facilities include picnic tables, fire rings, vault toilets, and drinking water. Leashed pets are permitted.

Reservations, fees: Reservations are not accepted. Camping costs $12. Open June-mid-September, depending on snow.

Directions: From Highway 191 in Pinedale, turn northeast onto Fremont Lake Road for four miles. Continue straight onto Skyline Drive for about 12 miles until the road's end. GPS Coordinates: N 43° 0.324' W 109° 45.151'

Contact: Bridger-Teton National Forest, Pinedale Ranger District, 29 E. Fremont Lake Rd., Pinedale, WY 82941, 307/367-4326, www. fs.usda.gov/btnf.

44 BOULDER LAKE (BLM)

Scenic rating: 5

in the Wind River Mountains

At 7,300 feet, the BLM Boulder Lake Campground is located at the foot of the four-mile-long Boulder Lake on the north side of the dam. Anglers can fish the creek below the dam and the lake, which is surrounded by dry sagebrush foothills broken by rocky outcroppings. You can launch hand-carried watercraft from primitive ramps, but larger boats must launch from the boat ramp on the west end of the lake accessed via the Boulder Lake Road. Boulder Creek, which flows west from the lake's dam, tumbles about 1.5 miles down to Stokes Crossing, located on the south side of the stream.

Both campgrounds are quite primitive and raw in comparison to the USFS Boulder Lake Campground at the head of the lake. The dirt sites at both campgrounds have full sun, territorial and water views, no shade, and are subject to wind. Rocks and sagebrush surround the campsites.

Campsites, facilities: Boulder Lake Campground has four RV or tent campsites. Stokes Crossing Campground has two campsites. RVs are limited to 40 feet. Facilities include picnic tables, fire rings with grills, and vault toilets. Bring your own drinking water, or treat lake and creek water. Pack out your trash. Leashed pets are permitted.

Reservations, fees: Reservations are not accepted. Camping is free. Open late May-mid-October.

Directions: From Boulder (south of Pinedale),

drive north on Burnt Lake Road for seven miles to Boulder Lake Campground. For Stokes Crossing, drive east on State Route 353 for 2.4 miles. Turn north onto the dirt and gravel Boulder Lake Road (Forest Road 125) for five miles. Turn left at the Stokes Crossing sign.

GPS Coordinates: N 42° 50.250' W 109° 42.303'

Contact: Bureau of Land Management, Pinedale Field Office, 1625 W. Pine St., Pinedale, WY 82941, 307/367-5300, www.blm.gov/wy/st/en/field_offices/Pinedale/recreation/developed_sites.html.

45 BOULDER LAKE (USFS)

Scenic rating: 7

in the Wind River Mountains in Bridger-Teton National Forest

At 7,300 feet, Boulder Lake Campground is located at the head of the four-mile-long Boulder Lake. But the campground actually sits on Boulder Creek, which runs into the lake. Anglers can fish the creek and the lake, which is surrounded by dry sagebrush foothills broken by rocky outcroppings. You can launch hand-carried watercraft into the creek or at the lake's head, but larger boats must launch from the primitive boat ramps on the west end of the lake. For access to the Bridger Wilderness, the Boulder Creek Trailhead with horse corrals sits adjacent to the campground. Trails loop to a myriad of lakes including Burnt, Blueberry, and Lovatt Lakes. Another trail wanders up the Boulder Canyon to the Continental Divide. Swimmers can enjoy the lake.

One campground loop circles through a mixed forest of aspens, lodgepole pine, and willows. A few of the grassy, private campsites have views of the lakes while others pick up territorial views. The location at the end of the road guarantees nighttime quiet.

Campsites, facilities: The campground has

20 RV or tent campsites. RVs are limited to 40 feet. Some pull-through sites are available. Facilities include picnic tables, fire rings, vault toilets, and lantern holders. Bring your own drinking water, or treat lake water. Pack out your trash. Leashed pets are permitted.

Reservations, fees: Reservations are not accepted. Camping costs $7. Open June-mid-October.

Directions: From Boulder (south of Pinedale), drive east on State Route 353 for 2.4 miles. Turn north onto the dirt and gravel Boulder Lake Road (Forest Road 125) for six miles. At a fork, veer right for 4.5 miles to the campground entrance across the creek.

GPS Coordinates: N 42° 51.406' W 109° 37.039'

Contact: Bridger-Teton National Forest, Pinedale Ranger District, 29 E. Fremont Lake Rd., Pinedale, WY 82941, 307/367-4326, www.fs.usda.gov/btnf.

46 SCAB CREEK

Scenic rating: 6

in the Wind River Mountains

At 8,200 feet in the southern Wind River Range foothills, the Scab Creek Campground is mostly used by those launching into the Bridger Wilderness. From the trailhead, the route bolts with a steep grunt for two miles, but moderates into more gentle grades after entering the wilderness. Anglers hike the 2.5 miles to Divide Lake for fishing, and horseback riders cruise farther to a series of high alpine lakes along the Continental Divide. Above the campground, a jumble of rocky buttresses provide habitat for marmots, and about 45 minutes up the trail, rock climbers scale a popular 400-foot granite slab known as the Scab Creek Buttress.

The ultra quiet campground gains partial shade from a loose lodgepole and aspen forest.

In early summer, elk frequent the grass, sagebrush, and wildflower meadows that surround the campground. A horse camp was added to accommodate those traveling with stock. Be prepared for heavy mosquitoes and black flies in summer, but enjoy the brilliant stars from this altitude.

Campsites, facilities: The campground has nine RV or tent campsites. RVs are limited to 31 feet. Facilities include picnic tables, fire rings with grills, and vault toilets. Bring your own drinking water, or treat creek water. Pack out your trash. Leashed pets are permitted.

Reservations, fees: Reservations are not accepted. Camping is free. Open May-mid-November, snow permitting.

Directions: From Boulder (south of Pinedale), drive east on State Route 353 for seven miles. Turn north onto the gravel Scab Creek Road for 1.4 miles. Veer left and go 7.3 curvy miles that climb to the campground at the road's end.

GPS Coordinates: N 42° 49.247' W 109° 33.162'

Contact: Bureau of Land Management, Pinedale Field Office, 1625 W. Pine St., Pinedale, WY 82941, 307/367-5300, www.blm.gov/wy/st/en/field_offices/Pinedale/recreation/developed_sites.html.

47 BIG SANDY

Scenic rating: 7

in the Wind River Mountains in Bridger-Teton National Forest

At 9,100 feet in the southern Wind River Range, remote Big Sandy Campground requires hours of laborious, bumpy dirt-road driving to reach it. Despite the rough roads, you'll arrive to parking areas brimming with 50-60 cars because of the popular trailhead, which accesses both the Bridger and Popo Agie Wildernesses, lakes for fishing, and the Cirque

High elevation Jackass Pass accesses Cirque of the Towers in the Popo Agie Wilderness.

© BECKY LOMAX

of the Towers rock-climbing area. Day hikes lead to three small lakes within 3.5 miles, Big Sandy Lake (5.3 miles), and Jackass Pass (7.7 miles), the latter with stunning views into the Cirque of the Towers. Horse facilities (corrals, ramps, and hitch rails) are available. Big Sandy River flows past the campground, offering wade-fishing for brook and Yellowstone cutthroat trout.

Despite the number of cars, the campground is quiet. Grassy campsites vary between sunny and open with views of vehicles to shaded under mature lodgepoles within earshot of the river. All have large flat spaces for tents. The three spacious campsites at the end of the turnaround may see each other, but not the hordes of vehicles, plus they are shaded from the late afternoon heat. Campers not acclimatized to high elevation will feel shortness of breath at the altitude.

Campsites, facilities: The campground has 12 RV or tent campsites. Some grassy parking pads can accommodate midsized RVs, but leveling is difficult and the access road brutal.

Facilities include picnic tables, fire rings with grills or fire pits, pit and vault toilets, and bear boxes. Drinking water is not available. Bring your own, or treat river water. Leashed pets are permitted.

Reservations, fees: Reservations are not accepted. Campsites cost $7. Cash or check. Open mid-June-early September.

Directions: From Highway 191 south of Pinedale, drive 19 miles east on Highway 353 to where pavement ends. Turn east onto Big Sandy Elkhorn Road for 8.6 miles. Turn east onto the Lander Cutoff Road for seven miles. Turn north onto Big Sandy Road for 10 miles. Plan on one hour to drive the rugged, narrow Big Sandy Road. From Highway 28 at South Pass, you can also drive the dirt Lander Cutoff Road for 25 miles to reach Big Sandy Road. GPS Coordinates: N 42° 41.258' W 109° 16.283'

Contact: Bridger-Teton National Forest, Pinedale Ranger District, 29 E. Fremont Lake Rd., Pinedale, WY 82941, 307/367-4326, www.fs.usda.gov/btnf.

© BECKY LOMAX

Brooks Lake sits high on Wyoming's Continental Divide.

48 BROOKS LAKE

Scenic rating: 10

in the Absaroka Mountains in Shoshone
National Forest

BEST (

Located at 9,100 feet, Brooks Lake sits on the
Continental Divide, squeezed between large
orange buttresses of rock. The campground
looks across the lake to the Pinnacles, spires
that capture the alpenglow of the setting sun.
The Continental Divide Trail departs from
the lake, and trails loop around the Pinnacles.
Trails also lead to Upper Jade Lake, Upper
Brooks Lake, and Rainbow Lake. At the
campground, a primitive boat ramp aids those
launching small boats (motors are okay) for
paddling the shoreline of the 234-acre lake or
fishing for rainbow and brook trout. The lake
has exceptionally clear water in early summer,
but as it overturns at the end of August, it takes
on a green cast from algae. Historical Brooks
Lake Lodge sits behind the campground, with
its horses grazing near the lake.

Recent thinning, to control fungus in the
pine trees at the ultra-quiet campground,
changed some of the campsites from deep
shade to partial shade. Two short gravel spurs
and one gravel loop make up the campground,
with the loop offering sites 10-13 overlooking
the lake and pinnacles. Most of the loop sites
are open, close together, and substitute privacy
for stunning location; the spur campsites are
more private. You will feel the high elevation
walking from the lake back to your campsite.
Campsites, facilities: The campground has
13 RV or tent campsites. RVs are limited to 32
feet. Facilities include picnic tables, fire rings
with grills, vault toilets, bear boxes, garbage
service, and campground hosts. Drinking
water is not available; treat lake water. (You
can also get potable water one mile east at
Pinnacles Campground.) Leashed pets are
permitted.
Reservations, fees: Reservations are not accepted. Campsites cost $10. Cash or check.
Open July-early September.
Directions: On Highway 26/287, drive 22
miles west from Dubois or 33 miles east from

Moran Junction. At milepost 33, turn north onto Brooks Lake Road (Forest Road 515). Drive four miles and veer left at the fork. At the signed junction, turn left for 0.6 mile, and turn sharp right at Brooks Lake Lodge, dropping 0.2 mile to the lake.

GPS Coordinates: N 43° 45.017' W 110° 0.320'

Contact: Shoshone National Forest, Wind River Ranger District, 1403 W. Ramshorn, Dubois, WY 82513, 307/455-2466, www.fs.usda.gov/shoshone.

49 PINNACLES

Scenic rating: 10

in the Absaroka Mountains in Shoshone National Forest

BEST

Located at 9,142 feet, Pinnacles Campground nestles below an orange butte of fantastical pinnacles—hence its name. The Pinnacles are a photographer's delight, best shot in late afternoon and evening light. The campground also sits on Brooks Lake and borders its outlet creek. The Continental Divide Trail departs from the lake, and trails loop around the Pinnacles. Trailheads within two miles also lead to Bonneville Pass and the Pinnacles. You can launch boats, canoes, and kayaks from Brooks Lake Campground one mile to the west. Both the lake and the creek have rainbow and brook trout along with splake, a cross between the two. The lake has exceptionally clear water in early summer, but as it overturns at the end of August, it takes on a green cast from algae. Be ready at this high elevation for afternoon thunderstorms.

In contrast to nearby Brooks Lake Campground, Pinnacles offers more private, shadier campsites spread out across a bigger area. The hilly campground has one loop with some campsites tucked directly under the Pinnacles (site 10 grabs a good view of them) and six campsites overlooking Brooks Lake (these can

be windy). The ultra-quiet campground in the mixed subalpine fir and pine forest has both gravel pull-through and back-in parking pads. Sites 1 and 2 are positioned for snippets of Pinnacle views, but with traffic at the entrance.

Campsites, facilities: The campground has 21 RV or tent campsites. RVs are limited to 32 feet. Facilities include picnic tables, fire rings with grills, vault toilets, bear boxes, drinking water, garbage service, and campground hosts. Leashed pets are permitted.

Reservations, fees: Reservations are not accepted. Campsites cost $15. Cash or check. Open late June-mid-September.

Directions: On Highway 26/287, drive 22 miles west from Dubois or 33 miles east from Moran Junction. At milepost 33, turn north onto Brooks Lake Road (Forest Road 515). Drive four miles and veer left at the fork for 0.3 mile. At the signed junction, turn right, crossing the bridge into the campground.

GPS Coordinates: N 43° 45.114' W 109° 59.740'

Contact: Shoshone National Forest, Wind River Ranger District, 1403 W. Ramshorn, Dubois, WY 82513, 307/455-2466, www.fs.usda.gov/shoshone.

50 FALLS

Scenic rating: 8

in the Absaroka Mountains in Shoshone National Forest, Wyoming

Falls Campground, elevation 8,366 feet, sits just east of Togwotee Pass on Wyoming's Centennial Scenic Byway. The campground is one convenient for cyclists touring the highway and those needing a campground before hitting Grand Teton National Park, 40 minutes west. An interpretive wheelchair-accessible trail leads to an overlook of the falls that gives the campground its name. Hiking trails, boating, canoeing, and fishing are available five miles to the north at Brooks Lake.

The campground's location on the busy highway explains the hum of vehicle noise. However, the road is not a major trucking thoroughfare, so traffic does quiet somewhat after dark. The partly shaded campsites tuck under a loose mixed forest of pines and subalpine firs in two loops. Neighboring campsites are visible, but not stacked close like a parking lot. Gravel back-in and pull-through parking spurs access the campsites, some of which grab snippets of views of the Pinnacles to the north. **Campsites, facilities:** The campground has 54 campsites. Loop A is geared toward RVs with 20 campsites with electrical hookups, and loop B is geared more toward tent campers with 34 sites, including five walk-ins. RVs are limited to 32 feet. Facilities include picnic tables, fire rings with grills, vault toilets, bear boxes, drinking water, garbage service, and campground hosts. Leashed pets are permitted. Wheelchair-accessible facilities include toilets and campsites.

Reservations, fees: Reservations are not accepted. Campsites cost $15, or $20 with electricity. Cash or check. Open mid-June-late September.

Directions: On Highway 26/287, drive 22.5 miles west from Dubois or 32.5 miles east from Moran Junction. At milepost 32.5, turn southeast off the highway onto the campground road. GPS Coordinates: N 43° 42.409' W 109° 58.248'

Contact: Shoshone National Forest, Wind River Ranger District, 1403 W. Ramshorn, Dubois, WY 82513, 307/455-2466, www. fs.usda.gov/shoshone.

51 DOUBLE CABIN

Scenic rating: 9

in the Absaroka Mountains in Shoshone National Forest

At 8,100 feet, Double Cabin Campground

enjoys seldom seen views of the Absaroka Mountains because it is long miles from the highway. But those who go here must be prepared for the tedious slow driving on the single-lane access road that is rough in places. The campground sits at the confluence of Frontier Creek and Wiggins Fork pour from the Washakie Wilderness, offering fly-fishing for trout. Several trails for hikers and horseback riders lead into the wilderness, which surrounds the campground. The Frontier Creek Trail #818 leads seven miles to a petrified forest.

For utter quiet far from a highway, the campground provides a remote hideaway. The campsites tuck under a forest of spruce and lodgepoles in one loop. Most of the campsites have spectacular views of the surrounding rugged peaks that climb more than 11,000 feet high.

Campsites, facilities: The campground has 14 RV or tent campsites. RVs are limited to 32 feet. Facilities include picnic tables, fire rings with grills, vault toilets (wheelchair-accessible), bear boxes, drinking water, garbage service, tent pads, and campground hosts. Leashed pets are permitted.

Reservations, fees: Reservations are not accepted. Campsites cost $15. Cash or check. Open late May-late September.

Directions: From Dubois, drive north on Horse Creek Road (Forest Road 285), which turns into a gravel road before four miles. At seven miles, veer right at the fork and continue for three miles. Turn right and drive for two miles. Veer right (Forest Road 285) and drive for 13 miles to the campground. GPS Coordinates: N 43° 48.396' W 109° 33.646'

Contact: Shoshone National Forest, Wind River Ranger District, 1403 W. Ramshorn, Dubois, WY 82513, 307/455-2466, www. fs.usda.gov/shoshone.

52 HORSE CREEK

🛶 🏕 ♿ 🚐 ⛺

Scenic rating: 7

in the Absaroka Mountains in Shoshone
National Forest

At 7,700 feet, Horse Creek Campground
flanks the arid southern slopes of the Absaroka Mountains. From the campground, you
can see only the lower sagebrush-, grass-, and
forest-covered rounded foothills rather than
the rocky peaks of the high Absarokas. Horse
Creek runs parallel to the campground, offering a place for anglers to go fly-fishing. The
stream usually clears of runoff sediments by
July, with the remainder of summer and early
fall offering decent fly-fishing.

With its location far from town and the
highway, the campground gives campers a
place to find quiet. The campsites have a mix
of shade and sun: some tuck into forested
nooks for privacy while others that are more
open garner territorial views. Lodgepole pines
and brush separate the campsites. Paths lead
to the stream for wading or fishing.
Campsites, facilities: The campground has
nine RV or tent campsites. RVs are limited to
32 feet. Facilities include picnic tables, fire
rings with grills, vault toilets (wheelchair-
accessible), bear boxes, drinking water, and
garbage service. Leashed pets are permitted.
Reservations, fees: Reservations are not accepted. Campsites cost $15. Cash or check.
Open late May-late September.
Directions: From Dubois, drive north on
Horse Creek Road (Forest Road 285) for 10
miles. (Around four miles, the road turns to
gravel and can be rough.) Turn north into the
campground.
GPS Coordinates: N 43° 40.003' W 109°
38.133'
Contact: Shoshone National Forest, Wind
River Ranger District, 1403 W. Ramshorn,
Dubois, WY 82513, 307/455-2466, www.
fs.usda.gov/shoshone.

53 WIND RIVER KOA

🏊 🛶 🏕 🚴 🚐 ⛺

Scenic rating: 6

in Dubois

At 6,917 feet, the Wind River KOA makes
a good base camp for exploring the Wind
River Mountains to the south or the Absaroka Mountains to the north. It also makes
for a place to camp en route to Yellowstone
and Grand Teton National Parks. The Wind
River flows past the campground, offering
trout fishing and riverside relaxation, and
with the campground's location in town, you
can walk to shops and restaurants. Dubois is
a cowboy town with rodeos, square dances,
and western celebrations during the summer.

Only a few small cottonwood trees for shade
cluster in a portion of the grassy campground
where narrow sites line up in parking lot fashion. The sunny campground affords an easy
place for satellite reception. Many campsites
capture views of the Wind River Mountains.
Campsites, facilities: The campground
has 43 RV campsites and 14 tent campsites.
RVs are limited to 80 feet. There are 17 pull-
though sites for big RVs. Hookups include
water, sewer, and electricity up to 50 amps.
Three RV sites cater to equestrians with horse
corrals. Two of the tent sites have electricity
and water. Facilities include picnic tables, fire
rings with grills, flush toilets, showers, launderette, drinking water, indoor swimming
pool (late May-early September), game room,
playground, wireless Internet, cable TV, camp
store, and firewood for sale. Leashed pets are
permitted.
Reservations, fees: Reservations are accepted
(800/562-0806). Hookups cost $48-54. Tent
sites cost $28-32. Rates cover two people. For
extra campers, add $4-6. Kids under six stay
free. Open mid-May-September.
Directions: From Highway 26 in Dubois, turn
south on Riverton Street and drive one block
to the campground entrance straight ahead.

GPS Coordinates: N 43° 31.949' W 109° 38.148'

Contact: Dubois/Wind River KOA, 225 Welty Street, Dubois, WY 82513, 307/445-2238, www.koa.com.

54 DICKINSON CREEK
🏃 🛶 🐎 🚐 ⛰

Scenic rating: 9

in the Wind River Mountains in Shoshone National Forest

At 9,358 feet, Dickinson Creek Campground sits just outside the Popo Agie Wilderness in Dickinson Park between Black Mountain and Dishpan Butte. Trails for hikers and horseback riders lead to high alpine lakes. Anglers head to Shoshone Lake to fish for trout. Access to the campground is over private Wind River Indian Reservation Lands. All persons in the vehicle are required to purchase tribal fishing licenses to cross the reservation. They are available at Hines Store. Stunning mountain views accompany the drive to the campground.

This little visited campground can guarantee quiet and solitude, miles from the hubbub of civilization. A loose forest of lodgepoles shades some of the campsites, and the campground forest is surrounded by the expansive meadows of Dickinson Park. Some of the campsites garner views of the wilderness peaks. Campers not acclimatized to high elevation may feel shortness of breath. Be prepared for voracious mosquitoes and daily afternoon thunderstorms.

Campsites, facilities: The campground has 15 RV or tent campsites. RVs are limited to 20 feet. Facilities include picnic tables, cook grates, and vault toilets. No drinking water is available; treat creek water. Pack out your trash. Leashed pets are permitted.

Reservations, fees: Reservations are not accepted. Campsites cost $15. Cash or check. Open May-November, snow permitting.

Directions: From Lander, drive Highway 287

northwest for 15 miles, or from Fort Washakie, drive 0.7 miles south. At Hines General Store, turn west onto Trout Creek Road for 5.5 miles. Go straight through the intersection and drive for 17 miles on Moccasin Creek Road. Veer left at forks to stay on Moccasin Creek Road, which turns into Forest Road 329 at the forest boundary. Through the Wind River Indian Reservation, the narrow, rocky dirt road with no turnouts can beat up RVs. Be prepared to handle flat tires and other vehicle emergencies. GPS Coordinates: N 42° 50.188' W 109° 3.423'

Contact: Shoshone National Forest, Washakie Ranger District, 333 E. Main St., Lander, WY 82520, 307/332-5460, www.fs.usda.gov/shoshone.

55 SLEEPING BEAR RV PARK
🏕 🚐 ♿ 🚐 ⛰

Scenic rating: 6

in Lander

At 5,491 feet, the Sleeping Bear RV Park and Campground sits on the southern edge of Lander, home to NOLS (Northwest Outdoor Leadership School). Visitors to Lander can explore the Museum of the American West, take in a rodeo, check out casinos, or hook up with guides for fishing, rock climbing, and horseback riding. Downtown Lander includes a few galleries, shops, and restaurants. The local 18-hole golf course flanks the campground, and Sinks Canyon State Park sits just southwest of town.

Given the highway location and the nearby airport, you'll hear traffic and airplanes in the campground. Gravel back-in and pull-through RV sites line up with minimal privacy in parking lot fashion, and tent camping flanks the north perimeter. Some permanent residents live in the campground. Grassy campsites have full sun; a few trees dot the center island of RV sites. Views span the Wind River Range and the lights of Lander at night.

Campsites, facilities: The campground has 45 RV campsites and 10 tent campsites. RVs are limited to 65 feet. Hookups include water, sewer, and electricity up to 50 amps. Facilities include picnic tables, fire rings, flush toilets (wheelchair-accessible), showers, launderette, drinking water, splash park, playground, wireless Internet, dog run, propane and firewood for sale, disposal station, and camp store. Leashed pets are permitted.

Reservations, fees: Reservations are accepted. Hookups cost $25-39. Tent sites cost $21. Rates cover two people. For extra campers, add $2-4. Kids under six stay free. Open year-round.

Directions: On Highway 287, drive south in Lander for 0.5 mile past Buena Vista Drive. Turn right into the park.

GPS Coordinates: N 42° 49.485' W 108° 43.139'

Contact: Sleeping Bear RV Park and Campground, 515 E. Main Street, Lander, WY 82520, 307/332-5159 or 888/757-2327, www.sleepingbearrvpark.com.

56 PIONEER RV PARK

Scenic rating: 6

in Lander

At 5,491 feet, the Sleeping Bear RV Park and Campground sits on the southern edge of Lander, home to NOLS (Northwest Outdoor Leadership School). Visitors to Lander can explore the Museum of the American West, take in a rodeo, or hook up with guides for fishing, rock climbing, and horseback riding. Downtown Lander includes a few galleries, shops, and restaurants. The local 18-hole golf course flanks the campground, and Sinks Canyon State Park sits just southwest of town.

At this location on the highway, you'll hear traffic and airplanes, as the airport sits nearby. The sunny, treeless campground consists of gravel pull-through RV sites lined up with minimal privacy in parking lot fashion, but the owners take great care to keep the lawns green and potted flowers blooming. A long strip of lawn flanks all campsites, and views span the Wind River Range.

Campsites, facilities: The campground has 22 RV campsites. RVs are limited to 90 feet. Hookups include water, sewer, and electricity up to 50 amps. Facilities include picnic tables, launderette, drinking water, and wireless Internet. No showers or toilets. Leashed pets are permitted.

Reservations, fees: Reservations are accepted. Hookups cost $28. Open May-September.

Directions: On Highway 287, drive one mile south of Lander to Sunflower Street and turn right.

GPS Coordinates: N 42° 48.879' W 108° 42.751'

Contact: Pioneer RV Park, 176 Sunflower Street, Lander, WY 82520, 307/332-0155 or 888/875-5238, www.pioneerrv.com.

57 SAWMILL

Scenic rating: 8

in the Wind River Mountains

At 6,200 feet in Sinks Canyon State Park, Sawmill is one of two state park campgrounds in the narrow, arid sagebrush canyon. Sinks Canyon, an Ice Age feature, acquired its name from the disappearance of the Middle Fork of the Popo Agie River (pronounced po-PO-zha). The river enters a limestone cave and sinks underground only to emerge 0.25 mile lower in a pool called The Rise. The park's visitors center (open Labor Day-Memorial Day) sits 0.5 mile up the highway, where hikers can access the one-mile Popo Agie Nature Trail and the four-mile Canyon Loop Trail. The Sinks area is near the visitors center; a 0.25-mile trail leads to The Rise. Fishing is available in portions of the Popo Agie River but not permitted in The Rise pond.

Tucked along the roaring, boulder-strewn river in the canyon bottom, Sawmill is a small, sunny campground right on the highway. However, traffic dwindles after dark, as the road is a forest access rather than a trucking route. A few cottonwoods lend partial shade, and several campsites are open to the road. Tent space is limited in the very small and cramped sites. The campground is best suited as an overflow site for Popo Agie Campground one mile southwest. A wildlife-watching area—visible from several campsites—sits on the opposite side of the highway. Look for bighorn sheep and golden eagles.

Campsites, facilities: The campground has four RV or tent campsites that can fit small RVs. Facilities include picnic tables, fire rings with grills, vault toilets (wheelchair-accessible), drinking water, playground, and garbage service. Leashed pets are permitted.

Reservations, fees: Reservations are not accepted. Campsites cost $10 for Wyoming residents, $17 for nonresidents. Rates include day-use fees. Cash or check. Open May-September.

Directions: From Lander, drive south on Highway 131 for six miles. At milepost 7, turn left into the campground.

GPS Coordinates: N 42° 45.423' W 108° 47.982'

Contact: Sinks Canyon State Park, 3079 Sinks Canyon Rd., Lander, WY 82520, 307/332-6333 or 307/332-3077, http://wyoparks.state.wy.us.

58 POPO AGIE

Scenic rating: 8
in the Wind River Mountains

In Sinks Canyon State Park, Popo Agie Campground (pronounced po-PO-zha), elevation 6,750 feet, is the largest of the two state park campgrounds in the narrow, arid sagebrush canyon housing the Middle Fork of the Popo Agie River. Sinks Canyon, an Ice Age feature,

acquired its name from the disappearance of the river, which enters a limestone cave and sinks underground only to emerge 0.25 mile lower in a pool called The Rise. The park's visitors center (open Labor Day-Memorial Day) sits 0.5 mile down the highway. The Sinks cavern is near the visitors center; a 0.25-mile trail leads to The Rise. From the campground, a bridge crosses the river to access the one-mile Popo Agie Nature Trail and the four-mile Canyon Loop Trail. Fishing for rainbow trout is available in portions of the Popo Agie River but not permitted in The Rise pond. Rock climbers tackle several routes in Sinks Canyon.

Set in junipers, cottonwoods, and sagebrush, the sunny campground squeezes in between the highway and the river. The roar of the river with early summer high runoff drowns out vehicle noise from the highway, which, as a forest access, is not used for commercial trucking. A paved road winds through the campground, connecting paved parking pads. Most sites can only accommodate small tents. The campground offers a mix of privacy, with some sites very open and others more sheltered with privacy. Sites 13, 15, 16, 19, and 20-23 overlook the river.

Campsites, facilities: The campground has 21 RV or tent campsites plus three walk-in tent sites. RVs are limited to 35 feet, although one site can fit a 45-footer. Facilities include picnic tables, fire rings with grills, vault toilets (wheelchair-accessible), drinking water, and garbage service. Leashed pets are permitted.

Reservations, fees: Reservations are not accepted. Campsites cost $10 for Wyoming residents, $17 for nonresidents. Rates include day-use fees. Cash or check. Open May-September.

Directions: From Lander, drive south on Highway 131 for seven miles. At milepost 8.2, turn left into the campground.

GPS Coordinates: N 42° 44.560' W 108° 49.206'

Contact: Sinks Canyon State Park, 3079 Sinks Canyon Rd., Lander, WY 82520, 307/332-6333 or 307/332-3077, http://wyoparks.state.wy.us.

59 SINKS CANYON

Scenic rating: 8

in the Wind River Mountains in Shoshone National Forest

At 6,850 feet in Sinks Canyon, Sinks Canyon Campground squeezes between the Middle Fork of the Popo Agie River and the canyon highway. Sinks Canyon, an ice age feature, acquired its name from the disappearing river, which enters a limestone cave and sinks underground only to emerge 0.25 mile lower in a pool called The Rise. The state park visitors center (open Labor Day-Memorial Day), The Sinks, and The Rise sit one mile down the highway. Fishing for rainbow trout is available along the river. From the campground, a bridge crosses the river to access the four-mile Canyon Loop Trail. From Bruces picnic area 1.5 miles southeast, a trail leads 1.6 miles to Popo Agie Falls, a series of roaring cascades. Bicyclists and scenic drivers also tour the Loop Road, which climbs above the campground in a series of switchbacks and continues 33 miles to Highway 28. The pavement ends after eight miles. Sinks Canyon also attracts rock climbers.

In a thin forest of aspens, lodgepoles, and junipers, the sunny campground tucks between the highway and the river. Most of the campsites are open to the highway, but the views also yield sights of the streaked canyon walls and the split habitat of the canyon's sagebrush north slopes and forested south slopes. The highway—a forest access road—sees traffic in midsummer but quiets after dark, as the route is not used for commercial trucking. The river, which is strewn with large boulders, roars in early summer. Tenters find more space here than at the two nearby state park campgrounds; sites 1-3 offer shaded walk-in sites for tents.

Campsites, facilities: The campground has 11 RV or tent campsites and three walk-in tent campsites. RVs are limited to 20 feet. Facilities include picnic tables, fire rings with grills, vault toilets (wheelchair-accessible), drinking water, bear boxes, garbage service, firewood for sale, tent platforms, and campground hosts. Leashed pets are permitted.

Reservations, fees: Reservations are not accepted. Campsites cost $15. Cash or check. Open May-November, but services are shut off October 1.

Directions: From Lander, drive Highway 131 eight miles southeast. Turn left into the campground at milepost 9.

GPS Coordinates: N 42° 44.197' W 108° 50.160'

Contact: Shoshone National Forest, Washakie Ranger District, 333 E. Main St., Lander, WY 82520, 307/332-5460, www.fs.usda.gov/shoshone.

60 WORTHEN MEADOWS

Scenic rating: 8

in the Wind River Mountains in Shoshone National Forest

At 8,850 feet, Worthen Meadows Campground sits on the south shores of cold Worthen Meadows Reservoir, which provides water for the city of Lander. Surrounded by large granite boulders and lodgepoles, the reservoir is named for the high elevation sagebrush and lupine meadows in the area. A trailhead accesses Roaring Fork, Stough Creek Lakes, and the Sheep Bridge Trail in Popo Agie Wilderness. Anglers go after brook and rainbow trout in the reservoir, best fished from a boat, and the small lake offers canoers and kayakers a place to paddle. Water levels can drop in the reservoir by late summer; call the Forest Service for status. Mountain bikers tour the dirt Loop Road (Hwy. 131) to Louis Lake.

The campground is divided into two sections—one sitting on each side of the boat ramp. The Lakeside loop has 20 campsites, with sites 9, 10, and 12-15 overlooking the reservoir. The partly shaded campsites tuck under aspens and lodgepoles with whortleberry and pine needle duff forest floors. Eight sites sprawl around the Hilltop loop on a peninsula, with sites 4 and 5 overlooking the water. Sites are spread out for privacy, but the lack of understory allows visibility of neighboring campers from some campsites. Both gravel pull-through and back-in sites are available. The campground is extremely quiet, except for the loud squawking of Clark's nutcrackers.

Campsites, facilities: The campground has 28 RV or tent campsites. RVs are limited to 24 feet. Facilities include picnic tables, fire rings with grills, vault toilets (wheelchair-accessible), drinking water, bear boxes, garbage service, tent platforms, and campground hosts. Leashed pets are permitted.

Reservations, fees: Reservations are not accepted. Campsites cost $15. Cash or check. Open July-September.

Directions: From Lander, drive Highway 131 (also known as The Loop or Louis Lake Road) for 16 miles south, climbing up the series of Loop switchbacks. Turn right at the signed junction and the end of the pavement onto Forest Road 302. Drive 2.4 miles, veering left at the youth camp and the unmarked entrance to the reservoir. Turn right into the campground. GPS Coordinates: N 42° 41.885' W 108° 55.721'

Contact: Shoshone National Forest, Washakie Ranger District, 333 E. Main St., Lander, WY 82520, 307/332-5460, www.fs.usda.gov/shoshone.

61 FIDDLERS LAKE

Scenic rating: 8

in the Wind River Mountains in Shoshone National Forest

At 9,400 feet, the remote 57-acre Fiddlers Lake houses a beaver lodge, yellow water lilies, brook trout, boat ramp, boat dock, and campground. The lake, which is stocked annually with rainbow trout, is cold, retaining ice often through May. It's best for small boats and canoes. With stock facilities, the trailhead to Christina Lake (#721)—a scenic popular fishing lake—is 0.5 mile south on The Loop. The 4.3-mile trail climbs to the lake. The same trailhead also leads four miles into the Popo Agie Wilderness to Upper Silas Lake. A 0.7-mile trail, one mile north of Fiddlers Lake, climbs to Blue Ridge Lookout, an abandoned fire lookout at 9,998 feet with views of the Wind River Range. Mountain bikers ride The Loop road.

If you're looking for solitude and quiet, Fiddlers Lake offers both in abundance. The campground sprawls along the north and west sides of the idyllic lake, with sunny or shaded campsites spread out for privacy; however, some sites are open to the campground road. Sites 5, 7, 8-10, and 18-20 overlook the lake. Many of the lake sites have pull-over gravel parking pads; the other campsites have back-ins. The surrounding lodgepole forest is broken by grassy meadows of purple lupine and white yarrow. Campers not acclimatized to high elevation will feel shortness of breath at the altitude.

Campsites, facilities: The campground has 16 RV or tent campsites and four walk-in tent sites. RVs are limited to 40 feet. Facilities include picnic tables, fire rings with grills, benches, pedestal grills, vault toilets (wheelchair-accessible), drinking water, bear boxes, garbage service, tent platforms, and campground hosts. Leashed pets are permitted.

Reservations, fees: Reservations are not accepted. Campsites cost $15. Cash or check. Open June-September, snow permitting.

Directions: From Lander, drive Highway 131 (also known as The Loop or Louis Lake Road) for 21 miles southeast. The last five miles are on a narrow dirt road. Turn right and drive 0.3 mile into the campground. GPS Coordinates: N 42° 38.047' W 108° 52.823'

Contact: Shoshone National Forest, Washakie Ranger District, 333 E. Main St., Lander,

WY 82520, 307/332-5460, www.fs.usda. gov/shoshone.

62 LITTLE POPO AGIE

🥾 🚴 🛶 🎣 ♿ 🚐 ⛺

Scenic rating: 7

in the Wind River Mountains in Shoshone
National Forest

At 8,800 feet, Little Popo Agie (pronounced po-PO-zha) sits on the east side of the Wind River Range. A long, rough dirt road drive is required to reach it. Compared to the other three developed lake campgrounds on The Loop, this one sits near the Little Popo Agie River, which spills from Christina Lake. Trout fishing is available a three-minute walk from the campground near the single-lane bridge crossing the river. Watch for black bears and moose along the river. Hiking trails are available within 2-3 miles at Fiddlers and Louis Lakes. One mile south of the campground, the adjacent Maxon Basin loops with mountain-bike and ATV trails.

The four sites are located around the circumference of a gravel parking lot of this older, quiet, little-used campground surrounded by lodgepole and aspen trees. Whortleberries and lupines cover the ground, and some willow brush grows nearby, but the partly shaded campsites are open to each other. Ponds in the area can produce prodigious mosquitoes in July, but they abate by the end of August.

Campsites, facilities: The campground has four RV or tent campsites. RVs are limited to 16 feet. Facilities include picnic tables, fire grates, vault toilet (wheelchair-accessible), and garbage service. Drinking water is not available. Bring your own, or treat creek water. (You can also get water at Fiddlers Lake Campground two miles northwest.) Leashed pets are permitted.

Reservations, fees: Reservations are not accepted. Camping is free. Open July-September.

Directions: From Lander, drive Highway 131 (also known as The Loop or Louis Lake Road) for 23.5 miles. The last 7.5 miles are on a narrow, rough dirt road. Turn right into the campground.

GPS Coordinates: N 42° 36.503' W 108° 51.298'

Contact: Shoshone National Forest, Washakie Ranger District, 333 E. Main St., Lander, WY 82520, 307/332-5460, www.fs.usda. gov/shoshone.

63 LOUIS LAKE

🥾 🚴 🏊 🛶 🚤 🎣 🎣 ♿ 🚐 ⛺

Scenic rating: 8

in the Wind River Mountains in Shoshone
National Forest

Remote small Louis Lake, elevation 8,600 feet, offers boating, fishing, and swimming, but be prepared for cold water. The high elevation lake retains ice until late May. A boat launch with a ramp, dock, and trailer parking is available on the campground entrance road, and picnic areas with sandy swimming beaches sit on the opposite side of the lake. The Louis Lake Lodge runs a tiny camp store on the lake's west shore, rents canoes, kayaks, and fishing boats, and guides horseback tours. A Forest Service guard station also sits on the lake. A trail leads 4.5 miles to Christina Lake and 1.7 miles farther to Atlantic Lake in the Popo Agie Wilderness. Two miles north, mountain-bike and ATV trails also loop through Maxon Basin.

The quiet campground tucks at the bottom of a tall talus slope in a loose forest of aspens and lodgepoles. The small sunny sites are clustered close together with sites 6 and 7 overlooking the lake. A trickling stream, which flows only in early summer, runs through the campground loop.

Campsites, facilities: The campground has nine RV or tent campsites. RVs are limited to 24 feet. Facilities include picnic tables, fire rings with grills, vault toilets (wheelchair-accessible), bear boxes, and garbage service.

Drinking water is not available; treat lake water. Leashed pets are permitted.
Reservations, fees: Reservations are not accepted. Campsites cost $10. Cash or check. Open June-September.
Directions: From Lander, drive Highway 131 (also known as The Loop or Louis Lake Road) 26.5 miles (the final 10.5 are dirt). Watch for ATVs on the road, which narrows to one lane frequently. Turn left and drive 0.8 mile through giant potholes into the campground. Trailers may have trouble with some of the deeper potholes. Louis Lake can also be reached via an eight-mile drive on Forest Road 300 from Highway 28.
GPS Coordinates: N 42° 35.522' W 108° 50.624'
Contact: Shoshone National Forest, Washakie Ranger District, 333 E. Main St., Lander, WY 82520, 307/332-5460, www.fs.usda. gov/shoshone.

64 THREEMILE

Scenic rating: 8

in the Absaroka Mountains in Shoshone National Forest

On the North Fork of the Shoshone River, Threemile Campground, elevation 6,700 feet, allows the quickest access into Yellowstone National Park from the Buffalo Bill Scenic Byway. Debating whether to camp here or push on into the park? Consider that the drive to Fishing Bridge Campground requires more than an hour. Threemile snuggles into the narrow canyon between the Absaroka Mountains and Washakie Wilderness. From the campground, anglers wade-fish the river for rainbow, brown, and Yellowstone cutthroat trout. Rafters and kayakers put in here to float the Class I-III white water. As the river level drops throughout the summer in front of the campground, sand and rock bars form beaches. Sitting one mile west, Pahaska Tepee Resort features a

lodge built by Buffalo Bill Cody in 1904. The resort offers trail rides and has a convenience store, gas, restaurant, bar, and gift shop. The 22-mile Pahaska Trail (#751) leads hikers and horse-packers into the Absaroka Mountains.

The campground was thinned to remove beetle-killed trees, leaving much of it wide open and sunny. Views from many of the campsites span the forested hills and the river; however, they also now include the highway and other campsites. Road noise is pervasive in the campground, but it does quiet down at night. Thick cow parsnip meadows surround the campground.
Campsites, facilities: The campground has 20 RV campsites. RVs are limited to 32 feet. With the prevalence of bears, only hard-sided camping units are permitted (no tents, tent pop-ups, or tent trailers). Facilities include picnic tables, fire rings with grills, vault toilets (wheelchair-accessible), drinking water, lantern poles, bear boxes, garbage service, and campground hosts. Leashed pets are permitted.
Reservations, fees: Reservations are accepted (877/444-6777, www.recreation.gov). Campsites cost $15. Cash or check. Open late May-early September.
Directions: On the Buffalo Bill Scenic Byway (Hwy. 14/16/20), drive three miles east of Yellowstone National Park or 47.5 miles west of Cody. Turn south into the campground.
GPS Coordinates: N 44° 29.783' W 109° 56.854'
Contact: Shoshone National Forest, Wapiti Ranger District, 203A Yellowstone Ave., Cody, WY 82414, 307/527-6921, www.fs.usda.gov/ shoshone.

65 EAGLE CREEK

Scenic rating: 6

in the Absaroka Mountains in Shoshone National Forest

At 6,500 feet on the North Fork of the

Shoshone River, Eagle Creek Campground allows quick access into Yellowstone National Park, about six miles west. The 10-mile Eagle Creek Trail (#755) departs from the campground, crossing the North Fork on a hiker and horse bridge, heading into the Washakie Wilderness. From the campground, anglers wade-fish both the river and Eagle Creek for rainbow, brown, and Yellowstone cutthroat trout. Rafters and kayakers drive 10 minutes west to put in at Pahaska Tepee to float the Class I-III North Fork of the Shoshone. As the river level drops in front of the campground, sand and rock bars form beaches.

Eagle Creek sits in a loose lodgepole and juniper forest with meadows of hollyhock, cow parsnips, fireweed, harebells, and black-eyed susans. Wild roses are thick enough to scent the air. The two loops are crammed in between the river and the highway, which, unfortunately, adds vehicle noise that you can hear above the sound of the river. You can also see the highway from a few campsites in the left loop. All of the campsites in the left loop have river frontage, although some of the views include cabins across the river. About half of the right loop's campsites overlook the river. You'll have your choice of sunny or partly shaded campsites. Recent thinning projects have removed many of the beetle-killed trees, giving the campground a fresher, more open appearance.

Campsites, facilities: The campground has 20 RV campsites. RVs are limited to 40 feet. Because bears are prevalent, only hard-sided camping units are permitted (no tents, tent pop-ups, or tent trailers). Facilities include picnic tables, fire rings with grills, vault toilets (wheelchair-accessible), drinking water, bear boxes, lantern hangers, garbage service, and campground hosts. Leashed pets are permitted.

Reservations, fees: Reservations are not accepted. Campsites cost $15. Cash or check. Open mid-May-September.

Directions: On the Buffalo Bill Scenic Byway (Hwy. 14/16/20), drive seven miles east of Yellowstone National Park or 43.8 miles west of

Cody. Turn south off the highway into the campground.

GPS Coordinates: N 44° 28.312' W 109° 53.298'

Contact: Shoshone National Forest, Wapiti Ranger District, 203A Yellowstone Ave., Cody, WY 82414, 307/527-6921, www.fs.usda.gov/shoshone.

66 NEWTON CREEK

Scenic rating: 8

in the Absaroka Mountains in Shoshone National Forest

Located at 6,300 feet along the North Fork of the Shoshone River, Newton Creek is the last campground en route toward Yellowstone National Park that allows tents, tent trailers, and bicycle-touring campers. All campgrounds upriver require hard-sided camping units. The campground is popular for fishing, rafting, and kayaking on the Class I-III North Fork of the Shoshone River; however, fishing is closed below Newton Creek April-June because of spawning trout. (Upriver, there's no closure.) The surrounding canyon walls often have bighorn sheep grazing in early summer. On a spur road one mile east, the Blackwater National Recreation Trail climbs four miles to a memorial for 15 firefighters who died fighting a blaze in 1937. The Mummy Cave archeological site is also nearby.

Newton Creek also defines the abrupt shift from the arid sagebrush and juniper forest to the thicker Douglas fir and pine forests of the Absaroka Mountains. Two gravel loops weave around the sagebrush, wild rose, grass, and pine needle duff floor. The spacious campsites include large flat spaces for tents, and a small creek bisects the left loop campsites. Over half of the campsites have river frontage, either sitting adjacent to it or overlooking it from a small bluff. Views include the dramatic pinnacles across the river. While this campground

Anglers head to campgrounds along the North Fork of the Shoshone River for its reputable fishing.

is popular for its ambiance, it comes with highway noise, which dwindles after dark.

Campsites, facilities: The campground has 31 RV and tent campsites. RVs are limited to 40 feet. Facilities include picnic tables, fire rings with grills, vault toilets (wheelchair-accessible), drinking water, bear boxes, garbage service, and campground hosts. Leashed pets are permitted.

Reservations, fees: Reservations are not accepted. Campsites cost $15. Cash or check. Open mid-May-September.

Directions: On the Buffalo Bill Scenic Byway (Hwy. 14/16/20), drive 14.5 miles east of Yellowstone National Park or 36 miles west of Cody. Turn south off the highway into the campground.

GPS Coordinates: N 44° 27.148' W 109° 45.472'

Contact: Shoshone National Forest, Wapiti Ranger District, 203A Yellowstone Ave., Cody, WY 82414, 307/527-6921, www.fs.usda.gov/shoshone.

67 REX HALE

Scenic rating: 7

in the Absaroka Mountains in Shoshone National Forest

At 6,100 feet, along the North Fork of the Shoshone River, Rex Hale is one of the last two campgrounds en route toward Yellowstone National Park that allows tents, tent trailers, and bicycle touring campers. The campground is popular for fishing, rafting, and kayaking on the Class I-III North Fork of the Shoshone River; however, fishing is closed along the campground section April-June because of spawning trout. The surrounding canyon walls often have bighorn sheep grazing in early summer. On a spur road 1.5 miles away, the Blackwater National Recreation Trail climbs four miles to a memorial for 15 firefighters who died fighting a blaze in 1937.

The wide, open sagebrush plateau blooming with yellow clover in July offers neither privacy nor shade, but it is popular because of the electrical hookups at the campsites. Only a few fir, pines, and junipers dot the campground, allowing every campsite to have big canyon views, which unfortunately includes the highway. Highway noise dies down somewhat at night as the route is not a major trucking thoroughfare. Ten campsites overlook the river, and large spaces for tents are available.

Campsites, facilities: The campground has 30 RV and tent campsites. RVs are limited to 40 feet. Facilities include picnic tables, lantern hangers, fire rings with grills, vault toilets (wheelchair-accessible), drinking water, hookups for electricity, bear boxes, garbage service, a group campfire area for interpretive programs, and campground hosts. Leashed pets are permitted.

Reservations, fees: Reservations are accepted (877/444-6777, www.recreation.gov). Campsites cost $20 for electrical hookups and $15 without hookups. Cash or check. Open late May-mid-September.

Directions: On the Buffalo Bill Scenic Byway (Hwy. 14/16/20), drive 16 miles east of Yellowstone National Park or 34 miles west of Cody. Turn south off the highway into the campground.

GPS Coordinates: N 44° 27.241' W 109° 43.745'

Contact: Shoshone National Forest, Wapiti Ranger District, 203A Yellowstone Ave., Cody, WY 82414, 307/527-6921, www.fs.usda.gov/shoshone.

68 CLEARWATER

Scenic rating: 8

in the Absaroka Mountains in Shoshone National Forest

BEST (

Along the North Fork of the Shoshone River, Clearwater Campground, elevation 6,000 feet, is aptly named, for after spring runoff, the river runs with very clear water. The river, which wraps under a rusty-orange cliff wall opposite the campground, attracts anglers wade-fishing for rainbow, brown, and Yellowstone cutthroat trout, but because of spawning trout, fishing here is closed April-June. As the river level drops during the summer, large sandy and pebble beaches form along the campground. The Class I-III river works for floating in a raft or kayak usually through July. The tent-only campground works well for cyclists touring the highway. The campground tucks next to the river on an open sagebrush plateau under a mix of limber pine, junipers, and cottonwoods. The sparse trees allow for big views of the dramatic canyon walls from many of the grassy, sunny campsites. Several sites overlook the river. The open campsites allow views of neighboring campers, and vehicle noise from the highway seeps into the campground.

Campsites, facilities: The campground has 11 tent campsites. Facilities include picnic tables, fire rings with grills, vault toilets, bear boxes, garbage service, and campground hosts. Drinking water is not available; treat river water. Leashed pets are permitted.

Reservations, fees: Reservations are not accepted. Campsites cost $10. Cash or check. Open late May-early September.

Directions: On the Buffalo Bill Scenic Byway (Hwy. 14/16/20), drive 20 miles east of Yellowstone National Park or 31 miles west of Cody. Turn south off the highway into the campground.

GPS Coordinates: N 44° 27.678' W 109° 40.101'

Contact: Shoshone National Forest, Wapiti Ranger District, 203A Yellowstone Ave., Cody, WY 82414, 307/527-6921, www.fs.usda.gov/shoshone.

69 ELK FORK

Scenic rating: 6

in the Absaroka Mountains in Shoshone National Forest

Located at 6,000 feet along Elk Fork Creek, Elk Fork Campground is popular with horse-packers and hunters. Across the Buffalo Bill Scenic Byway from Wapiti Campground, it also offers an alternative for tenters who may not want to be around so many RVs. At the back of the campground, a popular horse-packing trail follows Elk Fork Creek upstream into the Washakie Wilderness. Horse facilities at the trailhead include trailer parking, corrals, and a stock ramp. Elk Fork Creek is closed to fishing, but across the highway, anglers can wade-fish the North Fork of the Shoshone River for trout after July 1 (it is closed April-June for spawning trout). Rafters, kayakers, and skillful canoeists can float the river, which runs with Class I-III white water. Hunters use the campground in fall.

Surrounded by an arid sagebrush canyon, the grassy campground with junipers, willows, and fireweed contrasts with a lush cottonwood bottomland on the east side of Elk Fork Creek. The partly shaded or sunny campsites are spread out for privacy; however, many are open enough to see neighboring campsites. The paved campground road connects with paved parking pads, most of which are back-ins. With the campground's proximity to the highway, you'll hear traffic, but it does die down at night.

Campsites, facilities: The campground has 13 RV or tent campsites. RVs are limited to 22 feet. Facilities include picnic tables, fire rings with grills, vault toilets, bear boxes, garbage service, and campground hosts. No drinking water is available; treat creek water. Leashed pets are permitted.

Reservations, fees: Reservations are not accepted. Campsites cost $10 when services are available in summer; otherwise free. Cash or check. Open year-round.

Directions: On the Buffalo Bill Scenic Byway (Hwy. 14/16/20), drive 22 miles east of Yellowstone National Park or 29 miles west of Cody. At milepost 22.4 just east of the bridge over Elk Fork, turn south off the highway into the campground.

GPS Coordinates: N 44° 27.828' W 109° 37.701'

Contact: Shoshone National Forest, Wapiti Ranger District, 203A Yellowstone Ave., Cody, WY 82414, 307/527-6921, www.fs.usda.gov/shoshone.

70 WAPITI

Scenic rating: 8

in the Absaroka Mountains in Shoshone National Forest

At 6,000 feet along the North Fork of the Shoshone River, Wapiti Campground is named for the elk herds that inhabit the valley. Across the highway at Elk Fork Campground, a popular horse-packing trail follows Elk Fork Creek upstream into the Washakie Wilderness. The river attracts anglers wade-fishing for its wild trout (rainbow and Yellowstone cutthroat), but because of spawning trout, fishing here is closed April-June. The North Fork of the Shoshone River runs with Class I-III white water, navigated usually through July in a raft or kayak.

Surrounded by red canyon walls with dramatic eroded spires, the popular, well-maintained, partly shaded campground's two loops sit under tall cottonwoods and junipers on each side of the forest road that crosses the river. Campsites are spread out for privacy, plus tall brush makes some ultra-private. Ten sites overlook the river; for the remainder of the campsites, paths access the river. As the river level drops throughout the summer, sandy beaches grow larger. Passing vehicles on the highway can be heard, but traffic dwindles at night as the route is not a major trucking thoroughfare.

Campsites, facilities: The campground has 21 RV sites and 19 RV or tent campsites. RVs are limited to 50 feet. Facilities include picnic tables, fire rings with grills, vault toilets, drinking water, hookups for electricity, bear boxes, garbage service, and campground hosts. Leashed pets are permitted. Wheelchair-accessible facilities include toilets and campsites.

Reservations, fees: Reservations are accepted (877/444-6777, www.recreation.gov). Campsites cost $20 with electrical hookups and $15 without hookups. Cash or check. Open mid-May-September.

Directions: On the Buffalo Bill Scenic Byway (Hwy. 14/16/20), drive 22.5 miles east of Yellowstone National Park or 28.5 miles west of Cody. At milepost 22.5, turn north off the highway onto Sweetwater Creek Road (Forest Road 423) for 0.1 mile. Campground loops sit on both sides of the road.

GPS Coordinates: N 44° 27.932' W 109° 37.458'

Contact: Shoshone National Forest, Wapiti Ranger District, 203A Yellowstone Ave., Cody, WY 82414, 307/527-6921, www.fs.usda.gov/shoshone.

71 BIG GAME

Scenic rating: 7

on the North Fork of the Shoshone River in Shoshone National Forest

At 5,900 feet along the North Fork of the Shoshone River, Big Game Campground is surrounded by sagebrush hills broken by eroded orange pinnacles. The Wapiti Wayside, 0.5 mile west of the campground, offers interpretive information on grizzly bears. The river attracts fly-fishers for its wild trout, but because of spawning trout, fishing here is closed April-June. The river runs with Class I-III white water, runnable usually through July in a raft or kayak. Canoeists can paddle part of the river. As river levels drop during the summer, a large pebble and sand bar forms between the campground and the water.

Compared to the arid surrounding hillsides, the campground is lush—partly shaded by giant willow trees, junipers, and lodgepoles with privacy created by short brushy willows. This vegetation means none of the sites overlook the river, but paths weave through the brush to the bank. Some open, grassy sites have views of the pinnacles. A few pull-through gravel parking pads are available for RVs, and flat spaces are available for tents. Because the sites are squeezed between the highway and the river, the sound of passing vehicles enters the campground, but it dwindles at night as the route is not a major trucking thoroughfare. **Campsites, facilities:** The campground has 16 RV or tent campsites. RVs are limited to 32 feet. Facilities include picnic tables, fire rings with grills, pit toilets, bear boxes, garbage service, and campground hosts. Drinking water is not available; treat river water. (You can also get potable water 0.5 mile west at Wapiti Campground.) Leashed pets are permitted. **Reservations, fees:** Reservations are accepted (877/444-6777, www.recreation.gov). Campsites cost $10. Cash or check. Open mid-June-mid-September.

Directions: On the Buffalo Bill Scenic Byway (Hwy. 14/16/20), drive 23 miles east of Yellowstone National Park or 28 miles west of Cody. At milepost 23.1, turn north off the highway into the campground.
GPS Coordinates: N 44° 27.715' W 109° 36.439'
Contact: Shoshone National Forest, Wapiti Ranger District, 203A Yellowstone Ave., Cody, WY 82414, 307/527-6921, www.fs.usda.gov/shoshone.

72 NORTH FORK

Scenic rating: 7

in Buffalo Bill State Park

At 5,500 feet, North Fork Campground sits at the confluence of Trout Creek and the North Fork of the Shoshone River about 36 miles from Yellowstone National Park's east entrance station. Buffalo Bill Reservoir is less than one mile to the east. An east-end boat launch nearby allows for fishing, boating, paddling, and waterskiing, plus the reservoir's consistent winds make it popular for windsurfing. The campground's Trout Creek Nature Trail, a 0.25-mile walk, tours riparian habitat on Trout Creek. About four miles west, the Four Bears Trail explores the eroded badlands country for 4.5 miles to a ridgeline viewpoint below Four Bears Mountain. The North Fork of the Shoshone River contains Class I-III water for rafting, canoeing, and kayaking and is floated best in June. The river is closed to fishing April-June for spawning trout.

The North Fork campground with lush, mowed, green lawns is strikingly opposite from the arid North Shore Bay Campground, but as at its sister campground, every campsite has views of the surrounded eroded hills. A few short cottonwood trees rim the three paved loops, but the trees aren't tall enough to yield shade or provide wind breaks. Most of the campsites have paved pull-through parking pads. While the campground sits on the Shoshone River, none of the campsites overlook the water. You can hear the highway, but wind can drown out traffic.

Campsites, facilities: The campground has eight RV campsites with hookups for water and electricity, 55 RV or tent campsites, and six tent-only walk-in sites. RVs are limited to 50 feet. Facilities include picnic tables, fire rings with grills, vault toilets, drinking water, garbage service, playground, disposal station, and campground hosts. Leashed pets are permitted. Wheelchair-accessible facilities include toilets and three campsites with water and electrical hookups.

Reservations, fees: Reservations are accepted (877/996-7275, http://travel.wyo-park.com). Campsites cost $10 for Wyoming residents and $17 for nonresidents. Cash, check, or credit card. Open May-September.

Directions: From Cody, drive west for 13 miles on the Buffalo Bill Scenic Byway (Hwy. 14/16/20) toward Yellowstone National Park. At milepost 36.7, turn south off the highway and drive 0.1 mile. Turn right into the campground entrance.

GPS Coordinates: N 44° 29.174' W 109° 19.935'

Contact: Buffalo Bill State Park, 47 Lakeside Rd., Cody, WY 82414, 307/587-9227, http://wyoparks.state.wy.us/.

73 NORTH SHORE BAY

Scenic rating: 8

in Buffalo Bill State Park

North Shore Bay Campground, elevation 5,500 feet, sits on the north shore of Buffalo Bill Reservoir about 42 miles from Yellowstone National Park's east entrance station. Surrounded by eroded sandstone formations, the reservoir draw locals for its fishing, boating, paddling, windsurfing, swimming, and waterskiing. The campground's boat launch includes a cement ramp, dock, and fish-cleaning station. Anglers go after rainbow, brown, lake, and Yellowstone cutthroat trout. The wheelchair-accessible Eagle Point Trail, which will eventually traverse the north shore, is in the Eagle Point Day Use Area four miles east. Buffalo Bill Dam maintains a museum open to the public, and the walk across the dam lets you view the Shoshone Canyon gorge from above.

The campground, with a paved road and paved parking pads at most of its campsites, squeezes its three loops in between the reservoir and the highway. Even though the highway is a major traffic route into Yellowstone, it does not serve as a major trucking highway; much of the noise diminishes after dark. The arid campground sits on a natural sparse grass and sagebrush plateau exposed to the wind and sun with only a handful of small cottonwoods. Half of the campsites overlook the lake, which makes it popular, and all of the campsites have views encompassing the rock spires to the north. The tent-only sites sit on a terraced hillside with windscreens.

Campsites, facilities: The campground has seven RV campsites with hookups for electricity and water, 32 RV or tent campsites, and five tent-only walk-in sites. Large RVs are okay, although midsized and smaller ones will have more choices. Facilities include picnic tables, fire rings with grills, vault toilets, drinking water, garbage service, boat launch, disposal station, and park personnel on-site in the entrance station. Leashed pets are permitted. Wheelchair-accessible facilities include toilets and three campsites.

Reservations, fees: Reservations are accepted (877/996-7275, http://travel.wyo-park.com). Campsites cost $10 for Wyoming residents and $17 for nonresidents. Cash, check, or credit card. Open May-September.

Directions: From Cody, drive west for nine miles on the Buffalo Bill Scenic Byway (Hwy. 14/16/20) toward Yellowstone National Park. Locate the entrance to the campground at milepost 42 on the south side of the highway.

GPS Coordinates: N 44° 30.095' W 109° 14.234'

Contact: Buffalo Bill State Park, 47 Lakeside Rd., Cody, WY 82414, 307/587-9227, http://wyoparks.state.wy.us/.

74 CODY KOA

Scenic rating: 5

near Cody

At 5,097 feet just east of Cody, the KOA is convenient for visiting sights in town. Buffalo Bill Historical Center wraps five museums about the West (including the life of Buffalo Bill Cody) under one roof. The Cody Rodeo, the longest-running rodeo in the United States, runs every night June-August with bull riding, calf roping, and barrel racing. (The KOA provides a shuttle to the rodeo.) Cody also is home to local outfitters for white-water river rafting, fishing, and horseback riding. The Shoshone River, west of Cody, froths with Class II-III white water through Red Rock Canyon for rafters and kayakers, with water runnable through September. Nearby Beck Lake offers fishing for kids.

The open, sunny campground affords an easy place for satellite reception. Only a few small cottonwood trees cluster in the mowed lawn campground for a bit of shade. Located outside of town, the campground is removed from the hubbub of town but has highway noise, which does include some commercial trucking.

Campsites, facilities: The campground has 161 RV campsites and 12 tent campsites. RVs are limited to 80 feet. Hookups include water, sewer, and electricity up to 50 amps. Facilities include picnic tables, fire rings with grills, flush toilets, showers, coin-operated launderette, drinking water, playground, basketball, horseshoe pits, jumping pillow, swimming pool, hot tub, wading pool, game room, dog playground, wireless Internet, cable TV, patios,

camp store, firewood and propane for sale, and disposal station. Leashed pets are permitted.

Reservations, fees: Reservations are accepted (800/562-8507, www.koa.com). Hookups cost $45-70. Tent sites cost $29. Rates cover two people. For extra campers, add $4-6. Kids under six stay free. Taxes and a resort fee will be added on. Open May-September.

Directions: From Cody, drive three miles east on Highway 14/16/20, passing the airport. Turn left into the campground.

GPS Coordinates: N 44° 30.775' W 109° 0.487'

Contact: Cody KOA, 5561 Greybull Hwy., Cody, WY 82414, 307/587-2369, www.codykoa.com.

75 JACK CREEK

Scenic rating: 8

in the Absaroka Mountains in Shoshone National Forest

Located about 7,600 feet along the Greybull River, Jack Creek Campground sits in terrain that looks like the southwest. Cliffy and arid, large buttes of the Absaroka Mountains rise up above the forested river valley. One trail follows the Greybull River for miles upstream, eventually connecting into the Washakie Wilderness, while other trails climb along tributaries. The trails attract hikers, hunters, anglers, and horseback riders, and stock facilities are available at the trailhead. Anglers consider the Greybull River a fly-fishing mecca. The river harbors native fish such as Yellowstone cutthroat trout and mountain whitefish.

The campground sits literally at the end of the road; that alone guarantees night time quiet. A mixed forest provides shade, and many sites sidle up to the river.

Campsites, facilities: The campground has seven RV or tent campsites. RVs are limited to 30 feet, but most of the spurs are smaller. Facilities include picnic tables, fire rings, and vault toilets. No drinking water is available; treat river water. Pack out your trash. Leashed pets are permitted.

Reservations, fees: Reservations are not accepted. Camping is free. Open mid-May-October.

Directions: From Meeteetse, drive State Highway 290 southwest for 11 miles. Take the dirt and gravel Forest Road 208 east for eight miles and veer left at the junction for another eight miles.

GPS Coordinates: N 44° 6.606' W 109° 21.125'

Contact: Shoshone National Forest, Greybull Ranger District, 203A Yellowstone Ave., Cody, WY 82414, 307/527-6921, www.fs.usda.gov/shoshone.

76 BROWN MOUNTAIN/ WOOD RIVER

Scenic rating: 8

in the Absaroka Mountains in Shoshone National Forest

Located about 7,400 feet in the Wood River Valley, Brown Mountain and Wood River Campgrounds sit about two miles apart, cowering under the tall Absaroka Mountains. The pair of campgrounds attracts anglers fishing for trout in the Wood River, horseback riders, hikers, hunters, and ghost town fans. Nearby trails follow tributaries upstream from Wood River. Below 12,000-foot peaks, the ghost town of Kirwin tucks on a hillside just below timberline. Find it 16-18 miles west of the campgrounds on a rough road suitable only for four-wheel drives or mountain bikes. By the early 1900s, the mining town held 200 inhabitants. Today, historical preservation efforts work toward saving its remaining 38 buildings.

The long gravel drive to the campgrounds guarantees that you'll fall asleep to the sound

of the river rather than the sounds of civilization. The forested campgrounds provide shade with some campsites enjoying river frontage.

Campsites, facilities: Wood River has five RV or tent campsites with a maximum RV length of 30 feet. Brown Mountain has seven RV or tent campsites; most of the sites can fit RVs up to 16 feet, and one site has a 40-foot parking spur. Facilities include picnic tables, fire rings, and vault toilets. No drinking water is available; treat river water. Pack out your trash. Leashed pets are permitted.

Reservations, fees: Reservations are not accepted. Camping is free. Open mid-May-October.

Directions: From Meeteetse, drive State Highway 290 southwest for about seven miles. Turn left at Wood River Road (4DT) and drive 16 dirt and gravel miles to Wood River Campground on the left. Continue 2.5 miles further to Brown Mountain Campground on the left. Wood River GPS Coordinates: N 43° 55.923' W 109° 7.888'

Brown Mountain GPS Coordinates: N 43° 56.136' W 109° 10.756'

Contact: Shoshone National Forest, Greybull Ranger District, 203A Yellowstone Ave., Cody, WY 82414, 307/527-6921, www.fs.usda.gov/shoshone.

77 FOUNTAIN OF YOUTH RV PARK

Scenic rating: 6

outside Thermopolis

At 4,300 feet, Thermopolis is home to natural hot mineral springs. At the Fountain of Youth RV Park north of town, the Sacajawea Hot Springs flows at 128°F pumping out 1.3 million gallons a day. It feeds a large 235-foot-long and 75-foot-wide soaking pool, which is kept at 100°F. A bathhouse, lounge chairs, and benches flank the pool. Thermopolis State

Park sits about 2.5 miles south with a bath-house, outdoor hot pool, hiking, and fishing. Two private concessionaires run additional indoor and outdoor hot pools with waterslides.

Pull-through RV sites have gravel parking pads set amid grass and shade trees. The campground squeezes between the highway and the railroad tracks, so bring earplugs to aid sleeping. The Bighorn River flows on the other side of the railroad tracks.

Campsites, facilities: The campground has 62 RV campsites. RVs are limited to 50 feet. Tenting is available in an overflow area. Hook-ups include water, sewer, and electricity up to 50 amps. Facilities include picnic tables, flush toilets, showers, drinking water, playground, large mineral pool, launderette, wireless Internet, horseshoes, dog trail, and camp store. Leashed pets are permitted. A toilet and the pool are wheelchair-accessible.

Reservations, fees: Reservations are accept-ed. Hookups cost $39-42. Tent sites cost $35. Rates cover two people. For extra campers, add $6 each. Open year-round.

Directions: From Thermopolis, drive north on Highway 20 for 1.9 miles and turn east into the campground.

GPS Coordinates: N 43° 40.425' W 108° 12.330'

Contact: Fountain of Youth RV Park, 250 N. Highway 20, Thermopolis, WY 82443, 307/864-3265, www.fountainofyouthrvpark.com.

78 WYOMING GARDENS RV PARK

Scenic rating: 6

in Thermopolis

At 4,300 feet, Thermopolis is home to hot springs. At Thermopolis State Park, the natu-ral hot springs pumps out more than 8,000 gallons per day of mineral water. While the hot water steaming down rainbow-colored terraces reaches 135°F, water for bathing in the free bathhouse is 104°F. (Rental tow-els and swimsuits do have a fee, though.) With a bison herd on site, the park flanks the Bighorn River, crossed by a suspension footbridge, and 6.2 miles of hiking trails tour the grounds. Anglers fish the river for trout. Trails and a fishing pier are wheelchair-accessible. Two private hot spring businesses offer indoor and outdoor swimming pools, hot tubs, and slides. From the campground on the south end of town, you can walk down-town for shopping and restaurants, but the state park and hot pools sit 1.8 miles away on the north end of town.

Pull-through RV sites have gravel parking pads separated by grass picnic strips and shade trees. Each of the tent sites has its own water and electricity services, plus woods chips for tent pads. A Mexican restaurant is also on the premises.

Campsites, facilities: The campground has 11 RV campsites and four tent campsites. Large RVs are okay, but call to check avail-ability. Hookups include water, sewer, and electricity up to 50 amps. Facilities include picnic tables, pedestal grills (bring your own charcoal), flush toilets, showers, drinking water, sandbox, trampoline, and wireless Internet. A launderette sits across the street. Leashed pets are permitted.

Reservations, fees: Reservations are accept-ed. Hookups cost $28-31. Tent sites cost $18. Rates cover two people. For extra campers, add $2 each. Kids under five stay free. Open year-round.

Directions: In Thermopolis, go south on Highway 20 where it turns west into Shoshoni Street. Drive two blocks and turn right.

GPS Coordinates: N 43° 38.325' W 108° 12.910'

Contact: Wyoming Gardens RV Park, 720 Shoshoni Street, Thermopolis, WY 82443, 307/864-2778 or 307/921-0151, www.wyominggardensrvpark.com.

79 UPPER AND LOWER WIND RIVER

🛶 🎣 🚌 🚤 🏕 🚶 ♿ 🚐 ⛺

Scenic rating: 8

in Boysen State Park

In the southern Owl Creek Mountains, Boysen State Park—Wyoming's largest state park—sits on the Wind River Canyon Scenic Byway. It contains the 20-mile-long Boysen Reservoir spilling north through Boysen Dam into Wind River Canyon. The reservoir is popular for boating, water-skiing, fishing, paddling, and swimming. Anglers catch ling, walleye, perch, crappie, and trout. Fishing is available in the Wind River, too. Lower and Upper Wind River Campgrounds squeeze between the highway and the Wind River, tucked into the canyon below the dam at 4,600 feet. Lower Wind River Campground is the site where the original dam stood.

The campgrounds have lawns and some shade trees, but you can find open sites with views of the canyon walls and its geological features. The canyon is home to bighorn sheep, which you can sometimes see from the campsites. Expect to hear trucking and railroad noise drowning out the sound of the river, and prepare for strong winds through the canyon. Pull-through sites are available, and large RV parking areas can accommodate multiple rigs.

Campsites, facilities: Together, the two campgrounds have 100 RV or tent campsites. Large RVs are okay. Facilities include picnic tables, fire rings with grills, vault toilets, drinking water, garbage service, playgrounds, disposal station (at park headquarters), and campground hosts in summer. Leashed pets are permitted. Wheelchair-accessible facilities include toilets and four campsites (three in lower, one in upper).

Reservations, fees: Reservations are accepted (877/996-7275, http://travel.wyo-park.com). Campsites cost $10 for Wyoming residents and $17 for nonresidents. Rates include day-use fees. Cash, check, or credit card. Open mid-May–mid-September.

Directions: From Boysen Dam at the north end of Boysen State Park, drive north on Highway 20 for 1.4 miles to the upper campground or 1.9 miles to the lower campground. Find the entrances on the left.

Lower Campground GPS Coordinates: N 43° 26.478' W 108° 10.344'

Upper Campground GPS Coordinates: N 43° 26.044' W 108° 10.645'

Contact: Boysen State Park, 15 Ash Street, Shoshoni, WY 82649, 307/876-2796, http://wyoparks.state.wy.us/.

80 BRANNON/TAMARASK/ MARINA

🛶 🎣 🚌 🚤 🏕 🚶 ♿ 🚐 ⛺

Scenic rating: 6

in Boysen State Park

In the southern Owl Creek Mountains, Boysen State Park—Wyoming's largest state park—sits on the Wind River Canyon Scenic Byway. It contains the 20-mile-long Boysen Reservoir, which spills at the north through Boysen Dam into Wind River Canyon. Surrounded by arid sagebrush hills, the reservoir attracts boaters, water-skiers, anglers, paddlers, and swimmers. Anglers catch ling, walleye, perch, crappie, and trout. Brannan, Tamarask, and the Boysen Marina line up adjacent to each other along the northeastern shore of the reservoir, all three with camping zones. A sandy swimming beach is available along with full marina services, concrete boat ramps, docks, boat slips, moorings, fuel, and fishing licenses.

The campgrounds and marina overlook the reservoir, but back up to the highway and the railroad, which contribute a significant amount of noise. With virtually no trees in the sunny campgrounds, winds whip through the area. The campground sites vary between individual grass sites and large cement parking lots.

Campsites, facilities: The campgrounds

have 65 RV or tent campsites. Large RVs are okay. Facilities include picnic tables, fire rings with grills, vault toilets, drinking water, garbage service, playgrounds, disposal station (at park headquarters), and campground hosts in summer. Leashed pets are permitted. Wheelchair-accessible facilities include toilets and campsites.

Reservations, fees: Reservations are not accepted. Campsites cost $10 for Wyoming residents and $17 for nonresidents. Rates include day-use fees. Cash, check, or credit card. Open mid-May-mid-September.

Directions: In Boysen State Park, locate Brannon Drive on the east side of Highway 20 about 0.25 mile north of park headquarters or 0.8 mile south of the dam. Brannon Drive accesses the campgrounds and marina. Brannon GPS Coordinates: N 43° 26.478' W 108° 10.344'

Tamarask GPS Coordinates: N 43° 26.044' W 108° 10.645'

Contact: Boysen State Park, 15 Ash Street, Shoshoni, WY 82649, 307/876-2796, http://wyoparks.state.wy.us/.

81 TOUGH CREEK

Scenic rating: 5

in Boysen State Park

On the Wind River Canyon Scenic Byway, Boysen State Park is Wyoming's largest state park with the 20-mile-long Boysen Reservoir. Surrounded by arid sagebrush hills, the reservoir attracts boaters, water-skiers, anglers, paddlers, and swimmers. Anglers fish for ling, walleye, perch, crappie, and trout. Tough Creek Campground is located on the east side of the reservoir on a narrow long spit rimmed with sandy beaches. A concrete boat ramp and dock are available. Two other primitive overflow campgrounds sit west of Shoshoni: Poison Creek and Lakeside. Lakeside has a boat ramp.

Plan for strong winds to pummel this campground at times since it has minimal trees for wind protection. Contrary to the state park campgrounds further north, Tough Creek offers quiet. Pavement ends at the parking area with most of the campsites on dirt road spurs. Many campsites overlook the water; some have private beaches.

Campsites, facilities: The campground has 67 RV and tent campsites. Large RVs are okay. Facilities include picnic tables, fire rings with grills, vault toilets, drinking water, garbage service, playground, picnic shelters at 15 sites, and disposal station (at park headquarters). Leashed pets are permitted. Wheelchair-accessible facilities include toilets and campsites.

Reservations, fees: Reservations are accepted only for the group camping shelter (877/996-7275, http://travel.wyo-park.com). Campsites cost $10 for Wyoming residents and $17 for nonresidents. Rates include day-use fees. Cash, check, or credit card. Open mid-May-mid-September.

Directions: In Boysen State Park, drive 6.7 miles south from park headquarters on Highway 20. Turn right onto Tough Creek Road and drop 1.6 miles, crossing the railroad tracks and going to the end of the narrow peninsula. GPS Coordinates: N 43° 19.807' W 108° 9.144'

Contact: Boysen State Park, 15 Ash Street, Shoshoni, WY 82649, 307/876-2796, http://wyoparks.state.wy.us/.

82 BOYSEN WEST SIDE PRIMITIVE

Scenic rating: 5

in Boysen State Park

Boysen State Park on the Wind River Canyon Scenic Byway is Wyoming's largest state park with the 20-mile-long Boysen Reservoir. Surrounded by arid sagebrush hills, the reservoir attracts boaters, water-skiers, anglers, paddlers, and swimmers. Anglers fish for ling, walleye, perch, crappie, and several species of trout. Small primitive campgrounds cluster among the bays and peninsulas on the rugged west side of the reservoir. Cottonwood Bay, the furthest north, requires the longest drive and sits on the south shore of one of the reservoir's largest bays. Loop 1 road accesses campsites closer to reach in South Muddy, Fremont Bay, Libby Point, and Sandy Hills Loop; Loop 2 road scatters campsites in Trout Bay, Cottonwood Bay, Sand Mesa, Wilson Bay, and North Muddy. Fremont and Cottonwood Bays have the only boat ramps on the reservoir's west side. Fremont Bay, to closest to access, has a playground for kids. Stop at park headquarters to pick up a state park brochure with a map to help with locating west side campgrounds.

These quiet, primitive, sunny campsites offer a place to be off by yourself. Many have private beaches. Some have a few cottonwood trees for shade; others are dusty and dry. Tenters should choose locations with trees for wind protection.

Campsites, facilities: Loop 1 has 20 RV or tent campsites. Loop 2 has 30 RV or tent campsites. Smaller and midsized RVs are best. Facilities including picnic tables and fire pits are limited to specific locations. Toilets are only available at Cottonwood Bay, Trout Bay, Sand Mesa, North Muddy, South Muddy, Sandy Hills, and Fremont Bay. Drinking water is only available at Fremont and Cottonwood Bays. A disposal station is at park headquarters. Leashed pets are permitted.

Reservations, fees: Reservations are not accepted. Campsites cost $10 for Wyoming residents and $17 for nonresidents. Rates include day-use fees. Cash, check, or credit card. Open mid-May-mid-September.

Directions: From Shoshoni, drive four miles west on Highway 26 to the bridge over the head of the reservoir. From the bridge, continue west for one mile to Bass Lake Road and turn north. To access Loop 1, veer right. To access Loop 2, veer left, staying on Bass Lake Road for 8.2 miles to West Shore Drive. The loops are mostly gravel and dirt roads. GPS Coordinates of Fremont Bay: N 43° 15.871' W 108° 11.725'

Contact: Boysen State Park, 15 Ash Street, Shoshoni, WY 82649, 307/876-2796, http://wyoparks.state.wy.us/.

Index

YOUR ADVENTURE STARTS HERE

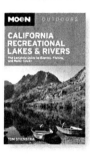 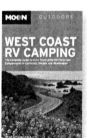  

MOON SPOTLIGHT YELLOWSTONE & GRAND TETON CAMPING

Avalon Travel
a member of the Perseus Books Group
1700 Fourth Street
Berkeley, CA 94710, USA
www.moon.com

Editors: Leah Gordon, Sabrina Young
Series Manager: Sabrina Young
Copy Editor: Carolyn Cotney
Production and Graphics Coordinator:
   Lucie Ericksen
Cover Designer: Lucie Ericksen
Map Editor: Mike Morgenfeld
Cartographer: Stephanie Poulain

ISBN-13: 978-1-63121-011-2

Printing History
1st Edition – 2001
2nd Edition – May 2014
5 4 3 2 1

Front cover photo: Grand Prismatic hot pool, Yellowstone © Becky Lomax
Title page photo: © Becky Lomax

Printed in the United States of America

ABOUT THE AUTHOR

Becky Lomax

© STACEY BENGSTON

Becky Lomax grew up camping. She cherishes fond memories of family camping trips in a yellow station wagon packed door-to-door with five raucous kids and their gear. Piled on air mattresses or cots in a canvas tent, she and her siblings woke each morning to their mom doling canned grapefruit and mandarin oranges into plastic camping bowls while their dad pumped the green two-burner Coleman stove to cook pancakes.

Like any camping family, they had their share of rain, mosquitoes, vehicle breakdowns, and siblings who strip-mined the chocolate from the gorp bag. Her brothers still swear they didn't put that frog in her sleeping bag – but she's not convinced.

Today, Becky's favorite kind of travel still involves backpacking, hiking, and camping – especially with her nieces and nephews. After 10 years as a hiking and backpacking guide in Glacier National Park, she now travels the Northern Rockies as a full-time professional outdoors writer and photographer. She uses her writing career as an excuse to camp, hike, mountain bike, kayak, and ski. Her favorite research involves wildlife: She has followed biologists into the field to band raptors and radio-collar bighorn sheep and grizzly bears.

Becky is also the author of *Moon Glacier National Park*. Her work has been published in various magazines, including *Smithsonian*, *Backpacker*, *National Wildlife*, *Cross Country Skier*, *Montana Magazine*, *Montana Outdoors*, and *Northwest Travel*.

CPSIA information can be obtained at www.ICGtesting.com
Printed in the USA
LVOW10n0901050614

388750LV00003B/9/P